THE NEW RULES OF WORK

THE NEW RULES OF WORK

**THE ULTIMATE CAREER GUIDE
FOR THE MODERN WORKPLACE**

ALEXANDRA CAVOULACOS
AND KATHRYN MINSHEW

themuse

*In collaboration with Adrian Granzella Larssen
and The Muse's writers, editors, and career experts*

First published in Great Britain in 2017 by Orion Spring
This edition first published in 2019 by Orion Spring
an imprint of the Orion Publishing Group Ltd
Carmelite House, 50 Victoria Embankment,
London, EC4Y 0DZ
An Hachette UK company

1 3 5 7 9 10 8 6 4 2

A CIP catalogue record for this book
is available from the British Library.

ISBN: 978 1 4091 6709 9
eISBN: 978 1 4091 6710 5

Book design by Andrea Lau
Jacket design by Tal Goretsky

Printed and bound in Great Britain by Clays Ltd, Elcograf S.p.A.

MIX
Paper from
responsible sources
FSC® C104740

www.orionbooks.co.uk

ORION
SPRING

To the Muse community, who made this all possible

CONTENTS

PART THREE

CHARTING YOUR COURSE THROUGH THE MODERN WORKPLACE

We believe you should love your job. In fact, we believe that you should be *thrilled* with your job. And more than thrilled—fulfilled by it.

We believe that you can find a career that gives you purpose, one that lets you use a set of skills that give you pride, and enjoy a day-to-day that gives you meaning. We believe that your work can—and should—be a part of who you are, what you value, and what you want for the future of the world.

And we truly believe that you—yes, you—can achieve all of this.

Decades ago, this would have been a revolutionary, even ridiculous, idea. For the vast majority of workers, a job was at best a means to a paycheck and at worst total drudgery. Work paid for your "real life," the one outside of a 9-to-5: your hobbies and pastimes, your families and friendships, your weekends. Free time was where you anchored your identity. Work itself was never a source of fulfillment.

You may still feel very much like this now. But you should also know there's another way.

We're not the first to say it, but the world of work is changing—in profound ways. The last twenty years have seen a massive shift both in terms of what work means to us, and in what it demands from us. We are connected by our smartphones twenty-four hours a day, seven days a week. Gone are the days when your clients or your boss couldn't reach you unless you were in the same room or at your desk next to a landline phone. Now not only can you take work home with you, but you're often expected to be in constant contact, available around the clock.

This dramatic shift—this ability to be constantly connected, this blurring our boundaries between "work" and "not work"—is exactly what makes it so crucial that your work is something that inspires and fulfills you. But luckily, these very same shifts also mean there is more opportunity for you to find a perfect fit between the things that fulfill you and how you make a living. That's in large part because the same internet that connects you to work long after 5 p.m. has also democratized access to information and people, meaning it is easier than ever to explore and pursue new career opportunities, acquire new skills, and connect with an ever-expanding network of individuals across the globe. Today, it's more feasible than ever to take control of your future and pave the way for change.

But there's more. In the past, people typically chose a career path when they were young and were generally constricted to a fairly limited set of options. Their opportunities were then further narrowed for the rest of their lives. Those who decided, at age twenty-one, to go to medical school or law school became doctors or lawyers—and remained such until they retired. And while there were always people who broke through barriers, or experienced a midlife career reinvention, the obstacles to changing careers later in life proved too steep for most to overcome.

But you, dear reader, have options your parents never dreamed of. The traditional paths—go to medical school, become a doctor; go to law school, become a lawyer—are giving way to an increasingly broad set of choices: a menu of options that actually *expands* as we gain new experience and new skills and access to new networks over the course of our careers. For example, a med school grad today may be weighing private practice against a consulting opportunity in the healthcare space, a chief medical officer role at a healthcare start-up, or a position advising hospital staff on safety and reducing medical errors. Down the road, that same individual may write a book or speak publicly about national healthcare issues, or even run for political office.

Our menu of options has expanded in this way largely because of the explosion of new jobs and fields that didn't even exist as recently as a decade ago. Today there are countless jobs that have only recently become viable career paths: social media manager, cybersecurity analyst, UX (user experience) designer, to name just a few.

It used to be you went to college, picked a field, found a good job at a stable company, moved up in your department, got your pension, and retired. You worked in a single industry, sometimes for a single company, and never questioned your next step.

Unlike the generation before, most professionals now change jobs—and even careers—every couple of years. They have many roles at multiple companies throughout their lifetimes, and some may even start their own businesses. What that means is that you will likely reinvent yourself many times over. This is an amazing freedom that our parents' generation never enjoyed.

With this expanded set of options comes the opportunity to find not just a "good on paper" job, but a job that is the perfect fit for *you*. Today you're able to weigh your choices not just in terms of the work itself—though that's important too—but also in terms of many other factors that have just as much, if not more, impact on your day-to-day job satisfaction. You can (and should), for example, factor in a company's culture and mission, and whether that aligns with your priorities and values. You can (and should) take into account workplace culture, flexibility of hours, and opportunities for learning. For you have your own dreams, needs, and motivations, and as you'll learn later in the book, finding a job or career path that best aligns with them will not only make you much happier getting up to go to work in the morning, but also help you thrive once you get there.

Put another way, picture a map with point A, which is where you are now, and point Z, which is where you retire after a long career. Twenty years ago, there might have been a reasonably finite number of straight lines connecting those two points. Now it's like a UV light has been turned on, illuminating dozens of previously hidden interconnected pathways that branch and diverge in many directions. And within this maze are any number of paths that may prove deeply fulfilling for you.

This isn't to say that you will love every job you have, or that you will love your job every day. In fact, a lot of people who love their jobs today had to go through difficult periods with terrible bosses, long hours, or unfulfilling work to get where they are now. And even those of us who love our jobs still have bad days from time to time! But we believe that, with the right tools and perspective, you can find a job that fills you with meaning and purpose more days than not, and moves you toward a goal that is resonant and rich.

To get there, though, you need to throw out all the old, traditional advice about what it takes to find, land, and thrive in the perfect job. The old rules no longer apply here. Instead, you need the New Rules— rules that will help you navigate the changing landscape of work and the unique career path you will build, not follow.

Given all the ways in which the world of work is changing, you simply *can't* plan your career using the same methods and approaches that may have worked before. Instead of climbing a predetermined ladder, you will be hiking a journey with many twists, turns, and forks in the road. So the New Rules necessitate a major mindset shift; one that involves looking at your career as a series of two- to five-year steps, rather than a single choice made up front.

And just as you can't approach career planning the same way, you can't be searching for jobs the same way, either. This is a good thing— because, let's be honest, the old way wasn't so great. Most of us have had the experience of going to a job site and coming face-to-face with that big, empty search box. It stares back at you, asking: *What do you want?* And even though you may not be sure, you pick something because you have to. Depending on what you enter into that box, you may get results that are extremely broad or extremely narrow, and most of them probably don't appeal to you in the slightest. That's not a surprise: The professional aspirations of most people don't fit cleanly in a search bar.

The problem with the traditional search box is that it assumes that you already know exactly what kind of job you want. If you know 100 percent that you want to be a sell-side analyst or a pediatric cardiologist or an exotic animal veterinarian—if you are one of the lucky few who have it figured out—then, sure, you can type those words into the search bar and find some great job opportunities for yourself. If, on the other hand, you're not quite sure what you want to do next (and most of us fall into this category!), then that big empty box is not going to help you at all.

In the new world of work, what many of us need is not a tool for job *search,* but tools for job *discovery*—tools to help you figure out what you, as a unique individual, really want. You need tools to help you understand what your professional strengths, skills, and values are. You need tools to explore the countless different options that are available to you. You need resources to research positions and companies—resources that will tell you not just how many employees they have or what their yearly operating budget is, but whether their culture is a fit for your work style, whether their workspace is inspiring to you, whether their employees are happy and fulfilled, and whether those employees are the type of people with whom you'd want to work. You need methods for career experimentation, the ability to try a few things and see when you're on the right track—and the wrong one. A lot of the rules are being rewritten as we speak, meaning that we all have the opportunity to contribute to the future of a workplace that will look remarkably different in five to seven years than it does now. We're pretty excited by this idea, and we hope you are, too.

This is exactly why we built TheMuse.com. Yes, we wanted to provide tools to let you search for jobs, if that's what you're ready to do. But we also wanted to provide tools to let you *discover:* to read stories of how other professionals found their paths, to watch videos that bring you inside the walls of a variety of different companies to see how they operate, to explore job opportunities based on values, skills, and interests that are unique to you.

The Muse is a different type of career site, in that we personalize the experience for you. We target and get to know specific companies and provide curated advice that helps you understand not only what a position entails in the context of a company, but also what you want from a job. We guide you through this process; we don't simply point you in the direction of hundreds of job openings. In short, we show you how to play the career game by the New Rules.

The book you hold in your hands is not only an extension of that philosophy, but a practical playbook—one that draws on our collective experiences helping millions of people find the perfect fit—for navigating the new world of work. In it, we will walk you through everything from how to create and narrow a menu of possible job options, to how to get your foot in the door at your dream company, to how to set a goal for the next stage in your career journey—and then achieve it. And we'll show you how to do all that by following the New Rules.

Wherever you are or whatever you're facing in your career right now, we believe that there is a way to move forward, and a destination that is right for you. Whether you've just graduated or are about to graduate from college and have no idea what you want to be "when you grow up"; whether you're midcareer with a decent job and salary but feel bored or stuck, and wondering what else could be out there for you; whether you are a parent reentering the workforce after a decade career break raising a family, only to find that the job landscape looks nothing like you remember it; whether you are nearing retirement but nowhere near ready to retire—only you've been "aged out" (read: replaced by someone younger) of the job you've had for thirty years with only a distant memory of what it even means to "look for work"—this book can help. We are here to tell you that whatever your current obstacle is, you can face it. The only thing you shouldn't be doing if you're feeling stuck or disillusioned or stressed out is *nothing*. There are always next steps to take, new strategies to try, and new skills to build, and we can tackle them together.

There isn't anything wrong with wanting more from work. Wherever you're starting from, banish forever the idea that just getting paid in exchange for your forty-plus hours a week is good enough value from your career path. Instead, know that you can choose a job where you can get paid *and* be mentored, get paid *and* develop new skills, get paid *and* be on a fast track toward your ultimate career destination, get paid *and* have phenomenal co-workers or perks or flexibility for your lifestyle (or—you guessed it—many of the above). The most important thing is being curious and open to exploring the many opportunities in front of you. This is what we mean by exciting!

MAKE A CONTRACT WITH YOURSELF

When you write down exactly what you're trying to accomplish and make it visible, you are making yourself more accountable to you—to your goals, your dreams, your passions. At The Muse, we are big believers in reminders that help us stay aware of our actions, our behaviors, and our attitudes, and whether they are moving us closer to our goals—in this case, to find a job, change careers, or grow personally and professionally.

So let's first agree to leave behind those usual excuses—I'm too busy, I'm just getting over a cold/flu/hangover, it's a bad time at work, etc. Taking control of your future is hard (though rewarding) work and you will always have a ready excuse to put it off until tomorrow (and then the next tomorrow and the next tomorrow). And if it's not excuses that are holding you back, but fear of getting started, try to set that aside for a bit as you work through this book. (We'll give you some tips on exactly how to do that, later on.)

The career coaches we work with at The Muse often share with us how impressed they are by the investments that people make in their own careers. They understand that when someone signs up for a thirty- or sixty-minute coaching session, they have already demonstrated a concrete kind of commitment to their own growth—personal and professional. But not everyone needs a coach. In fact, we want this book to offer you much of what you might gain from working one-on-one with a coach. Either way, the big takeaway for you is this: identifying your passion and purpose means stepping up to the plate and truly taking responsibility for your own career path.

One way to formalize this commitment to yourself is by creating a contract. Take five minutes right now to think about why you picked up *The New Rules of Work*. What do you hope to come away with from reading these pages and where do you hope to be at the end of this process?

Now we invite you, at the start of this journey, to write your own contract and print it out. Post it in an easily visible location (on your night table, taped to the bathroom mirror or on the refrigerator). It might feel a little cheesy, but having a constant visual reminder of your motivation is a powerful force for change. And identifying the challenges you might face—anything from obligations with family and friends to your own fear of making a career shift—up front will make sure you think ahead of time about exactly how to address them.

Here is a sample template you can follow:

MY CONTRACT

As I read *The New Rules of Work*, I hope to learn more about
_____ and
_____

Some challenges I may face: _____
_____
_____
_____

To deal with these challenges I plan to _____
_____
_____
_____
_____
_____

I commit to putting time aside for myself, because I want to achieve my goal of _____

_____ and I deserve the care and commitment I am putting toward my career.

My signature:

Date:

You'll encounter challenges along the way that may deter you from achieving your goals—it's important to identify what they are and think about how to overcome them. But slipups are a normal part of this process, so don't be hard on yourself. Just get back on that horse.

IN THE MIDDLE OF AN OCEAN OF POSSIBILITY, HOW DO YOU KNOW WHICH WAY TO SWIM?

So, new workplace, New Rules. But where to start? Don't worry, we'll walk you through it.

The pages ahead, Part 1: What Do I Actually Want?, will set the stage for figuring out what drives you and what key skills and qualities you have to offer your dream employer. You will discover how to identify, sift through, and narrow your options to make your next move, whether it's to land a new job, to shift careers, or to make big or little changes in your current role. It can be easy to get stuck and become resigned to staying on the path you chose years ago, even if it's no longer feeling like a fit. But many people don't realize that there are absolutely ways to get unstuck and redesign your own career from an expanded set of diverse options—and beyond that, most people don't realize how exciting it is! But to do so, we believe that your very first step, wherever you are in your career, begins with learning more about yourself. This kind of check-in with who you are, where you are, and where you've been makes moving forward much, much easier.

The chapters in Part 1 will take you through what we call the Three R's—Reflect, Research, and Refine—a series of steps that will enable you to navigate this preparatory stage of your process. We will help you answer some grand but empowering questions: What are my real passions? What really gets me out of bed in the morning? What do I really want from work? Knowing the answers to these questions helps to narrow your options, understand your real choices, and get ready to make your move.

Some of you may be confused (and a little intimidated) about how to take the first step in your career, while others of you may have a solid grounding in the workplace but feel that something is missing and are seeking a different way to think about your options. We'll introduce our belief that the job search is akin to the scientific method: you first have a hypothesis about what you want to do with your career, and then you take steps to prove or disprove whether you're headed in the right direction—that is, the right direction for you. In other words, you don't have to "have it all figured out" to make the next move, but you do need a solid footing—and this section will help you get one.

Once you've gained a solid understanding of what your dream job or career could look like, Part 2: Making Your Move will show you how to start tackling the nuts and bolts of getting a job. First, we will show you how to communicate who you are, how you can contribute, and why your experience is so valuable. Remember that under the old rules, if you were an elementary school teacher you'd look for a position in an elementary school; if you were a lawyer you would look for a job at a law firm; if you were an engineer at Intel you would look for a job higher up the ladder at Intel . . . or maybe at Dell. This would mean that you'd likely have a certain set of expected skills, education, and experience for such jobs, and you might not have to work all that hard to explain what those skills and experience were, or to sell yourself, your talents, and their relevance to employers.

Playing by the New Rules looks very different. With the expanded menu of career options comes an expanded menu of skill sets, but if you can't communicate that skill set—what your job experience really means—your options will be limited to existing jobs in whatever field you are currently in.

If you understand the New Rules, however, you can chart your own course. You can design a very different kind of resume from the resume of yore that contained only a past-tense description of tasks assigned. Instead you can describe the impact your skills have had in a way that is clearly transferable to the job you are trying to land. Part 2 of this book will show you exactly how to do this—so that any of those professional options you'd like to pursue will become well within your reach.

Then we will show you how you can craft compelling applications based on quality, not quantity, and ace every step of the interview process, from getting your foot in the door to getting what you want in the salary negotiation.

Finally, remember that the New Rules don't only apply to presenting yourself in such a way as to get that job, but also to what comes afterward: to acclimating at that job, thriving in that job, and then understanding where you want to go next. This is what's covered in Part 3: Charting Your Course Through the Modern Workplace, where we will show you how to control your destiny. Once you've landed the job you've been looking for, Part 3 covers the core "soft" skills you need to do the best work you can, regardless of what you do or where you are in your career. First impressions, communication, presenting to a group—these are the things you need to know, and we'll give you tricks and tips to enhance your value in the workplace and make it so much more obvious to your boss or employer that whatever level you're currently at, you're already getting ready to move ahead to the next one. You will learn how to build your confidence and your brand, enabling you to stand apart from other candidates, employees, managers, and leaders to thrive at the job of your dreams.

Throughout this book, you will hear stories from our community of Musers—what we call our loyal subscribers to The Muse—and from our own careers. You'll also find many exercises designed to guide you toward exploring your strengths and what you want in your career and to help keep you organized along the way—so don't hesitate to mark up these pages, or designate a notepad, or file on your phone or computer, as your Muse Notebook, and keep it handy so you can write things down as you go along.

Yes, it will be work, but wouldn't you rather dig in and invest in yourself now, knowing that the effort and work will pay dividends later? *The New Rules of Work* is all about knowing and believing that your career is in your hands. You are not a puppet on someone else's string. You are not a passive employee lying in wait for that one-of-a-kind boss to suddenly discover you and your hidden talents. No: *you* have the power, the know-how, and the drive to create the life you want. You can choose—and succeed at—a job that you truly love.

So welcome to the first day of the rest of your life. We are thrilled that you picked up this book: It's the first sign that you are committed to taking charge of your career and your future. It's a sign that, like most Musers, you are a go-getter, a participator, a person who wants to be a maker—not simply a bystander, watching the world whiz by. You want work to be a meaningful part of your life. You want to enjoy what you do. You want to feel empowered by your job. You want to make a difference.

Yes—we are making a lot of assumptions here. But we're standing behind them. And we want you to know at the outset of this adventure that the process you will undergo here is not just about getting a job—it's about developing some of the most important skills that will empower you for the rest of your life.

So buckle up for a great ride. We're going to take the future by storm, together.

—Kathryn and Alex

PART ONE

WHAT DO
I ACTUALLY
WANT?

CHAPTER ONE

Reflect: Understanding Yourself

THE OLD RULE: You graduated from high school, got into college, and chose a major that led to a specific career path. If, for example, you were an English major in college, you would go into book or magazine publishing, journalism, or teaching, or apply to law school. If you were an econ major, you more than likely planned on a job in finance. End of story.

THE NEW RULE: Your education taught you skills and gave you experiences that brought you to where you are today—but now your past is a platform to spring forward from, not a ball and chain. Plus, your career path can be plotted from not only your education, but also your strengths, innate talents, personal interests, and core values. Maybe you'll use the communication skills you picked up as an English major, your attention to detail, and your love for creativity and design to land a job in event planning. Or social media and community management. Or as a museum curator. The choice is yours.

THE KEYS TO YOUR KINGDOM

In the old world of work, the decisions you made at age seventeen or eighteen years old—like choosing a college and a major—dictated not only your first job but likely your entire career path (just think about how crazy that is!). Moreover, the trajectory of that path was assumed to be linear: that as time passed, you would naturally get promoted, sometimes move between companies, and eventually reach a high position from which you would someday retire. You probably followed that path blindly; since it so clearly dictated your direction, you didn't need to stop and think about what *you* wanted. As a result, there were few opportunities to change or adjust course based on your unique values, skills, and aspirations. Like in kindergarten, you were assigned a seat, and you were required to sit there for the rest of the year.

It seems pretty clear that that concept of a predetermined career path has outlived its relevance. Some years ago, it was briefly challenged by an overly expansive (and somewhat ungrounded) "follow your star" approach, where people were advised to "live their dreams and the money will follow." There was a sense that instead of a rigid, cookie-cutter plan, you didn't need any plan; that over time, as you moved from job to job, you would gain more and more self-knowledge, culminating in steady promotions and raises, and one day, the holy grail: comfortable retirement.

If only that always worked out.

The New Rules ask us to answer alternate questions that stem from a radically different point of view. Instead of assuming the path is preordained or that it will appear miraculously by simply wanting it to do so, we need to understand—and accept—that *we are in charge* of our own path. No major, no degree, no parental connections, no industry, company, or proverbial north star is going to determine or decide where we are going. It's up to us to choose the destination that is right for us and then design the path that will make it happen. Unlike in kindergarten, if we don't like the seat we've been assigned, we can get up and move to another. In fact, we can even pick up and switch to a new classroom or school altogether. We're in charge of ourselves.

And this is great: What freedom! What possibility! What self-empowerment! But we also know that with all of this potential for great success and happiness comes something else: What terror! What pressure! What stress! What if we make a mistake? A wrong move, a poor choice, a stupid decision? We'll be destined to wallow in a career we hate forever, right?

Wrong. Because here's another great thing about the New Rules: we live in a culture where the world of work will continue to change rapidly. That's why we think of career planning as a series of two-to-five-year steps, to make thoughtfully and one at a time. So you are here now, trying to figure out your path for just the next two to five years. Not for the rest of your life. Sure, if you have long-term plans, we will help you tailor your Now Plan to your Big Plan, but in general, the advice in this book is going to be focused on that two-to-five-year horizon; on getting you ready to make the most of what you are doing today and for the next few years. The best part is, you can return to it again and again—the practices and thought exercises we're doing here will serve you not only now, but next time you're ready for another step, shift, or reinvention in your career.

WHO ARE YOU NOW?

Of course, it's hard to shake off the urge to try to determine your life as soon as you graduate from college. We get it, because we've been there. Take Kathryn, for example. After majoring in international relations and French, she always dreamed that she would end up in foreign service or become a diplomat. Her interest in travel, her love of languages, and her natural inclination to jump in and solve problems seemed to fit exactly with the career she had imagined for herself. Yet a few weeks into what had seemed like a dream position working at the US embassy in Cyprus, Kathryn felt that interest wane. The problems her team was tackling were important, but solutions moved the needle by inches and progress could sometimes take years, requiring unbelievable patience. When colleagues noticed her penchant for offering to roll up her sleeves and get to work right away, they would laugh and suggest she consider a different field where she could make an impact more quickly. Kathryn's expectations ran smack into the realities of working in the foreign service, and she suddenly realized it might not be such a solid long-term fit after all.

It was as if a tether to her mental image of career satisfaction had been severed and she was totally adrift. "It was incredibly frustrating," she remembers. "I thought I had it all figured out, and suddenly I realized that I didn't know what I was doing for the next year, let alone for the rest of my life. I'd invested so much in a career path I was about to walk away from. It's funny to look back and remember how much I was worried I'd 'wasted' that time. But now I realize that those years were anything but. They were useful—time to test myself—and I'm not sure I'd be where I am today without them."

Alex had a similar experience. Growing up in France, a country where your high school choices still guide much of your career opportunity, she was forced to pick a direction at the age of fifteen. Between the sciences, literature, and economics, she picked the sciences. She was good at them, and they were valued highly in the French education system. Two years later, she again had to choose, this time between math, physics, and biology for her senior-year specialization. Alex chose biology and started learning about genetics by mating strains of fruit flies. She applied to college in the United States and moved across the Atlantic to start her studies, where she declared a major of molecular, cellular, and developmental biology (a fancy term for genetics). But after many long hours spent toiling in the lab her freshman year, Alex realized that as much as she loved *learning* about genetics, she didn't enjoy the day-to-day lab work that would be a big part of her job if she continued down this road. Genetics was an interest, yes, but not the right career for her. Facing this fact was hard, but it was also a pivotal moment that forced Alex to question her assumptions and embark on a journey of exploration and learning that brought her to the consulting company where she met Kathryn. Without these two diverging paths and the twists and turns we took, The Muse might never have come to be.

The point is: often what we *think* we want in our heads is actually very different from what we can learn we want in the day-to-day experience of actually living our careers. So even if you think you have your dream career all figured out, it's really important to go through the steps outlined in the next few chapters. The goal is to dig deep enough to have a clear understanding of what kind of job or career will make you truly happy.

What's different about today's rules is that they are all premised on your having a much keener, more concrete, and more nuanced under-standing of your values, interests, and motivations. This requires not only understanding what you enjoy and what you're good at, but also how these interests and skills stack up against other important personal pri-orities. How much money do you need to live comfortably? How much flexibility do you want in your weekly schedule? How important is your job title, the name of your company, the size of your office? What kind of impact do you want to have on the world? We're going to help you zero in on all of these variables so that you can not only succeed at defining your path, but enjoy getting to know yourself a bit better in the process!

Knowing yourself in this way is a huge part of finding the right job, by which we mean, the right job for you, right now. So in this chapter we'll address the first of what we call the Three R's: *Reflect*. And by the time you complete the exercises and steps in this chapter, you will feel much more confident in your understanding of what you are looking for in a ca-reer or job. Even if you have absolutely no idea what you want to do with your life, these tools can help point you in the right direction. Of course, if you've picked up this book already knowing who you are and what kind of job you are looking for, that's fine, too. You will still benefit from the exercises, as the reflection will only serve to underscore your confidence and sharpen your drive. *Wherever you are, we're here to take you forward.*

> It's time to develop a special kind of self-awareness:
> you are going to come to know yourself in an introspec-tive yet objective way. We are big believers in looking
> inward before you can expect to create the outward
> success you aspire to.

To start figuring out what you want in a job or in life, it helps to start by reflecting on who you are today. One of the early steps of this process is being brutally honest with *how* you are feeling (frazzled and fearful, confident and competent, muddled but also excited?) and *where* you are (in a current job that you despise, in a current job that's fine but not quite right, out of a job, living with your parents and unable to pay rent on your own place, in between a rock and a hard place?). You're going to ask yourself a couple of hard questions, but trust us, it'll be worth it.

QUESTION 1: WHAT DO YOU VALUE?

 Back in the 1970s, a few social scientists came up with a way for people to deepen their understanding of themselves by "clarifying their values." You can probably hear a bit of that seventies vibe in the language alone. But they were onto something: clarifying our values really helps when we are trying to figure out what we want in our lives.

In the context of creating a successful career plan, the word *values* refers to what in your work provides you with meaning and purpose. That might be a deep sense of creativity, or it might be making a positive contribution to society. In many ways, your values are more important than the type of work you're actually doing; in fact, numerous studies have shown that most people who pursue work that aligns with their values feel more satisfied *and* successful in their careers.

When it comes to charting a professional path, clarifying our own values can feel confusing. There are so many outside voices and perspectives that can clutter this very personal process: parents' expectations and advice, friends' choices, society's collective ideas about the "right" path. It's time to shut all those out. Remember, we're talking about *your* life— and *your* values—not your well-meaning mom's or dad's, not your favorite professor's, not your brilliant roommate's. They're yours, and yours alone.

The following exercise can help. We've created a list of personal values that often accompany work life; assign each value a number from 1 to 4.

1: Absolutely essential to me
2: Desirable, but not essential
3: Of neutral value—neither important nor unimportant to me
4: Not of value to me; I would prefer to avoid

Don't worry about spreading the numbers out evenly among the different categories—this isn't an exact science—but do try to keep the number of 1's to around three (which will help you with an exercise we'll walk you through later on!). Most important, though, just be honest and candid with yourself.

MISSION AND IMPACT

___ Social change: I want to make a contribution to society at large.

___ Service: I want to be directly involved in helping individuals.

___ Influence: I want my work to shape and influence the thinking of others.

___ Decision making: I want to have a meaningful role in deciding direction and policy in my field.

___ Ethics: I want my work to connect directly with my own principles and morals.

___ Community: I want my work to be of direct benefit to the community in which I live.

SOCIAL INTERACTION, COLLABORATION, AND TEAMWORK

___ Sociability: I want to engage regularly with people as part of my daily work.

___ Solitude: I want to work alone or mostly alone, without substantial engagement with others.

___ Teamwork: I want to work as part of a collaborative team on projects and assignments.

___ Management: I want to lead and directly supervise the work of others.

___ Autonomy: I want to work independently, with minimal direction or supervision.

ROUTINE

___ Deadlines: I want to work under time-sensitive conditions, where there is pressure to deliver.

___ Variation: I want my tasks and responsibilities to vary regularly.

___ Consistency: I want a routine of tasks and responsibilities that remains largely the same.

___ Detail: I want to engage in work where attention to detail, precision, and/or accuracy matter a great deal.

___ Flexibility: I want the ability to influence my schedule in a way that works for me.

___ Travel: I want to travel regularly for work, experiencing new places.

REWARD

___ Acknowledgment: I want to receive public acknowledgment for my professional accomplishments.

___ Compensation: I want my work to deliver significant financial reward.

___ Security: I want a position and a salary that are likely to remain secure.

___ Prestige: I want to work in a role or at a company that is valued by others.

CHALLENGE AND EXPRESSION

___ Expertise: I want to work hard toward expertise and mastery in my field.

___ Creativity: I want my work to have a strong element of creativity.

___ Competition: I want to work in an environment where my skills are tested against the skills of others.

___ Risk-taking: I want to experience a sense of risk and adventure in my work.

___ Thrill: I want my work to be exciting on a regular basis.

___ Physical engagement: I want my work to involve being physically active and using physical skills.

Take all the values you've ranked as 1, or essential, and list them:

_____   _____

_____   _____

_____   _____

_____   _____

These are the values that are most significant to you at this stage of your career. We say "at this stage" because our values don't remain static throughout our lives. When we are in our twenties, things like glamour and thrill, a company's mission, and opportunity for creative expression might be of the utmost importance. As we get older and maybe have a partner or children, security, flexibility, compensation, and a company's culture might become more critical. Remember that it's totally okay and normal for your priorities and preferences to change over time, so it can be helpful to revisit this exercise every two to five years to make sure your current path aligns with who you will have become.

QUESTION 2: WHAT'S YOUR CURRENT FRAME OF MIND?

When people sign up at The Muse, they are usually looking for something specific, whether it's a job, contacts, opportunities, or advice. Musers are often at some turning point in their lives and are in the midst of a bit of soul-searching. From speaking to them, we've found that in addition to taking stock of who you are from a personality perspective, it's also really helpful to know how you are feeling. Forgive the mini-therapy, and just hang with us for a few minutes as you respond to the following questions that are meant to tease out your frame of mind and take your emotional temperature:

1. On a scale of 1 (low) to 5 (high), how would you rate your confidence level? Perhaps you feel confident about some parts of your life or self and less confident about others. Feel free to give yourself multiple scores for a couple of different areas of your life.

   _____

   _____

   _____

   _____

2. How do you feel today? Use three adjectives to describe how you feel physically, emotionally, or spiritually.

_____

_____

_____

_____

3. What was the last thing you did or accomplished that made you feel proud of yourself? This can be as simple or profound as you'd like. Maybe you helped bring on a new client last week. Maybe you showed up for your best friend or your grandmother. Maybe you sent out three resumes. These are all actions that one can be proud of. Don't judge yourself. Simply write down what comes to mind.

_____

_____

_____

_____

_____

4. When did this event/achievement occur? Was it yesterday? Last week? Last month? Or years ago?

_____

_____

_____

_____

5. Do you feel the urge to change some aspect of your life? Your job? Yourself? Obviously, this is a big question that you can answer in many different ways. For your purposes right now at the beginning of this process, keep your response simple and choose one thing you wish to change. Be specific.

_____

_____

_____

_____

_____

> If you are feeling anxious or doubtful about a decision or job choice you've made in the past, don't ignore those feelings. Listen to yourself, your gut, and pay attention to what your misgivings are telling you. And if they're telling you you've made a mistake, don't panic. Remember: nearly everyone you admire has made career mistakes at one time or another. It's never too late to change courses. This process is all about learning how to adjust and pivot with wisdom and grace.

———

We know this process isn't easy! Self-awareness is hard. And the truth is, when it comes to deeply knowing and understanding who you are, there is no *one* right answer. But as you get closer and closer to *a* right answer, you'll start to know it. If you're still feeling confused and want to take an even deeper dive into your values, check out our list of the best career assessments or search TheMuse.com for "career quizzes."

In the next chapter, "Research" (the second of the Three R's), you are going to use the values we talked through above to guide your exploration of possible career paths. You won't have to dive in blindly; your values (and the exercises in the next chapter!) will help you break this task down into manageable steps as you narrow your interests, identify your priorities, and begin to make some practical decisions to guide your job search.

Onward!

Research: The Muse Method

for Laying Out a Full Set of Choices—Including Those You May Not Know You Have

---

THE OLD RULE: Traditionally, there were very few methods of getting career information or advice. During your college years, you relied upon a guidance counselor (or some lame, generic pamphlets) to help pick a major and then get you your first job. These choices were heavily influenced by who was around you—if one of your parents was an accountant, you were more likely to consider finance as an option. Once you landed at a company, you relied upon your manager or HR department to tell you what next role would be best for you. You could only see as far as the world you knew, and so the choices were limited to those handed to you.

THE NEW RULE: Now information is at our fingertips. The internet has made it easy to reach anyone and learn almost anything about a possible career. Even if no one you know is a comic book designer, for example, you can follow your favorite artists on their websites and social media platforms to learn about exactly what their job entails, and what education and career path they took to get there. Whether you're just starting your professional life or contemplating making a pivot, the options are truly unlimited, and all it takes is a web browser and a bit of curiosity and determination to explore them.

One of the rules of today's workplace is that the industry you're working in right now is not necessarily the one you'll stay in forever—in fact, it's easier than ever before to shift gears in your career. Moreover, the menu of possible roles you could have at any given company (what we'll be calling "functions" in this chapter) has been expanding rapidly over the past few decades, as the ever-increasing integration of technology in virtually every company or workplace has given rise to (technical and nontechnical) roles that never before existed. And, as technology gets more specialized and nuanced, so are the roles companies are looking to fill. In other words, today it's not unusual to find postings for jobs like "mobile designer" or "business systems analyst" or "web content director"—not just at technology companies and start-ups, but in just about every industry you can think of.

In this new landscape, if you think about a job as the combination of the function you perform for a company (for example, sales or marketing or project management) and the industry you've chosen (say, financial services or healthcare or media), then the choices have just multiplied, and the process of choosing a single job has gotten a whole lot more complicated!

That's exciting, but it's also pretty anxiety inducing. At each career decision point, you will encounter a large number of potential jobs—a combination of industry and function you could be in—that could be viable next steps for you. So how do you even get started sorting through all these options?

Essentially, you need one key thing: information. And lots of it.

In this chapter, you are going to take the new self-knowledge you gained in the last chapter and apply it directly to your job search.

But first, you need to do some homework; hence the name of the chapter: Research. Because how can you begin to think about what kind of job you want before getting clear on what exactly that job entails? And again, we're talking not just about the work itself here, but also how a given role lines up with your identified values and priorities.

That's why the research phase of this process is so crucial. This chapter will show you how to do this kind of background work before launching your resume out into the world.

THE MUSE METHOD: HOW IT WORKS

The Muse Method is designed to help you narrow down a seemingly infinite list of industries and functions to a manageable set of choices. You'll start by creating your own Muse Grid, which we'll explain in detail below. But before we get there, a few words about the mindset you should be in to get the most out of this first step of the process.

First of all, as you start organizing your thoughts, don't be afraid to be messy! When you make your Muse Grid, it can be as scribbly and filled with notes as you need it to be. In this phase we want you to think about things as freely as possible and explore to your heart's content.

As you're going through this process, we suggest looking back to your list of values regularly, reminding yourself of what's at the top of your Most Important list. As you begin this messy phase of researching your options, you may realize that your values have shifted a bit—and that's okay! Feel free to edit your list as needed as you learn more about yourself.

Finally, don't get too far ahead of yourself. Remember, right now, you should be thinking about the next two to five years of your career. Yep, only two to five years! A whole lot can change in even a few years (remember when there were no social media managers?), so there's no sense in trying to predict what the job landscape is going to look like a decade out. Right now, you're aiming to learn about what's possible for you in the *current* job market.

HOW LONG WILL THIS PROCESS TAKE?

Keep in mind that we don't want you to rush this process. You can be efficient, yes, but you must also be thoughtful. Gaining a true understanding of the industries and specific roles that you're considering requires significant background research. In most cases, especially if you're really unclear on your desired path, it may take about two months to do all the legwork required. Of course, if you have a rough idea of the field you want to be in and know a bit about it already, you might be able to knock your Muse Grid out in a couple of weeks (or one action-packed weekend!).

No matter where you're at, though, take your time! Think of the research stage as an investment in the future; the more you put in, the more you stand to gain later. The great thing about the research project is that not only will it help you narrow down your sea of options to find the job that's best, but you'll also meet people who can help you land the next step and may even end up being valuable contacts or mentors as you move further along in your career.

CREATE YOUR MUSE GRID

The goal of your Muse Grid is to keep this part of the research process organized, finite, and pointed toward a single goal: actually helping you make decisions about your career. In four steps, we'll go from a massive crawl of options out there to a manageably sized grid lining up those that hold the most appeal for *you*. Remember, here we'll be looking at both a job's **Function** (e.g., sales, product management, marketing) and the **Industry,** or sector (e.g., healthcare, tech, government). Later we'll worry about the specific **Companies** you might want to work for (e.g., Facebook, the Gates Foundation, Pfizer). Trust us, it will be much easier to identify companies once you've narrowed down your search by industry and function.

Think of the intersection of function and industry like choosing a restaurant. Picking an industry is like deciding to go out for Chinese food instead of French or Italian. Picking a function is like deciding you're in the mood for soup—but that could be ramen at the Japanese place or a French onion soup at the bistro. Choosing the perfect meal requires making both these decisions.

By the way, if you think you already know what specific field you want to be in, we still really encourage you to go through these steps to validate your hypothesis and learn more about that field in the process. The clearer you are on *why* you're interested in an industry or role, and the more knowledgably you can speak about it, the more convincing you will be when networking and interviewing.

Moreover, sometimes going through the grid-making process unearths doubts or questions that lead you to realize that you're perhaps conflating different interests: Maybe you aren't that interested in coding after all—you've been focused on it because you're after the energy of a start-up, but never considered that a product management role might be a better fit. Or maybe you've had your eye on working for a nonprofit because you want to feel like your career is making a difference—but you never considered that a for-profit education technology company might fulfill that same need.

One of our Musers, Sarah, shared with us how, after majoring in English lit and art history as an undergrad, and then earning an MA in literary studies, she thought the perfect industry for her would be book publishing, which would enable her to read, write, and interact with intellectuals from all walks of life. But after a year, she realized the job, at least for a few years, would be more about pushing paper and answering phones than it would be getting to know authors and engaging with their work. She felt stuck—like everything she had worked for was for naught—until she started researching other options. Now she's heading up business development for a start-up that specializes in self-publishing, working directly with authors to get them on the platform. It's an option she had never considered before, but one that's a much better fit for her values—and one that leaves her feeling far more fulfilled and challenged every day than a job at a traditional publishing house ever could.

CREATE YOUR MUSE GRID EXERCISE

STEP ONE

Consider the two lists below and circle all of the options for functions and industries that appeal to you in some way. Keep in mind there may be some overlap; for example, if you love finance, you might want to work in the accounting or financial planning division of a company in any industry, or you might want to work in the finance industry, in a number of functions. In cases like this, go ahead and circle them all. Our goal here is to cast the net as wide as possible. (Note: After this we'll use the shorthand "F&I" for functions and industries . . . but you'll know what we mean.)

As you review these lists, remember: these don't have to be functions you're currently qualified to do, or industries in which you already have experience—this is simply where you think you might *like* to be and what sort of skills you might *want* to possess. We all need to start in a new industry sometime, and it's entirely doable to transfer your existing skills into an entirely new realm or acquire brand-new ones as your career progresses. Truly. If you realize, for example, that you're passionate about a company's mission to connect produce farmers around the globe, but your background is in accounting, it's not too late to take a class on global agriculture, do an internship at a start-up, or get trained on a new skill that utilizes your accounting savvy!

Also note that this list includes just general categories; you can add to or adapt it to suit your needs. For example, say you're already pretty sure you want to be in sales in some capacity—you might want to add another layer of more specific functions to include inside sales, outside sales, account management, and sales training. Or if, for you, working in the fashion industry is a no-brainer, breaking that down to accessories, footwear, beauty, or men's fashion might be helpful.

Finally, if you're not sure what a role or function entails, look it up! We'll get to tools and resources to help you do that in just a minute. But for now just remember that the *Research* phase is crucial, so don't rush through. Be open-minded, too—you'd be surprised how many of us have stereotypes in our minds about a job (like what it means to be in "sales") that couldn't be further from the truth, and these preconceptions can keep us from exploring paths that might be fulfilling. Even if you're only mildly curious about a particular job, keep it on your list long enough to learn more about it. This stage of the process is all about keeping your options open, and there will be plenty of time later on to consolidate and narrow down.

Okay, so now it's time to get out your marker or your pen and select the functions that spark your interest. To make the process easier, also cross out anything you're pretty positive does *not* interest you.

FUNCTIONS

- ☐ Academics & Teaching
- ☐ Administrative & Support
- ☐ Business & Strategy
- ☐ Consulting & Advising
- ☐ Creative & Design
- ☐ Customer Service
- ☐ Data Analytics & Data Science
- ☐ Editorial
- ☐ Education
- ☐ Engineering (Software, Mechanical, Electrical, etc.)
- ☐ Entrepreneurship & Innovation
- ☐ Finance & Accounting
- ☐ Fundraising & Development
- ☐ General Management
- ☐ Healthcare & Medical Practice
- ☐ HR & Recruiting
- ☐ IT
- ☐ Legal
- ☐ Marketing or Advertising
- ☐ Operations
- ☐ PR
- ☐ Product & Project Management
- ☐ Sales (Corporate, Retail)
- ☐ Science/R&D
- ☐ Social Media & Community

INDUSTRIES

- ☐ Advertising & Agencies
- ☐ Architecture & Design
- ☐ Arts & Music
- ☐ Client Services & Consulting
- ☐ Consumer
- ☐ Education (K–12, Higher Ed)
- ☐ Energy & Natural Resources
- ☐ Entertainment & Gaming
- ☐ Fashion & Beauty
- ☐ Finance
- ☐ Food & Beverage
- ☐ Government & Policy
- ☐ Healthcare
- ☐ Journalism
- ☐ Law
- ☐ Law Enforcement & Security
- ☐ Manufacturing & Industrials
- ☐ Media & Publishing
- ☐ Military
- ☐ Nonprofit and/or Social Good
- ☐ Pharma & Biotech
- ☐ Real Estate
- ☐ Social Media
- ☐ Staffing & Recruiting
- ☐ Tech
- ☐ Telecommunications
- ☐ Travel & Hospitality
- ☐ Transportation & Logistics

STEP TWO

Now that you've circled the areas of interest, your next step is to **come up with seven F&Is** to put into your Muse Grid (below). Each of the seven can be a function or an industry—it's best to have a mix, but it's okay if the list isn't perfectly balanced. Obviously, you should pick the items that are most compelling or provoke the most curiosity. You may have to rely on your gut a little bit here, and that's okay. It's all part of the process.

Again, you should also feel free to add any F or I to our list, or to re-phrase or narrow an F or I that's on there—say, to narrow "Nonprofit" to "Global health nonprofit"—especially if you know specifically what you want to research. This is supposed to be an exploratory phase, so in general we recommend not getting too narrow too fast! But it's your grid, so the most important thing is to set it up in a way that's most useful to you.

If you have more than seven options at this point, we suggest going back through your master list and eliminating the ones you're least excited about. You can keep these "B-listers" on the sidelines for now—if you find yourself wishing you hadn't crossed one of them off, you can always bring it back later.

1. _____
2. _____
3. _____
4. _____
5. _____
6. _____
7. _____

FUNCTION SHORTLIST	#1: Flexibility	#2: Compensation	#3: Creativity
1: Sales			
2: Marketing			
3: PR			
INDUSTRY SHORTLIST			
4: Journalism			
5: Tech			
6: Finance			
7: Travel			

YOUR GUT CHECK

What's a gut check and why is it important? In short, it's about learning how to pay attention to your instincts and trust yourself. It's not an excuse to skip research; instead it's a way to pair how you feel about something with what you know about something. We'll have more to say about this later, but for now, just know it's okay to listen to your intuition. You want a job that feeds you as a whole person, so you have to use your whole person to find that job.

STEP THREE

Return to your notes from Chapter 1, pull up your list of values, and select the four or five that are most important for you at this time (any more and it's hard to optimize for all of them, though if you've narrowed your values to two or three, that's fine too!). Now enter them in the boxes that run across the top of the Muse Grid, as shown opposite.

Below is an example of what the Muse Grid should look like at this point. This is a real-life example from a friend of ours named Chloe who has graciously agreed to let us use her Muse Grid and her experience with the Muse Method to show you how it works. Thanks, Chloe! (For a blank copy of the chart see pages 38–39, or download one from themuse.com/thenewrules.)

In the first column, Chloe has listed the top seven F&Is of interest. And across the top row, she's penned in her top three values—flexibility, compensation, and creativity—which she narrowed down from the larger list she made in the last chapter.

At this point you should be ready to follow Chloe's lead and create your own grid. The next step? To fill all those empty squares in! Each box is the intersection between one of your seven F&Is and one of your values, and you are now going to dig in and do research to figure out how each F&I lines up with each of them. (Don't worry—we'll walk you through the process.)

At this point, you may feel like all you have are questions, especially if you've included functions or industries that you're not currently in (which we encourage you to do!). This is a good thing, because having specific questions will be very helpful when it comes time for the next step—information-gathering. So write down those questions right in the margins of your Muse Grid, or jot them down in your Muse notebook.

PASSION OR PROFESSION?

You may have noticed that we haven't touted the "Follow your passion" mantra yet in this book. Not because we don't believe that's important. We very much believe in being passionate about your work! We just believe that finding your passion isn't just about looking at what you love doing—it's about assessing what your values are and

aligning your career wants with what will practically bring you fulfillment and purpose in your day-to-day.

In fact, it's important to distinguish between professional passions
and hobbies. Say you studied ballet for ten years, and as you've been
plotting your career next steps, you've realized that anything to do
with ballet and dance still gets you excited and energized. While you
fill out your Muse Grid, you should take some time to learn about what
career paths look like in those fields—say, an event planner at a the-
ater or dance venue, or in an administrative or PR role with a dance
troupe. But you should hold these fields to the same scrutiny you hold
everything else to: Do the realistic jobs out there match up with what's
important to you? If they do, great! If they don't, that's okay, too—it's
just a sign that dance should probably stay a hobby, not a job.

Of course, sometimes the decision won't be quite so clear-cut, and
may require a little thinking outside the box. That's fine! Remember,
your love of cooking doesn't need to lead you into a restaurant kitchen
or a catering company. The creativity and improvisational skills you've
developed experimenting with recipes might find a different outlet in
advertising or even sales. Or your love of bringing people together for
food and drink could be a sign that you're primed for a career in event
planning.

Again, though, when you think about passion, it helps to think
about activities at work that have gotten you excited and engaged.
Maybe the most fun you've had at your job is when you got to collaborate with the marketing team on an ad campaign, or when you
were on point for organizing a big conference and pulled it off without
a hitch. Or let's say you work in sales and currently have clients in several industries, but realize that all the most exciting work you've had
has come from your music industry clients. In this case, following your
passion isn't about making a radical change from the 9-to-5, but about
making a career pivot (maybe small, maybe big). It could be to a role in
the marketing department where you focus just on the music service
accounts, or maybe another sales job, but this time at a company that

manages record labels. Make sure those functions or industries are on your Muse Grid! After all, the point of doing the grid in the first place is to overturn assumptions, explore functions and industries you may not even have known existed, and help you gain insight into how well each of these career moves might actually suit you.

STEP FOUR

In this step, you are going to fill out as much of your Muse Grid as you can with as much information as you can about roles, companies, and even big influencers in each F&I, as they pertain to each of your values, using two simple tools. What should you be looking for? Well, that's exactly where your values come in. There are an infinite number of things you could learn about a specific field, but the purpose of your Muse Grid is to make sure you learn about the aspects most important to you, and to focus your efforts.

For example, Chloe's top value is flexibility, so she's going to spend a lot of time learning about the day-to-day work schedules for roles in each of her F&Is. She may fill in things like, "Hours can be long close to a product launch, but seems cyclical" or "High geographic flexibility—can work from anywhere!" in her grid. Perhaps flexibility isn't as important to you as upward mobility—in which case, you'll spend time learning about people's career paths, and filling in your Muse grid with things like how quickly employees tend to be promoted and the training and experiences that are required to get there.

As you do this, don't worry if some squares have more info than others, don't worry if some are blank for now, and don't worry if you're writing down your "best guess" or notes to yourself to come back to later.

———

Okay, so how will you find all of this information? By working through the two tools below.

FUNCTION SHORTLIST	*Value 1*
1.	
2.	
3.	
INDUSTRY SHORTLIST	
4.	
5.	
6.	
7.	

Value 2	Value 3

TOOL 1: ONLINE IMMERSION

Luckily, you're not looking for a job before the internet existed! You're likely already quite skilled at Google-stalking and other forms of gathering information online (we know what you're capable of on Facebook!), so this is a great place to put those skills to work.

Here are some tips for where to start.

DIVE INTO INDUSTRY, COMPANY, AND BRAND WEBSITES

Look at the industries that you put on your list. Use resources like Bloomberg's *Industry Market Leaders* or even a Google search to identify the top companies in a given industry, from large to small. You can also use industry websites, the regular "Best Companies" articles in *Forbes* and The Muse, or the Inc. 5000 list for smaller, fast-growing companies for inspiration.

Pick a few interesting companies for each of your functions or your industries, and then spend ten minutes on each company's website to look at how it describes itself and what job listings are available. Now, don't stress about picking the "right" companies—these aren't places you're committing to work for or even apply to. This activity is all about using some top, highly researchable companies as tools to help show you the kinds of services they provide, the jobs they may have listed and their requirements, the backgrounds of top employees, and anything else that helps add to your understanding of the industry as a whole.

Note: The photo and video "behind the scenes" profiles of companies on TheMuse.com are a great place to start! Also, you may want to use your Muse Notebook to write down any additional notes you want to make—whether it's companies you want to look up, to-dos for your next research session, or anything else that is helpful to you.

As you browse, this is a chance to dig up clues as to how each F&I matches your values. So Chloe might ask herself, do the job descriptions at each company give insight into flexibility, compensation, or opportunity to be creative? For example, if a job description for a customer service position details specific hours you'll need to work, that suggests that flexibility could be low for that sort of role. On the other hand, if you see on a medical start-up's "contact us" page that they seem to have employees based all over the country, that could be a sign that this is an industry that is flexible about telecommuting. Or, if the job descriptions for a particular role tend to use words like *innovative, self-starter,* and *problem-solving,* there's a good chance that this is a job in which you'll get to showcase your creativity (that goes double for companies who announce having just won the "most innovative X" on their home pages).

The point is, be a career sleuth and find the nuggets of information relevant to you. As you see patterns, you can start forming hypotheses (to be tested later!) as to what that function or industry is like, along each of the dimensions you care about.

LEVERAGE LINKEDIN

In the days before LinkedIn, it was much more difficult to find out someone's career history without asking him or her directly. Now that we have this monster database of personal and professional information, we can save the face time for even more meaningful conversation. So where do you start when using LinkedIn?

First, look up the profiles of individuals you respect or admire whom you've connected with in your career—or who you just think are interesting—to see what roles they've had on their way to success. This could be a former boss or colleague, someone you knew from college or maybe met at a party, or even a name you know by reputation only. Take note of any details that catch your interest or raise questions, and add these to the master list on your grid. For example, Chloe had the idea to look up a high school classmate whom she always thought of as a creative type, and found that he was now working in consultative sales—an industry she'd never even heard of! One of his LinkedIn recommenders praised him for his creativity, which really caught her interest, as Chloe hadn't previously thought of sales as a very creative field. She wrote down on her grid to find out more about consultative sales.

To follow the trail further, you can also look at the "People Also Viewed" feature. This is a good way to explore jobs in similar but slightly different functions and industries than those you might have had on your list; for example, if you are viewing the profile of someone who does graphic design for apps, the LinkedIn algorithm might suggest you view the profile of an art director at a mobile advertising company. Or, if you are looking at the profile of someone who does consulting for a global financial institution, the algorithm might suggest you view the page of a chief strategy officer at a small venture capital firm or start-up. Either way, it will broaden your knowledge and your horizons!

USING LINKEDIN IN PRIVATE MODE

If you aren't sure you want other LinkedIn users to be able to see that you have viewed their profiles, you can sign out of your LinkedIn account and use the site anonymously, or do so through your settings. Or you can leave yourself signed in so that when your prospective contact sees you have viewed his or her profile, your name can make its first impression.

As you're exploring, you'll also notice that some industries seem to have their own language and jargon. Don't be intimidated, though: if you come across a phrase or word that seems unfamiliar, take the opportunity to research what it means and how it's used. Exposing yourself to the vocabulary and vernacular of a particular role or field will only help you when it comes time to build your personal brand and enhance your networking skills (both of which we get to later on in the book).

As you browse, keep a running list of people who are in interesting positions, or contacts of friends or colleagues who might be helpful to talk to. Make notes to yourself about these people in your Muse Notebook—they're perfect candidates for the one-on-one conversations you'll be setting up shortly!

Once you've spent some time doing your online immersion, add a High/Medium/Low score to each box on your Muse Grid as a rough measure of how enticing the function or industry is to you in each dimension; that is, how well it appears to be lining up with each of your values. You don't have to know everything yet—remember, you are still in the research stage of the process. For now, just put down a score that reflects your best guess based on what you've learned at this point.

After a couple of hours of online immersion, Chloe felt ready to start filling in her grid. Specifically, it had become clearer that her so-called dream job in journalism—what she had been telling people recently she wanted to do with her life—wasn't matching up very well at all with her top three values. A job as a writer or reporter might offer some outlet for creativity, she was learning, but it didn't offer much in terms of flexibility or compensation. After a gut check, she was able to be honest enough with herself that her true priorities didn't mesh with the reality of journalism, and she decided to turn her research focus to some of her other options.

HOW LONG WILL ALL THIS RESEARCH TAKE?!

All of this exploration takes time, and if you are really serious about launching the next phase of your career, we recommend devoting a minimum of ten hours a week to the research phase. We know that can sound a bit like having a second job (and in some ways it is), and if you are currently employed, or in school, you may feel that you don't have that luxury. But think about it this way: what if putting the effort into really thinking about your options could save you the headache—not to mention the heartache—of finding yourself in the wrong job altogether and having to do it all over again? Plus, when you think about it, isn't ten hours a week a pretty small investment to make in your future happiness?

Of course, it's easy to make excuses and keep pushing off career exploration for "just another day" until months have passed. To avoid this, we recommend a technique called calendar blocking to organize yourself. If you're finding that time just keeps getting away from you as you try to start this process, read more about calendar blocking and how to do it on page 276.

TOOL 2: MINING THE FIELD

Once you've spent some time immersing yourself in online research, you may have reached some conclusions about your F&Is, but you'll likely have generated quite a few questions, as well. And one of the most effective tools for getting answers, and for filling out those F&Is you're stuck on, is, quite simply, to talk with people who are actually working in them.

We're sure that you've heard of the "informational interview," which is not really an interview in the traditional job-hunting sense, but rather a meeting with the purpose of learning more about a given career path, company, or job. This can be a great tool for networking and getting your foot in the door once you're a bit further along in your job search, and we'll talk more about that process in Chapter 5. But for now, think of them for the purpose of uncovering more details about the career paths you're exploring: to test the hypotheses you formed during online immersion, to get answers to questions that surfaced, and to update your Muse Grid with a more complete picture of how your F&Is and values are aligning.

Okay, before we go any further we want to acknowledge that this might sound a little scary. The prospect of reaching out to strangers (especially impressive strangers, who have jobs you admire!) can be intimidating. But there are a couple of things to keep in mind. First, trust us when we say that most people are *happy* to share their stories and experiences with others, especially if you ask in the right way (more on that in a sec). Because the truth is, no one got to where they are today without help from someone, and each person you are about to reach out to probably went through the same process at some point!

Second, meeting new people and asking for their advice will definitely get easier as you go along. Really. Once you start doing it and seeing just how nonscary (and helpful!) it can be, you'll be that much more confident and inspired to keep going.

Now that we have the pep talk out of the way, let's look at some initial steps.

CHOOSE THE RIGHT PEOPLE

So you know you should get out there and start talking to people—but who? Through your online immersion, you likely came across people whom you know somewhat or have a loose connection to. These people are a great place to start! You don't have to know every person you reach out to, but people you have some kind of connection to are generally more likely to respond.

When narrowing down your list of people to talk to, try sorting them by function and industry—the ones who are a fit in both categories, or are in a category you have the most questions about, are likely to be most helpful. For example, Chloe had formed the hypothesis, which she was eager to confirm, that the compensation for PR jobs was best at big firms, so she prioritized connecting with people who were working at major PR companies. She was particularly thrilled when she found she had a LinkedIn connection who now did PR in the tech industry, so she could ask questions about both PR and tech at the same time.

If you have access to a relevant alumni community or other network—say, a women-in-communications group, or local meetup for engineers—you can also peruse these sources for people who might be helpful to you. Generally these types of groups post their members' profiles publicly, so as with LinkedIn, you'll often have the opportunity to look at where these people started their career and what moves they made along the way (not to mention the fact that networking and meetup groups will often post the email or contact information you're looking for).

And even if your college days are by now a distant memory, alumni groups in particular can be great resources, since sharing a common alma mater (or better yet a common major or athletic or student group) will increase your chances of getting a reply—and likely when you do meet, you'll forge a stronger bond, which will make them more eager to help with your job search down the line. For example, as Kathryn was considering next steps after leaving McKinsey (and before starting The Muse), she connected with a former colleague who was in the early stages of starting a business himself, and who was able to talk to her honestly about the ups and downs of entrepreneurship. After a few conversations, she even ended up joining him on several sales trips for his nascent company's products, giving her even more insight into the day-to-day of an early-stage start-up CEO.

Note: While you might be tempted to reach out to high-level executives or the most impressive people you can find, it's often a better approach to look for people who are just one or two steps above where you want to be. They're more likely to give you information that will be helpful to you (remember, we're looking at where you want to be in two to five years, not twenty)—plus, they're usually a lot less busy!

SEND THE RIGHT EMAIL

While it's smart to use your networks and LinkedIn to find people, we recommend reaching out to them over email rather than messaging them through the site. While you may be checking LinkedIn every day, most people aren't, so you're more likely to get a quick response over email.

What should that email look like? Basically, you'll want to do three things—and you'll want to do them as clearly and concisely as possible:

- Introduce who you are
- State exactly why you're reaching out and what you're hoping to learn
- Make a request for a brief conversation

Here's a template that one of our contributors, Aja Frost, created for our job seekers on The Muse:

Dear [first name],

My name is [your name], and I'm a [job title] who works in [your location]. I'm reaching out because [reason why you want to speak with this person]. I'd love to learn more about [two or three things you'd like to learn from the person].

I'm sure you're busy, so even 20 minutes would be appreciated.

Thanks so much,

[Your name]

It's brief, it's specific, and it tells the recipient exactly what you're looking for. Easy enough, right?

Note: Not everyone will respond, and that's okay—people are busy! Depending on the industry and seniority of whom you're reaching out to, you can expect anywhere from a 30 to 80 percent success rate. If yours is on the low end, please don't take it personally. Just focus on making the most of your time with the people who graciously agreed to meet.

MAKE THE MOST OF YOUR TIME

So someone's agreed to sit down with you. What now?

Well, you certainly don't want to waste time talking through questions you can get answered on LinkedIn! Go in with a list of questions for each person that's specific to the gaps in your knowledge and what you want to know most.

Here are a few to get you started:

- What's different about working at your company than most companies in the industry?
- As a [job title], what are you working on right now? What's the best part of your day, and what's the least exciting?
- What should someone who wants to break into the field be doing now?

- Who would do really well in this field? Who wouldn't?
- What are the most annoying parts of your job? What parts of your job make everything else worth it?

Take extensive notes, and learn as much as you can. Then stay in touch with your new contact! We'll go into this more in later chapters, but for now know that this is an important relationship you'll likely want to maintain for the long haul.

MOVING FROM 7 TO 3:
TIME TO NARROW IT ALL DOWN!

After a month of online immersion and mining the field, Chloe was pretty surprised by what she'd learned. Her completed Muse Grid is below, so you can see where she landed.

Like Chloe, you began the *Research* phase by combing through some very long lists of functions and industries, which you narrowed down to a master list of seven. Through online immersion and mining the field, and a whole bunch of hard work, you've now gotten insight into what each F&I is really like. You put hypotheses in your Muse Grid, talked to people to test them, and now have a much clearer idea about how each F&I matches up to your values and priorities.

Now the fun part: it's time to go back to your messy, marvelous Muse Grid and decide what you can cross out (trust us, this is going to feel great, kind of like checking something huge off your to-do list). In addition to asking whether each path lines up with your values, you need to ask yourself if you'd really want to pursue it as a career. For Chloe, journalism was easy to cross off once she saw that it wouldn't offer her flexibility or compensation, two of her three top values. But she still wondered if there might be a career in the travel industry— maybe being a travel writer—that would be a good fit.

Just like Chloe, you might easily see a number of F&Is that you can cross out, whether they seem unrealistic, a poor fit with your values, or just not that interesting now that you know more about them. Do any of your F&Is have mostly "Low" scores in the value columns? Probably not a good fit! If some F's or I's in your grid are looking borderline— you aren't sure you want to pursue them but aren't ready to give up on them yet, either—see what you can do to research them further. Have you tapped all your contacts and the contacts of contacts? Done all the informational interviews? Read enough about the leading companies?

Your goal at this point should be to get your list down to a maximum of three F&Is or career paths, since you want to be really focused as you enter the next phase. You'll be mapping the path to each career and coming up with an action plan—which is exciting stuff! But you're likely to feel spread too thin and overwhelmed if you're trying to map out five career paths instead of two to three. So do yourself a favor and spend as much time as you need now in the *Research* phase to get that list whittled down. The more information you gather, the more you will be able to narrow. And if your chart still doesn't clearly present you with the top three options, it's okay to walk away from it for a bit, do a gut check, and come back later. We know it can feel nerve-racking to limit your options, but just like before, you can keep those "B-listers" that don't make the cut on the sidelines, and bring any one of them back later if you want to.

Now it's time for the action plan. For some of you, it might be very clear what to do next. But for others, you might need to gather more information to narrow down your remaining choices into actionable next steps. That's where we're going next.

CHLOE'S MUSE GRID

SHORTLIST	#1: Flexibility
1: Sales (Function)	High geo flexibility (can usually find work anywhere), remote & flex work usually possible
2: Marketing (Function)	Medium. Most companies have marketing staff but switching jobs can be harder. Consulting work definitely possible
3: PR (Function)	Medium. Hours can be long close to a launch, but seems cyclical. Also pretty high geo flexibility for companies (not so much for PR firms—big cities mostly)
4: Tech (Industry)	Medium to High. Geo isn't all that flexible, but day-to-day hours are. Long hours but can make your own schedule
5: Finance (Industry)	Medium/Low: Finance jobs often require long hours in the office, though there are exceptions
6: Travel (Industry)	Medium: lots of travel flexibility, which is cool! But not a huge number of companies I'd be interested in working for
7: Rejected: Journalism (Industry)	Medium/Low: Journalism jobs often require long hours, though there are exceptions

#2: Compensation	#3: Creativity
High compensation: Sales are usually some of the highest paid employees within a company, though starting salaries can be low, and you have to earn commission	Medium to low: Many salespeople don't get to create products, only sell them. Start-ups are pretty similar—though sometimes have opportunities to work with product team on product updates/features, which is cool. Consultative sales can be pretty creative
Low: Marketing is usually lower compensated until senior leadership is reached (unless you have a sought-after specialization)	High: Marketing allows for a high degree of creativity in most jobs
Medium: PR firms pay reasonably well, but PR at a company might not	Medium: Seems to depend a lot on the company, job can be very schedule/organization oriented, or work more closely with creative/marketing teams. Not sure where to put this, but also get to work with journalists . . . sort of cool since I no longer think journalism itself is an option
Medium: high compensation in some larger tech firms but lower salary for start-ups. Best-paid employees seem to be engineers	High: Tech allows for a high degree of creativity in most companies; a lot of innovation in this space. Lots of opportunity to build things at start-ups
High: overall, high compensation across the board!	Low: seems like a pretty traditional industry
Medium: depends on role, but isn't a big perk across the board	Medium/Low: seems like a pretty traditional industry, unless you're at a newer/smaller company
Low: Journalism is not a career most people enter for the money!	Medium: Writing is inherently creative, but depending on the type of journalism some journalists report they feel like they are too beholden to the 24/7 news cycle or to press releases

CHAPTER THREE

Refine: Choosing (and Trying Out) Your Next Steps

THE OLD RULE: Your passions and motivations didn't matter in career decisions. You were practical, and followed a well-trodden path. If you enjoyed doing something other than the career you chose for yourself at age eighteen or twenty-two, that could become your hobby, or just another "what if" dream that was never pursued.

THE NEW RULE: What you want matters. Choosing the right next step for your career is a deeply personal decision and it's not one you can make overnight. It's now not only okay, but also essential to experiment with multiple options before committing yourself.

Congratulations! You've gone through some great Reflection and Research and now you are ready to *Refine* your Muse Grid. While you spent a lot of time in Chapter 2 doing homework, seeking out information, and talking to people, this phase of the process is when you dig deep, take a long hard look at your grid, understand what it will take to pursue your top options, perhaps do some experimentation, and use your gut check to home in on what you want and what you don't want.

Remember, this isn't about finding the perfect career forevermore—it's about finding a job that's the best fit for you right now. Maybe your choices will be obvious, but maybe they won't. There's no magic formula to get from a few options to one action plan, but this chapter will walk you through what you need to do in order to get there.

But first, we want to remind you that just as you can't expect to find a soul mate on the first date, finding work that fulfills you doesn't always happen on the first try, either. Understanding what's meaningful to you takes time, and answers may not truly emerge until you've been out in the world testing and experimenting, trying out different options, and challenging yourself at different levels. And that's exactly what we'll talk about next.

GIVING IT A WHIRL:
TEST-DRIVING YOUR CAREER PATHS

Throughout this process, you've spent a lot of time talking to people, but you've also spent a lot of time in your head. And the truth is, even if you think you would be happy in a particular career path, sometimes you don't know until you try it. Which is why we recommend, once you've narrowed your grid down to a few options, that you start taking small steps that'll help you test-drive those potential career paths.

This has an added benefit of giving you real-life experience that you can put on your resume and talk about when you're applying to jobs. We'll talk about this in detail in a few chapters, but your resume actually doesn't have to only include full-time positions! Part-time jobs, freelance gigs, internships, and even volunteer and pro bono work can go a long way in showing an employer that you don't just have the desire to work in a particular field, you've taken real action steps to get there.

Here are a few test-drive options to consider:

BE A SHADOW

Take the informational interview one step further, and ask a contact if you can shadow him or her for a half day at the office. Seeing what a day of work looks like can be a whole different ball game than being told!

TRY AN INTERNSHIP

Many people believe that internships are just for college students, but in reality, anyone can get a part-time or summer internship. We've had several interns at The Muse who've been working for a while but who are changing career paths, and a part-time internship outside of their current job has helped them make that shift. No matter where you are on your career journey, a few months actually working in a field you're interested in can tell you a lot about whether you're excited by the day-to-day job duties.

TAKE A CLASS

There are countless options for education these days, particularly on-line, with sites like Udemy and Coursera, and MOOCs (massive open online courses) from top-tier universities offering courses on literally thousands of professional topics—from interior design to programming languages to accounting and finance—and often for free. Yes, you'll gain knowledge from these courses and can put those credentials on your resume, but often the real benefit is understanding whether or not you truly get excited over the subject matter. If you're pumped to do your homework, or are driven to do additional "recommended reading" listed on the course syllabus, that's a pretty good sign that this is an area in which you'd like to work.

IMMERSE YOURSELF IN THE FIELD

Industry blogs, newsletters, conferences, events, podcasts . . . no matter what job you're interested in, there are so many options for learning more about an F or I. Again, maybe you'll find yourself geeking out over the topics you're learning about, or maybe you'll want to turn on Netflix instead—but either way, you'll have more insight into whether it's the path for you.

TAKE ON A PROJECT AT YOUR CURRENT JOB

Okay, this isn't an option if you're currently an engineer and you want to be a nurse practitioner, but in many situations, you might be able to find someone who does what you want to do without looking further than your own office! Ask if you can sit in on some of their meetings, join a project team, or see if there's a project that no one's really tackling that you could pick up on the side. We once had an employee at The Muse who was working in operations but wanted to learn more about PR. At the time, we didn't have anyone doing PR, so she asked to take it on, on top of her current responsibilities. How could we say no? Jumping in feet-first like she did forced her to learn a whole lot about the day-to-day realities of the role—and fast. And not only did she learn that she did enjoy it quite a bit, but she ended up being so helpful to the company that PR soon became a big part of her full-time job.

VOLUNTEER OR FREELANCE

Unless your employer has a restriction against it (and yes, some do, so you should check out your employment agreement and employee handbook!), there's a good chance you can test out certain career paths on the side, by volunteering at a nonprofit or helping out small businesses on a freelance basis. For example, a friend of Kathryn's was looking to transition to a career in social media. Instead of making a full-time leap right away, she volunteered to take on social media for a small local organization for a few months. By the end, not only did she confirm her hypothesis that this was what she wanted to do with the next few years of her life, but she was able to make a better leap to a new position based on real results she could show from that experience.

NEED MORE HELP? TALK TO SOMEONE

If you're really struggling to plot your next steps, know that you're not alone. Many people get stuck at this stage of the process, especially if they're just starting out on their career or making a dramatic change from what they were doing before. It's daunting! If you're really not sure how to move forward, it might be helpful to talk to a trusted mentor or advisor, or even a career coach. Many of our readers come to

The Muse's Coach Connect when they're feeling unsure and walk away with an action plan that helps them move forward.

IDENTIFY YOUR DREAM COMPANIES

As you've been researching companies, reading, volunteering, and talking to people to get a better sense of the industries you're interested in, you will likely start coming across employers you'd love to work for someday. No, you're probably not ready to start applying to jobs just yet—or maybe you're not even totally sure of what you want to do—but it can still be helpful to keep a running list of possible dream companies. It'll make life easier once you do start sending out applications, and it'll also help you keep refining your hypothesis about the type of work you want to do, the type of employers that are interesting to you, and the type of people you want to work with.

At this stage in the process, don't be afraid to think big! What brands do you love? Where have you always thought about working? Zappos? Disney? Facebook? Apple? Ralph Lauren? Of course, don't make the mistake of considering only the most famous employers, or most popular brands you love; also keep an eye out for lesser-known companies your contacts are working at and pay attention to new players in the space. Also think about the companies you browsed while creating your Muse Grid. Jot all of these down below.

And remember, you don't have to have a complete list now! The key is to begin keeping notes, adding more as you come across new employers that interest you. Later, you'll have a targeted list of companies that you regularly check in on, and learn more about by following their key players in the press, online, and through their websites.

_____   _____

_____   _____

_____   _____

_____   _____

_____   _____

PLOT YOUR PLAN

As you're thinking about your passion and trying out some of the things you're interested in, it's also smart to look practically at what steps you'll need to take to land that role.

For some, it's a matter of identifying your relevant transferable skills, starting to build your personal brand in a field, and networking with contacts who can help you get your foot in the door (more on this in the coming chapters). Often, your existing skills are more transferable than you think; as an example, on our sales team at The Muse, we've had people come from retail, government, and financial positions—and they're all top performers!

But for other career paths, there are additional necessary steps to take before you can start applying for positions. Graphic designers and developers, for example, need not just familiarity, but experience with all kinds of different software programs. Some community service jobs require a degree in social work or psychology. And you can't exactly become a surgeon or a financial planner or a human rights lawyer overnight! Many jobs very well might require specialized training, a certification, or a graduate degree—all steps that'll require quite a bit of time, money, and planning.

Throughout the process of creating your Muse Grid, researching various career paths online, and talking to people about how they got to where they are today, you likely gathered some of this information. But if you haven't already, it's time to really nail down what moving toward the path or paths you're considering may look like. You may want to add another row to your Muse Grid, or create a new document with your narrowed-down option set, and map out the logistics. What is required to launch a career in this field? What will that cost in time and money? Do you need to pursue education full-time, or can you take classes and gain skills while you're working?

Note: It's easy to get frustrated at this step of the process, especially if one of your dream careers seems like a lot of work—or even out of reach. But it's important to take things one step at a time and remember:

You're not making any decisions yet! You're still in research and refining mode.

Plus, though the road to your dream position may seem long, if it's the right path for you, it's definitely worth it. Take one of our Musers, Rick, who always thought he wanted to spend his career doing scientific research. Many of his peers headed to medical school right after college, while he accepted a full-time research job with a pharmaceutical research organization. After a couple of years, though, he realized that he hated sitting at a desk all day long and wanted to be more hands-on with patients, so he decided to go back to med school—from which he graduated in another three years.

It was no easy feat! In his mid-twenties, he quit his job, moved back to his hometown to live with his parents, and spent a year shadowing doctors, volunteering at a hospital, studying for the MCAT, and ultimately applying to and enrolling in medical school.

At the time, it seemed like a big step backward for him, and there were moments, especially looking around at his former classmates who were moving up and up in their careers, that felt disheartening. But today Rick works as an emergency medicine resident, a job that aligns much more with his work values than his research position did. Taking that initial step back was incredibly difficult, but if he hadn't done it, he'd still be in a job that wasn't right for him. It was an investment in his future that made his ultimate career goals possible.

Our point is, if it seems like a lot of work to start your desired career path, or pivot from one field to another, don't be discouraged. Certainly, you should weigh the costs of the time, energy, and money each step will require. The commitment of years in school and thousands of dollars in student loans is nothing to take lightly! But if you truly want to pursue something, it's worth exploring the path it will take to get there.

FACE YOUR FEARS—AND MOVE BEYOND THEM

Many people don't ever pursue the work that truly lights them up because they're afraid. Afraid of failing, afraid of not knowing how things will turn out, afraid of being afraid. It's easy to let fear get in the way of change. But you don't have to!

Conquering fear isn't about being the bravest person who ever lived. It's about knowing how not to let fear stop you from moving forward in pursuit of your goals. These steps can help.

1. IDENTIFY THE AREAS WHERE YOU NEED HELP

Rather than getting stuck because of the gaps in your skills and experience, address those gaps head-on. There's nothing to be ashamed of, and no reason to be held back by not being great at or experienced in everything. What's important is the ability to know where you're vulnerable, and find ways to help you become stronger. Here's an exercise that can help: Write down a list of your gaps or challenges, and then identify one person you could talk to about each—whether it's a friend who's recently made a job transition or someone who works in that industry. Then reach out to them for ideas on what steps you can take to start beefing up your knowledge or experience in those areas.

2. RECOGNIZE YOUR STRENGTHS

Just as important as knowing your weak spots is knowing where you shine—and being able to give yourself credit for those skills and attributes at which you excel. When fear and insecurity creep in, these are the points of pride you can turn to for a shot of confidence and courage. If you're not sure what your strengths are, we recommend (again!) reaching out to people you know and asking their thoughts (we have an exercise that may be able to help on page 68.) Sometimes we're so familiar with our own abilities that we don't even notice them, and having an outside perspective can be key.

3. GO OUTSIDE YOUR COMFORT ZONE

This is where so much real growth happens. It's also the place where you meet fear and overcome it. Challenge yourself regularly, whether it's by initiating a conversation with the senior vice president who intimidates you, or offering to play on the company softball team when you're more at home reading a book in the bleachers. What you choose doesn't have to be career related; the goal is simply to stretch yourself a bit.

4. DEAL WITH YOUR INNER CRITIC

We all can be our own worst enemies and our harshest critics. Even if your head and heart are firmly aligned in pursuit of your goals, you're still likely to have to contend with that critical inner voice telling you that it's foolish, or frivolous, or just plain impossible. We don't suggest you listen to that voice—but don't simply ignore it, either. Take a moment to think about the fear that underlies that voice—and address what it's saying, whatever that may be. Ask yourself how likely it is that whatever you are afraid of will actually become a reality—or try to step outside yourself for a minute and look at things more objectively. If you need extra help here, it's worth talking to a coach or mental health professional.

CELEBRATE HOW FAR YOU'VE COME

By this point in your process, you likely have a pretty good sense of what career path you'd like to pursue for the next two or five years—or at least have narrowed the list down to a couple of options. Pat yourself on the back, and throw your completed Muse Grid on the fridge or bulletin board—you've gotten further than most people ever do in really defining what you might like to do with your life!

You're also now far ahead of the game in a couple of other ways: You know more clearly what your priorities are, and whether the job you are about to pursue aligns with them. But having identified your next career move isn't actually your main accomplishment. The real accomplishment is that you learned a whole lot about your values—and you're now holding yourself accountable to your values. Of course, you want a job that pays the bills—who doesn't? But maybe you learned you have a lingering desire to be your own boss one day that keeps putting itself front and center, and you may just be willing to compromise on the dough for that extra flexibility. Or you've realized that you'd go mad if your intellect wasn't challenged every single day, no matter what you were paid. This is valuable self-knowledge that will put you on the path to a job that fulfills you and brings you joy.

And for those of you experiencing FOMO (*Wait! What if I change my mind and really do want to go into real estate? What if there's something I haven't even thought of!*), remember: we're only talking about what you want to do for the next handful of years, not forcing you to settle on what you want your career to be like in ten or twenty. Those choices will continue to evolve, just as you will certainly continue to evolve!

You will continue to learn along the way, too, exploring these options more deeply and refining your hypotheses further, but you have made one heck of a start. What you've done here is a micro-version of what a modern career really is, by the way. It's a process of gathering more information, widening a network, and creating opportunities.

So now it's time to rally. In the next section, we'll look at the steps you need to take to start to refine and communicate your skill set, grow personally and professionally, and build a network that is going to open the door to opportunities and help you find, and thrive in, that perfect job—whatever it is.

PART TWO

MAKING
YOUR MOVE

CHAPTER FOUR

The New Rules of Building Your Personal Brand

THE OLD RULE: Branding is for products. This dates back to the Industrial Revolution, when companies started enlisting the help of advertisers to build identities that communicated a distinct image for a product. Campbell's Soup. Domino Sugar. Wheaties. Kellogg's Corn Flakes. The old rules of branding were all about creating iconic images and clever messaging for the purpose of selling *stuff*.

THE NEW RULE: Today, brands aren't only associated with products, but with people—and your personal brand can make a big difference in helping you launch a career and land a job. Employers are looking for individuals who know who they are and are able to present themselves as attractive employees and colleagues. A strong personal brand can help you establish yourself as an expert in your field, provide hiring managers with insight into your personality, and give you that extra edge you need to snag your dream job.

Whew! You've done the hard work required in Part 1—work that's led you to a well-researched, carefully refined goal for what you want to pursue over the next two to five years of your career. And now you're probably ready to get moving toward it. Or you might also be thinking— Wait, I still don't know exactly what my goal is! That's okay, too. By the end of Part 1, you narrowed the list of possible career paths down to at most three. At this stage, it's okay to still have more than one option on the table. As we move forward, you may find that you want to do some of the exercises twice—for example, craft different variations of your brand statement for each of your potential career paths, especially if they are very different from each other. While it may seem like extra work in the short term, taking these extra steps is likely to shed light on which career path is ultimately the better fit and actually gets you more excited (Which one do you always want to do first? Which one just "makes sense" to you?). And while you're still on that journey—hang in there, it'll be worth it.

In this chapter, we'll equip you with the first of two important skills you'll need to do just that: personal branding and networking. Think of them as your secret weapons—the ones that will make all the difference between simply daydreaming about your dream career and taking real, actionable steps toward it.

PERSONAL BRANDING 101

So what is your personal brand, anyway? Put another way: What do people say about you when you're not in the room? What impression do you give your colleagues, boss, or potential employers? What's your reputation, both online and off?

We're not asking these questions to make you anxious, but the truth is, people *do* talk about you when you aren't in the room. Which means that if you don't define and articulate your own brand, others will do it for you. Put another way, if they don't have a clear picture of how you are, they'll write the story of who they think you are, without your input or consent. Rather than leave it up to chance, wouldn't you rather be in control of how the world perceives you?

Having a personal brand is no longer a luxury reserved for big businesses, mass-market products, and celebrities. Under the New Rules, no matter who you are or where you are in your career, understanding how you're perceived and how you stand out from the crowd of other professionals is absolutely essential to your success.

The personal branding process starts with being aware of who you are and what you have to offer potential employers. In this chapter, you'll take everything you've learned about yourself and desired career path so far and begin to cultivate an image that reflects your authentic voice, your most deeply held values, and your unique strengths, interests, and skills—in other words, your brand.

THE FIVE STEPS FOR SUCCESSFUL BRAND BUILDING

So how do you get started? Whether you're building your brand from the ground up or just need to give your existing identity a bit of a facelift, here's an overview of the five steps that you can use at any point in your career or job search—all of which we'll cover in more detail below.

1. **Determine Your Brand Attributes.** We know you've already done a lot of self-reflection in this last section. Now you'll decide on the three or four descriptors that best define your personal brand, which will be key to developing a tagline that is powerful, memorable, and truly *you*.

2. **Draft Your Branding Statement.** Before you panic, know that we won't be asking you to write a novel—just one or two sentences that capture who you are based on the attributes you chose in Step 1.

3. **Refine Your Profiles.** At this point, you'll update your social media profiles to reflect your newly drafted brand statement. The objective here is to make your online presence consistent *and* compelling (we have advice that can help!).

4. **Create Your Personal Website.** You may not think you need your own personal website, but under the New Rules of Work, we beg to differ. No matter who you are or what industry you're in, a website is the perfect vehicle to display your work, connect with others, and establish yourself as an expert in your field.

5. **Activate Your Brand.** In this final step, you'll pull together every element of your personal brand and begin to put yourself

out there by creating content, participating in conversations, and carving out your unique voice.

STEP ONE: DETERMINE YOUR BRAND ATTRIBUTES

Identifying the attributes that define your brand involves understanding not only yourself but also how you are perceived by others. You might *think* you know what your greatest strengths and attributes are as a professional, but do you, really?

It can be challenging to objectively identify your own strengths and personality traits, but you can learn a lot about yourself by getting feedback from the people who know you best.

To start, choose eight to ten trusted friends, peers, and mentors and ask or email them the following questions:

- How would you describe me in three words?
- If you had to introduce me to a new professional contact or colleague, what would you tell him or her about me?
- What traits do you most admire or enjoy about me?
- What makes me different from other people you've worked with in the past?

Listen and take notes. It can be helpful to do this with two different groups—one made up of people who know you more intimately (such as close friends or family members) and one made up of more distant acquaintances (like former colleagues, mentors, professors, or bosses).

Now look again at all the descriptions you gathered. What are the three to five descriptors that people seemed to agree upon? Circle those that seem like strengths, and underline those that could have a negative connotation, so you have a better sense of the whole picture you're working with.

Now in your own words, write down the five words or phrases that you agree are accurate (try to be as objective as possible!) *and* that you'd like to convey to a potential employer. Feel free to rephrase these in a way that would be most appealing to someone you aspire to work for.

_____   _____

_____   _____

_____

For example, when Jennifer, a project manager, asked these questions to a group of her peers, friends, and mentors, they described her as:

"Super nice"
"Easygoing"
"Always willing to help others"
"Puts others before herself"
"Reliable and friendly"
"Easy to get along with"
"Likes to smile a lot"
"Follows through on tasks"
"Works hard for others"

From these descriptions, it sounds like Jennifer is personable, friendly, and altruistic; she's also a hard worker and reliable. So here's one way Jennifer might describe her attributes: "Affable, agreeable, and gets along well with others."

But wait, here's an equally accurate description: "Relationship builder, strong follow-through, and motivated to collaborate."

So which should she lead with? The first describes someone you'd probably want to be friends with, while the second is someone you'd want to hire on your team. In terms of branding herself professionally, Jennifer should probably opt for the latter.

But what if the feedback you get back isn't so clear-cut? Or what if some of it is critical or negative? Here's how Zach, a sales manager, handled this. When he asked his group of friends and colleagues the same batch of questions, their responses were:

THE NEW RULES OF WORK

"Smart and occasionally irreverent"
"Determined and hard-charging"
"Passionate and occasionally stubborn"
"Willing to take risks"
"Authoritative, loves to take charge"
"Intelligent and ambitious"

With Zach, a different kind of profile is emerging: he comes across as smart, motivated, and risk-oriented, but not as collaborative. In fact, based on this feedback, you might even describe him as brusque or overbearing.

But again, would those descriptors appeal to an employer? Probably not. Zach would benefit far more from positioning himself as an ambitious leader and confident go-getter who will go the extra mile to achieve a goal.

As you see in these cases, defining your brand isn't just about describing yourself. Yes, you need to home in on words that capture you, your strengths, what motivates you, and your aspirations—but you also have to put it through the filter of "Would someone want to hire or work with this person?"

So, for example, rather than saying "enjoys helping others," you might write down "natural mentor" or "problem solver."

STEP TWO: DRAFTING YOUR BRANDING STATEMENT

Disclaimer: The branding statement you are about to write today is not carved in stone! In fact, from month to month and year to year, you should continue to refine how you define and brand yourself. But for now, let's create that first draft.

The basis for your branding statement will be the attributes you defined in the first step. But you don't have to stop there; consider adding a few elements that are more tailored to you and your mission—for example, the skills and attributes more specific to your target industry, the service or expertise you offer, or that describe how people benefit from working with you. Note that, if you're still juggling multiple career path options, it may be helpful to craft a slightly different brand statement for each.

Of course, your brand statement should communicate not just who you are today, but who you want to *become*. So come up with a few words that describe who you'd like to be (but be realistic; if you know you're a card-carrying introvert, don't put down "social butterfly"). If you are drawing a blank, look at your Muse Grid and see if you notice a pattern. Maybe, for example, your top functions all included telling stories or translating complex information into easily understandable language. That's a pretty good sign that your goal is to be known as an eloquent communicator. So go ahead and add that to your list.

You might also want to draw inspiration from people who have attributes that are similar to yours, or who work in jobs like the ones you're after. What words do they use to define themselves? (LinkedIn is a good place to look for this.) What common terms do you find in their personal profiles? How are they separating themselves from their competition? If you come across words or phrases that resonate with you and your vision, add them.

Now that you have all your key terms phrased in a way that will paint you in the most positive light, it's as easy—and, well, as difficult—as combining it all together in one or two brief sentences.

For example, after going through these steps, here's what Jennifer came up with: "Consensus builder with keen people skills; project management expert who seamlessly works across large organizations to get big things done."

Zach's brand statement became: "Driven leader who excels at leading sales teams to achieve aggressive goals—and keeping everyone laughing along the way."

Now give it a try:

_____

_____

_____

_____

_____

HOW YOUR RESUME FITS IN

This is going to sound like a crazy statement to make in a career book, but we actually don't want you to worry so much about your resume at this stage in the game. Don't worry, we'll get there eventually; we've designed a full resume workshop in Chapter 7. For now, we want you to zero in on creating and finessing a narrow, focused brand statement that captures the essence of you in just a few lines of text—think of it as your personal elevator pitch. Eventually, you will use this statement to craft and refine your resume, cover letter, and other application materials for maximum impact—but we're not there just yet!

STEP THREE: REFINE YOUR PROFILES

Now that you have a branding statement, it's time to start communicating it to the world. Of course, you won't always use it exactly as it looks above—later on, you'll learn how to tailor and refine it to specific employers or jobs—so think of it more as a cheat sheet to help you craft everything you use to present yourself, including what we'll cover next: your social media presence.

Surely it won't surprise you to learn that these days most job searching is done online, and that goes not just for job seekers, but for employers and recruiters as well. Trust us, while you are scouring the web for jobs, recruiters are scouring the web for qualified candidates, which means that a strong social media presence—with profiles that not only clearly communicate your brand but do it using the right keywords and language—not only gives you an opportunity to impress employers or professional contacts when they check you out online, but also makes them that much more likely to find you in the first place.

Now, you probably have a number of social media profiles, and to some extent, they can all be used to showcase your personal brand. But for the purpose of establishing yourself in the professional arena, we

BUT I STILL HAVEN'T PICKED A SINGLE CAREER PATH!

If you're at a point where you haven't landed on a single career path yet, you have two options for what to do in this step. If the career paths are even somewhat similar, the same personal branding may apply to both—for example, if your brand statement emphasizes being a go-getter and a team leader, it may not matter whether you decide you want to land at a start-up or a PR firm. But if your career paths are far enough apart that you're not ready to commit to a brand that you'll share with the world, feel free to bookmark the rest of this chapter and come back to it when you're ready—maybe after some of the networking you'll do in Chapter 5!

recommend focusing on LinkedIn. Under the New Rules of Work, a LinkedIn profile that accurately communicates your brand and career goals is pretty much a must; as the largest professional social network out there, LinkedIn is the ideal place to establish your professional identity, network with professionals who are in your desired career path, and connect with future employers.

CRAFTING YOUR LINKEDIN SUMMARY

Your LinkedIn summary is the best real estate you have for communicating your personal brand, not to mention being one of the first things people will read when they view your profile. So you'll want to spend some time making your summary engaging, informative, personal, and impactful.

To make this process a bit easier, one of our top Muse contributors, Aja Frost, developed these five LinkedIn summary templates that you can choose from, depending on how you want to highlight your experience, accomplishments, skills, and goals. But whichever of the below you decide to use, remember to work in the personal brand statement that you came up with above.

Five Templates That'll Make Writing the Perfect LinkedIn Summary a Breeze

by Muse contributor Aja Frost

1. THE MISSION-BASED SUMMARY

Every brand has stories to tell—stories that will not only engage, inform, surprise, delight, and impact their audience, but that will also deliver on measurable business goals. I am the conduit between brand and consumer. I help clients find the subject and medium that best fits their unique identity, and then I produce high-quality content that meets their objectives.

Currently, I am a content strategist at Alliance Media, where I've collaborated with companies such as Tiffany & Co., Burger King, and Netflix. My specialties include digital media, consumer behavior, brand awareness, and omni-channel marketing campaigns.

The mission-based summary opens with a broad description of what you do—what your mission is—then gets more and more specific. This is a great choice if you're casting a wide net in your job search. After all, someone who's unfamiliar with the field is probably hazy on what "content strategy" means—but everyone understands "telling stories for brands."

It also shows that you get the bigger picture. You understand why your job encompasses more than your daily to-do list. You want to have real impact, make a difference. And as you can see from the example, you don't have to be "increasing literacy rates in third-world countries" or "building prosthetics with near-natural motor capability" to be contributing something valuable to the world.

2. THE PERSONALITY SUMMARY

When I was 21, I climbed Mount Everest. Not metaphorically—I literally climbed the highest mountain on Earth. While I was hiking, I thought about quitting approximately 5,000 times. (And that's a lowball estimate.)

But despite the high winds, low oxygen, mental and physical fatigue, and trail mix overdose, I kept going. I'm that person. Once I say I'll do something, it will happen.

Now, I put that perseverance to work as a senior account manager for Polar. I don't have to climb any mountains . . . but I do have to move them. I'm well-versed in negotiations, planning and development, relationship management, operations, and logistics coordination and scheduling. If you're interested in grabbing coffee and talking shop (or to hear how I almost fell off the mountain at 27K feet), please send an email my way.

If you're really looking to hook people, begin with a memorable anecdote that demonstrates one or two key personality traits—and then show how you apply those same traits in your job or career.

Because this type of summary focuses more on personality than on hard skills, it's ideal for two types of people: the networkers and the less experienced. If you're using LinkedIn primarily to meet new people, rather than get a job, this type of summary is great because it makes you seem like an interesting person to know. As a result, you'll likely see an increase in the number of connections you make, as well as the number of people who accept your coffee invites.

It's also great if you're still a student or relatively new to the professional world. Since you won't have a lot of work experience to include in your summary, you can flesh it out by writing about character traits to help people learn more about you.

3. THE SHORT-AND-SWEET SUMMARY

I have over 15 years of experience working in data science. Currently, I work as Asana's Senior Data Manager, improving products and services for our customers by using advanced analytics, standing up big-data analytical tools, creating and maintaining models, and onboarding compelling new data sets.

Previously, I was the Chief Data Scientist at Guru, where I analyzed data from some of the biggest enterprises and networks in the world to educate the market on long-term internet trends. Competencies: data science, machine learning, cloud computing, Hadoop, Python/Java/R, network protocols.

The short-and-sweet summary is a smart choice for professionals in more conservative, traditional, or technical industries. For example, if you're a lawyer, you want to make it easy for employers to get the key facts: how long you've been practicing law, what your qualifications are, and the type of work you specialize in, without the distraction of anecdotes or stories. (Plus, getting too creative might undermine your credibility.)

This approach is also a good one for active job hunters. Why? It allows you to get a lot of keywords in, which will help advance you in the search results when a recruiter looks for someone who fits your profile.

Whatever the case, a short-and-sweet summary should include your current role, previous positions (if they're relevant or notable), and your more relevant skills.

4. THE BLENDED SUMMARY

I'm a talent acquisition specialist with an interest in building the most effective workforces possible. For over 20 years, I've been helping businesses find their perfect hires. I also do consulting on compensation and benefits, new hire processes, and company culture.

When I'm not on the job, I love hiking with my dog, working my way through every recipe in the family cookbook, and indulging my love for seeing new places. If you'd like to learn more about how my services can help your company, please reach out via email (janedoe@gmail.com).

As the name suggests, this summary is a blend between the short-and-sweet and the personality versions. It's perfect if you want to get straight to the facts, but you *also* want some levity in your description. I'd suggest it for professionals in more creative industries and people whose work involves lots of other people (think sales reps, managers, or HR specialists).

To make this work, begin with a one-line description of your current job and a couple of work accomplishments or highlights, then add some "fun facts." However, make sure they're not *too* fun; "I love karaoke (ask me about my Mariah Carey cover)" is probably fine. "My personal motto is 'It's 5 PM somewhere!'" is almost certainly not. When in doubt, leave it out.

If you need more help nailing the perfect tone for this one, imagine you're talking to someone you just met at an industry event. Keep it light, fun, but also *professional*.

5. THE ACCOMPLISHMENTS SUMMARY

I'm a freelance multidisciplinary graphic designer who's delivered creative and engaging solutions across brand identity, print, packaging, and digital media. In 2013, my online brand campaign for the Dorsey Children's Hospital won a GDUSA Award, one of the most prestigious honors in the graphic design industry.

My work has also been featured in Creatique Bloq, Compound Magazine, *and on the* Creative Review *blog. Skills: logo design, web design, branding and identity, typography, UI design, packaging, CSS, HTML, InDesign, Photoshop, Illustrator. If you have a project I can help with, please get in touch.*

I love the accomplishments summary for those who are actively seeking work—either a full-time position or freelance gigs. It tells potential employers or clients exactly why you deserve the job, as well as the (high) caliber of work they can expect from you.

And by the way, you don't have to limit yourself to awards, speaking engagements, or positive press. Something like "I planned and implemented a new social media strategy that tripled our online engagement in six months" works, too.

As you're drafting your summary from these examples, pay attention to the words you use. If you're pursuing a specific position, look at the job description for words and phrases that tie directly to the role—those are terms a recruiter might search. Again, you can also look at the profiles of professionals who are in your ideal role to get an idea of the language they use.

And remember, the path to an awesome summary often includes iteration—so start writing now, and don't be afraid to edit later.

YOUR LINKEDIN CHECKLIST

In addition to the summary, what does a full, complete, and compelling LinkedIn profile include? Here is a checklist of the basics that every professional profile should have:

☐ A summary that showcases your personal brand and includes keywords from the job descriptions of the roles you're considering. A great way to do this is to add a "Skills" line at the bottom of your summary, and list the keywords there. Be as concrete and specific as possible.

☐ A creative headline. Here it pays to think beyond your current job title. Here are two eye-catching examples:

- Instead of: Content Marketing Manager for Health Systems, PA: "Content creator who knows what it takes to make health and wellness media go viral."

- Instead of: Fundraising Manager, Goodness Knows Nonprofit: "Fundraiser who specializes in grants programs and donor outreach to help nonprofits do their best work."

☐ A professional profile picture (no selfies or cropped-out friends!) that aligns with how you want to be perceived. That could be friendly or serious, creative or buttoned-up—the most important thing is that it is appropriate for your specific field. If you're not sure, take a look at how others in similar roles brand themselves, and try to match that tone.

☐ Endorsements. Ask former colleagues or supervisors to write recommendations for you, which can back up the brand you've outlined in your headline and summary and serve as compelling proof of your talents. To make it easy for them, make your ask specific: "Would you mind writing a short LinkedIn recommendation about my project management skills, particularly as related to our last product launch?" or ". . . focused on my graphic design work?" is a lot easier than just asking for a plain old recommendation.

☐ Next steps for the people who view your profile. For example, if you're looking to build more connections through networking, you might add "Interested in chatting over coffee? Email me at Jennifer@gmail.com." Or, if you're openly searching for work, you could include "I'd love to help your company take your sales team to the next level. Get in touch by emailing me at Zach@ gmail.com."

Even though this list is specific to LinkedIn, you can—and should—use several of these elements across your other social media profiles. For example, you can use your same LinkedIn headline and photo for your Twitter or Instagram bio, or maybe include a version of your summary in your Facebook profile. This will help keep your brand consistent—and professional—which is important because today, potential employers aren't just looking you up on LinkedIn—they are looking up your Facebook and Instagram and Snapchat and Twitter profiles, too. If you're not on these platforms—or don't want to use them professionally—that's okay. Just make sure that you keep them set to private. Operate under the assumption that if Google can find it, your potential dream employer can, too.

Curious to see an example? Take a look at Muse expert Aja Frost's LinkedIn profile below, for a real-life version of our tips in action!

Finally, before you move on to Step Four, compare your updated social media profiles to the branding statement you wrote earlier. Do they sound like they're the same person? If not, go back and revise. If they hit the mark, you're ready for the next step.

STEP FOUR: CREATE YOUR OWN WEBSITE

So far, you've focused on building your brand by *telling* your audience the value you bring to the table—but with a personal website, you can actually *show* potential employers and contacts what you can offer through links, videos, photos, and samples of your work.

People often assume that only people in artsy fields—like graphic designers or photographers—need websites, but nowadays, that's not the case. No matter what industry you're in, and whether you consider your work to be "visual" or not, you can likely display some aspect of that

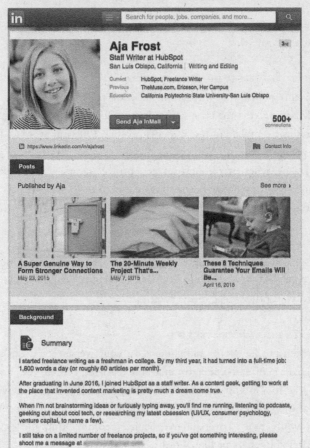

work online, whether it's a video of a speaking engagement, a list of projects you've worked on, a handful of testimonials from past clients, or even a video, word cloud, or some other creative visualization of your skills.

Beyond that, a website can help you in several ways:

IT CAN HELP YOU STAND OUT FROM OTHER JOB APPLICANTS

Almost every job seeker that you'll be competing with will be equipped with a resume and cover letter—so it's pretty easy to get lost in the shuffle. A personal website can be the element that sets you apart from the pack.

IT GIVES YOU FREEDOM AND CONTROL

Up to this point, your expression of your personal brand has been somewhat limited—the information had to fit within the constraints of your resume template or social media profiles. On your website, however, *you're* in control. You get to decide how to display your work experience—whether through images, project samples, or something else entirely—and that gives you the freedom to really let your personality and unique traits shine through.

IT HELPS BUILD YOUR NETWORK

A personal website opens up possibilities for you to connect with others in your field—especially if you include a regularly updated blog and links to your other social media profiles.

IT MAKES YOU EASIER TO FIND

With the right keywords and content on your website, you can boost your chances of a recruiter finding and reaching out to you—which could lead to a job opportunity. How do you find the right keywords? Look at the job descriptions of the positions you're considering and see which words are used over and over again. (Pro tip: Dump the text into a word cloud generator like Wordle, and see what stands out!) And if you are able to get your name as a URL for your personal website, all the better, because you will be more visible if someone is googling you.

———

On The Muse we've published several examples of people landing their dream jobs thanks to having a personal website, and one of our favorite examples is Jillian Youngblood, who wanted to pivot her career from politics to a more tech-focused role. So she created a site, which she used to demonstrate her web development and technical abilities. Eventually, the head of a development team discovered it and asked her to come in for an interview—a connection she likely wouldn't have made otherwise.

Do you have to know how to code to build a website? Or have the cash to hire a top-notch developer? Definitely not. There are several user-friendly website creation platforms available that even the least tech-savvy among us can master, such as Wix, WordPress, or Squarespace (which Alex used to build her personal website, acavoulacos .com!). If you're feeling intimidated, many of these platforms even have the option to create a simple landing page, which is more than enough real estate to house the "essentials"; that is, a photo, a short bio, and links to your social media profiles.

For more inspiration and step-by-step details of how to build a website, just do a quick search for "personal websites" on TheMuse.com /advice. There are many articles that'll walk you through the process from start to finish, and you'll also find dozens of examples of personal websites we love, which you can use for inspiration as you get started.

STEP FIVE: ACTIVATING YOUR BRAND

Now that you have a brand statement—and a social media presence and personal website to go with it—it's time to take active steps to get your brand out there. Think of activating your brand as akin to publishing a book or releasing an album or distributing a film: your creation could be a true masterpiece, but what good is it if that work of genius never sees the light of day? Just as you would put effort into getting that book, album, or film in front of an audience, think of the goal of activating your brand as getting that brand in front of as many eyeballs as possible (or at least the *right* eyeballs!).

Here are some ways to do exactly that:

BE A JOINER

Join LinkedIn groups or communities online that interest you or are relevant to your job, function, or industry, which can help you network with others in your field and stay informed about what's going on. (We'll go into this more in the next couple of chapters!)

FOLLOW INDUSTRY INFLUENCERS

Stay connected to your industry on a larger scale by identifying and following influencers online. LinkedIn has a community of official "Influencers" you can follow who regularly publish articles on industry-related and other topics. You can also follow and interact with industry leaders on Twitter, Facebook, and other social networks. This will not only keep you up-to-date on the trends and issues of the moment, but also give you the opportunity to share *your* thoughts, participate in conversations, and potentially get on the radar of your role models.

CREATE ORIGINAL CONTENT

Think about starting your own newsletter or blog based on your target industry and career goals—essentially, you want to offer whatever content is valuable to people in your field consistent with your brand and voice. If you're pursuing a career path in advertising, for example, this could be a monthly roundup of your favorite commercials or branded content campaigns. If you're a recruiter, you could include commentaries on new sourcing tools. Your content can live on your personal website, but you should also share it via Facebook, Twitter, LinkedIn, Instagram, etc. But note that before you start a blog or newsletter, you should be prepared to commit to posting or emailing content regularly; you might even set up a schedule for yourself of when you're going to write or post on their platforms, which will help you stay on top of it and organized!

GIVE TO RECEIVE

Personal branding is no longer a one-way street. As you interact with the people in your industry—both online and in person—look for ways that you can help *them.* Let's say, for example, that you are able to help one of your contacts by sharing a strategy you used to solve a problem similar to one he is currently facing—now suddenly you have the reputation for being helpful, knowledgeable, and a creative problem solver. Remember, your true brand is what people say about you when you aren't in the room. Helping other people is the one surefire way to make sure they say something positive about you.

———

These five steps are a great foundation for your personal brand—but even after you work your way through them, that doesn't mean you're done. Activating your brand isn't a one-and-done activity; it's an ongoing process that requires work on a weekly, monthly, and yearly basis. But the effort is worth it, because the more time you spend on it (through the duration of your job search *and* beyond), the more likely you are to get noticed—and regarded as a true expert in your field.

This requires continually refining your social media profiles, being active and engaged within your networks, and updating your personal website as you further develop your skills and experience and rack up new achievements. As you evolve, you'll need to manage your brand proactively, making sure that all aspects of the image you present to the world evolve as well.

In short, don't let your personal brand be an afterthought—and certainly, don't let someone else define it for you! By intentionally establishing and communicating your unique value, vision, and persona, you'll be much more likely to stand out from the rest of the pack and position yourself to discover and seize new opportunities.

So what's next? Let's move on to taking that personal brand out far and wide—through the power of your network!

CHAPTER FIVE

The New Rules of Networking

THE OLD RULE: Networking has always been considered a part of any strong action plan to get a new job or stay updated and valuable in your current career. But it used to be an awkward affair, limited to organized job fairs, industry conferences, alumni events, and other formalized get-togethers where you were invited and expected to shamelessly self-promote—something many of us don't enjoy doing. Cue: mental images of a used-car salesman handshake. No thanks!

THE NEW RULE: Although some of the old rules on how to build a relationship with someone remain viable, networking has become much more nuanced, common, and expected due to social media; it's no longer reserved primarily for the conference circuit or big industry events. From casual email or Twitter interactions, to coffee dates and informational interviews, to joining Facebook groups, you need to learn the New Rules for how to expertly build and manage a network—both online and off.

In Part 1 of this book, you saw how helpful it was to have others in your camp when you were researching various career directions. And in this chapter, we're going to take this idea a few steps further, showing you the power of building and using your network throughout the rest of your job search—and your career.

The great thing about networking in our golden age of social media is that it allows you to not only activate, but also *amplify* your personal brand on a scale that simply wasn't possible just ten years ago. But before we get started, we'll put this out there: *We know* networking can be intimidating, and sometimes feels like one more thing to jam into an already hectic schedule. Plus, if you're moving into a new field where you don't know a lot of people, it can be that much more daunting. Who should you connect with? How do you find networking events in the first place, and what do you do when you get there? How can you start non-awkward networking conversations? What about the follow-up?

But keep in mind that these questions are a lot easier to answer if you reframe how you think about networking according to the New Rules.

Under the New Rules, here's what networking is not: It's not about meeting people who can get you a job today or tomorrow. It's not about instant gratification. And it's not something you do only when you need something.

Networking *is* about meeting interesting people (anywhere—not just at events you dread attending, and all the time—not just when you are job searching) who could turn into long-term friends, contacts, or colleagues. These relationships could be the ticket to getting your foot in the door at a new company, introducing you to a future mentor or potential client, solving problems at work, and so much more. But this won't happen overnight. Like any worthwhile relationships, these require commitment and nurturing over time. For example, Alex met a writer at a conference, hit it off, and stayed in touch. They'd catch up when they were in the same city, and Alex offered her advice and an outsider's perspective when her contact was going through a career transition. Years later, this contact had switched industries and was working for a major social network—and when Alex was trying to find an "in" at that social network to help solve an access problem for The Muse, her contact was more than happy to step in and save the day.

Similarly, Kathryn didn't know a single person in the tech industry before starting a company and showing up alone at tech meetups. Those first few conversations were really intimidating, but slowly, over a series of weeks (and many, many cheese plates!), she built up a small group of people she knew in the industry who were rooting for her, and by extension The Muse, to succeed. Trust us when we say that many of those relationships will grow in ways you never could have dreamed, leading to introductions, referrals or references, advice in both directions, and in some cases, deep and long-lasting friendships that transcend work.

If you look at networking as building relationships that grow over time, rather than a business transaction when you need something, its value multiplies. That's because people are not too inclined to jump through hoops for someone they haven't heard from in ages and who is clearly only reaching out because they need something. Case in point: ever get one of those "it would be great to catch up" emails out of the blue, followed promptly by the real request? (Could they *be* more obvious?) The best network-building relationships are ongoing and mutual—they don't just surface when it's time for a favor.

BUILDING YOUR NETWORK: HOW TO MEET NEW PEOPLE

If you are just starting your career, actively looking for a new job, or transitioning to a completely different field, there's no two ways about it: you're going to have to meet new people. There are plenty of ways to do this, but we'll start with one of the most common: events. Whether it's alumni mixers, conferences, meetups, or industry happy hours, it pays to go to functions where you'll have access to a large number and wide variety of people.

Take it from Kathryn: In the early days of The Muse, when she was trying to make connections to help her recruit a team, discover new partners, and build the company's reputation in the start-up space, she would go to five or six events *per week*! It was exhausting, but also an incredibly efficient way to build a network of tech, media, and HR contacts that have repaid the effort many times over in the last few years. You definitely don't have to be *this* aggressive, but even showing up to events once a week or month can help you meet a lot of new people in a short amount of time.

With that said, you have to do more than just show up and stand in the corner eating the free snacks. You have to be strategic about really using the time to make a connection with—and hopefully leave a lasting (good) impression on—the people you most want to meet. To that end, we're going to break the art of mastering the networking event into three areas: pre-event prep, starting the conversation, and wrapping up. And we'll give you strategies for combating anxiety and intimidation that will help you show up as your most confident, dazzling self.

GO BIG OR GO HOME? NOT QUITE

If the idea of standing in a sea of other professionals at a crowded bar or convention center gives you social anxiety (or just sounds boring), you're not alone. Luckily, there are plenty of ways to avoid those big to-dos and still build a solid network.

Look for smaller get-togethers. Remember, the name of the game here is quality, not quantity. It's fine to eschew the major events and look for smaller groups to connect with—for example, a book group on Meetup.com or an intimate discussion group. One of our Musers, Victoria, once met some fascinating people in her field at an Indian cooking class!

Create your own group with a few friends and colleagues. Thomas Jefferson was famous for his legendary dinner parties, where he'd invite a variety of fascinating people and then pose deep, philosophical questions for everyone at the table to answer; a habit adapted to modern times by LinkedIn founder Reid Hoffman. Be the Thomas Jefferson (or Reid Hoffman). You can do something similar; each month, choose three interesting people, and ask each of them to invite three of their friends to convene at a coffee shop or someone's house. You never know whom you'll meet or what you'll learn.

Participate in Facebook or Twitter chats. This is a great way for quieter, more introverted types to chime into a real-time conversation . . . while sitting on your couch in PJs. (No one has to know!)

Search LinkedIn for an active group relevant to your industry, profession, or interests. There are groups out there of all sizes, so start small if you're new to these kinds of forums; in a smaller group you'll stand out more. Join a discussion to offer your perspective or start your own thread. Just make sure your comments are professional, relevant, and add value. ("I agree, John!" isn't going to get you noticed.)

PRE-EVENT PREPARATION
THAT WILL CALM YOUR NERVES

If that image of the used-car salesman just popped back into your head, banish it immediately. Because the truth is, networking doesn't have to be slimy, as long as you do it in a way that's true to your authentic interests and personality. The less nervous you are, the more genuine and authentic you will be, so here we're going to cover three steps to help put you at ease. The best part? Those can be done before you get to the event, so you'll feel (at least a little bit) calmer from the moment you walk in the door.

BE COMFORTABLE

The more comfortable you feel, the more confidence you'll exude, and the more successful you'll be. But if the very thought of working a room of strangers gives you hives, don't worry. Here are a few of our very favorite tried-and-true tips:

DRESS COMFORTABLY!

This sounds pretty basic, but it's important. Don't wear a suit if you never wear suits, save the five-inch heels for Saturday night, and check your coat so you're not stuck lugging it around while trying to simultaneously balance a drink and pass out your business card.

BRING A WING MAN OR WOMAN

It's so much easier to walk into a room when you're not solo. Invite a colleague or friend to join you at the event. For example, Kathryn once invited a fellow entrepreneur to join her at a small party hosted at SXSW, where she didn't know anyone but the host. Not only did they end up becoming fast friends (to this day!), but that other entrepreneur happened to know and introduce her to an investor at the same event—and a year later, he became one of The Muse's early backers.

VISUALIZE A COMFORTABLE SETTING

Think of a social setting where you're totally relaxed, like at a dinner party with your closest friends. Pretend you're there, and just be yourself.

———

Yes, putting yourself out there can be really intimidating. It's easy to feel outnumbered—like everyone else in the room has been trained to small-talk their way to a new job, and you somehow missed the memo. But chances are the person lingering by the food, looking very intently at her phone (along with the majority of attendees), is right there with you. Reminding yourself that *everyone* is a little nervous makes it easier to approach someone and get the ball rolling.

HAVE YOUR ELEVATOR PITCH READY

A networking event can feel like the Wild West if you go in without a game plan. The more prep you do, the more successful (and comfortable) you will be. The key to being prepared in these kinds of scenarios is having talking points up your sleeve. Most important, when someone asks you what you do, you should be ready to confidently tell your story, in thirty to sixty seconds. This "elevator pitch"—a concise, easy-to-understand snapshot of who you are—should feel natural, not forced.

THREE STEPS TO WRITING AN
UNFORGETTABLE ELEVATOR PITCH

Try this exercise to create a succinct speech that will leave a lasting (and awesome) impression. Even better—it will come in handy well beyond networking events, like when you're writing cover letters, interviewing, trying to explain to your grandma what you do, or even just chatting with a potential partner or hire.

Step 1. Turn to a blank page in your Muse Notebook or open a new Word doc, and write down every single thing you want someone to know about you. Don't hold back—you'll edit it down later. If you're feeling stuck, ask yourself questions like: How do you stand out in your field? What benefit would you like to bring to the world? How do your current skills and experiences ladder up to where you want to be? Remember that brand statement you wrote in the last chapter? Go ahead and use that as a starting place here.

Step 2. Now take what you've come up with and try to fit it onto a square sticky note. This forces you to choose information to prioritize and determine what's not crucial to share in a first interaction. If you're having a hard time narrowing it down, a good framework to use is simply: your job title + company + what that means in layman's terms + why you love it. When Alex goes to events, she uses: "I'm Alex, cofounder and COO of The Muse, a career platform that helps over sixty million people advance in their careers or find a job they love. Right now, I'm working on adding a CFO to our executive team and building the team in our New York headquarters—we just crossed one hundred and fifty people last month!" (Note: Putting your goals out there, as Alex did with her comment about hiring a CFO and growing the team, can open up the floor for someone to offer a useful tip or introduction.) If you're currently unemployed, try writing something that highlights your specific skills and experience, like "I love designing beautiful, easy-to-use websites and I'm passionate about social good. I'm currently looking for something that'll help me connect both of those things."

Step 3. Read it out loud to make sure it sounds like something you'd actually say in a conversation, not something you're reciting from a piece of paper. And cut the jargon! Lofty industry phrases like "strategic insight" and "leveraging influencers" won't help your case here. Find a simple, straightforward way to describe what you do so it's relatable and easy to understand.

Once you have a solid elevator pitch, hold on to that sticky note and keep it on your desk or in your wallet. Give it a daily glance so it stays fresh in your mind, and start integrating it into your conversations when possible. And remember that, just like your career, your pitch is a work in progress, so you'll continue to tweak it as you develop new skills and goals. Or you might reframe it a bit based on whom you're speaking with.

SET NETWORKING #GOALS

Another tactic for making the most of a networking event is to go in with a goal (or goals). Pinpoint your reason for being there: having a mission helps you focus and forces you to break out of your comfort zone. If you're new to networking, your goal might be simply to talk to two or three people to get the lay of the land. Other goals may be:

SETTING UP ONE INFORMATIONAL INTERVIEW

Who can you meet that you'd like to talk to further about a company, industry, or potential job opportunity?

LEARNING SOMETHING NEW

Can you take the opportunity to listen to a fascinating speaker or strike up a conversation with someone who writes a great blog? How can this event help you expand your skill set? Or inspire you to take a class? Will you be able to put together a short event recap and share with your co-workers (to teach them something new and impress your boss by taking the initiative)?

MEETING THREE NEW PEOPLE WHO WORK FOR COMPANIES YOU'RE INTERESTED IN

The timing may not be right for an informational interview, but it's always beneficial to swap contact information with people who work at companies that pique your interest, whether you're actively looking for a job or not. Who can you talk to for an insider's view of the office vibe, types of colleagues, perks, and management style?

GETTING YOUR FOOT IN THE DOOR: HOW TO MAKE THE MOST OF AN INFORMATIONAL INTERVIEW

So all of this networking is really paying off . . . and you've secured an informational interview with someone who works for a company you think you might want to work for. While not an official interview, think of this as an opportunity to make an impression and get your foot in the door. So even though these types of sit-downs are casual, you still need a game plan to ensure you make the most of the conversation and leave with concrete next steps.

Before you meet, do your research. Learn everything you can about the person you're going to meet with. Get up to speed on her career path, where she went to school, and professional groups she's part of (you can find this all on LinkedIn). You might find things you have in common that could serve as a great conversation starter when you meet. If she's active on Twitter, check out her latest tweets, and reference something you found interesting related to the industry. Use Google to discover links to articles or blogs she wrote for a deeper dive into her work.

Ease into the conversation. Kick things off by getting the other person to do most of the talking. Ask about his career experiences, such as:

- Why did you choose this field?
- What's the most rewarding thing about working in this industry? What would you say is the biggest challenge?
- What projects are you working on right now?
- What do you think about [piece of industry news]?

Make an impression. Be ready to talk about your previous experiences and career goals. (That elevator speech will come in handy here!) Although you're seeking advice, don't hesitate to show your expertise. That said, keep it brief—you can always go deeper if they ask follow-up questions.

Get what you came for. What's the insider industry information you hope to learn or the advice this person is particularly well suited to offer? Make sure you get it. Or, if you're seeking a specific position at your contact's company or want interviewing tips, ask pointed, specific questions like:

- Do you know of any positions available right now that might be a fit for me?
- What does your company look for in new hires? Any tips for standing out?
- Do you have any advice on how to best prepare for an upcoming interview in [X field]?
- What job search advice would you have for someone with my background?

Go with the flow. Let your contact initiate offering to connect you with the hiring manager or forward your resume. And if he or she doesn't? That's okay. The goal here is to make the connection, get helpful advice, and see what transpires from the conversation, either now or down the line. (In fact, we've had informational interviews with people interested in working for The Muse who weren't a fit for us at the time, but who impressed us so much that we introduced them to other companies when we heard about job openings that might fit their background.) Whatever you do, just don't be pushy.

Make another new connection. As you're wrapping up the meeting, ask your contact if he or she knows anyone else who would be good to talk to as you continue building your network. Hey, it never hurts to ask, and sometimes it'll pay off big-time. Kathryn and Alex both do this regularly, and the question has led to introductions to potential investors, partners, and employees.

Follow up. After the meeting, send a thank-you note, and keep this contact updated as your job search progresses. In particular, if any leads or advice she gave you during the interview ended up helping you land your next gig, write her to say thank you! We receive these kinds of emails from people we've given career advice to over the years, and nothing makes us happier than knowing that we played a role—however small—in their success.

Now that you are comfortable, prepared with an elevator pitch, and have your goals in mind, it's time to kick things off. But how do you just walk up to someone you don't know at an event—and *start talking*?

CONVERSATION STARTERS WAY BETTER THAN "SO DO YOU COME HERE OFTEN?"

Unless Snowmaggedon is fast approaching, no one really wants to talk about the weather while sipping the watered-down happy hour special (and maybe not even then). But aimless chitchat with total strangers at a networking event can feel pretty awkward if you're not armed with a few conversation starters. Here are a few of our favorite types, which don't involve the weather:

A SIMPLE INTRODUCTION

Just because it's a networking event doesn't mean you need some clever or witty icebreaker. A simple, straightforward, "Hi, I'm _____. Nice to meet you" is a light, friendly introduction. The other person will probably be relieved that you got the conversation going.

TALK ABOUT THE HERE AND NOW

These people may be strangers, but you do both already have one thing in common: the event experience. So say something about it!

- "That speech was fantastic! What did you think?"
- "These sliders look awesome. It's always a fun surprise when events actually have something edible, right?" (Note: Kathryn loves this type of opener. Talking about food is always fun!)
- "What a cool event space. Have you been here before?"
- "This event is packed! Can I join you over here where it's a bit quieter?"

GIVE A COMPLIMENT

Flattery pretty much always works like a charm. Say something nice to start a conversation, such as, "What a beautiful necklace. Where is it from?" Even better, if you know someone has given a presentation or played some role in organizing the event, walk up to them and compliment them on that! Alex loves to seek out speakers and organizers at conferences to thank them and try to engage them to talk more about the event's theme. It's an easy way to start a conversation, and, as a bonus, they're often well positioned to introduce her to other attendees they think would be interesting for her to meet.

OWN YOUR ROOKIE VIBE

If you're a newbie to the networking world, or that particular industry event, say something like "I've never been here before. Are the panels always this awesome?" Or "I just joined this organization, do they hold other events you'd recommend attending?" Most people love sharing recommendations or giving advice—it makes *them* feel special—so this type of conversation starter will endear you to them immediately while also potentially resulting in some useful information.

———

Once you've broken the ice, here's how to turn small talk into a really fulfilling (sometimes even fascinating!) conversation.

GET *THEM* TALKING

Ask open-ended questions to elicit more than the "yes/no" response; instead of "Do you like working at Google?" try "What's it like working at Google?" Inquire about their perspective on something relevant to your industry, and don't be afraid to get specific:

- "I hear they have amazing perks at [insert company]—what are some of your favorites?"
- "What's the most interesting thing about your current job?"
- "If you could be doing anything in five years, what would it be?"

Note: If you're shy, this one has an added bonus: the more they talk, the less you have to!

BE READY TO SHARE

On the flip side, if someone asks you a question, have open-ended responses ready. Don't respond to "How are you?" with "Okay, you know: long week." Instead try something like: "Actually—I just spent six hours delayed at the airport on my way home from meeting with a client. Let's just say I'm happy to be here! Was your day a little smoother?" By sharing a bit about yourself, then pivoting back to a question about them, you've instantly become relatable and more memorable, and you've opened the door for them to continue the conversation.

PRETEND YOU'RE AT HAPPY HOUR WITH A FRIEND

If you approach networking as just talking to someone you could be friends with, it takes the pressure off and makes things feel more authentic, and well, *normal*. Sometimes you'll realize that you have nothing in common, and that's perfectly okay. Other times, you may find yourself bonding over a love of the same book or a shared taste in bad reality TV.

———

Whichever approach you choose, you'll want to come away with a few things:

- An understanding of what the other person does
- Giving them an understanding of what you do
- Learning something memorable about the person (to talk about in future interactions)
- Contact information (or their name so you can connect later on LinkedIn)

If you have trouble remembering names or to follow up, try adding people on LinkedIn on your phone right then and there, rather than exchanging business cards.

As we said earlier, networking is all about the long-term connection. At the end of the day, people are attracted to those who are friendly, interested, and genuinely listen—not such a tall order! So think of these starters as laying the foundation upon which you will continue to build up that relationship.

Kathryn grew up believing that everyone has a story to tell. Learning those stories—and being genuinely interested more in hearing from the other person than pushing any agenda of her own—has led to some of the most rewarding conversations and relationships in her career.

WRAPPING UP THE CONVERSATION

Ironically, sometimes ending a conversation gracefully can be harder than initiating it. But to avoid spending half the night talking to one person, or taking up too much of someone else's time, have a few closing lines ready for a pleasant exit. The "compliment + honest excuse" is a great combination. Don't overthink it. Simply say, "It's been great talking—I have some other people to connect with," or "This has been so interesting, but it's getting late; I'd love to chat in detail when we have more time." Kathryn is always snacking, so she often goes with a food-related sendoff, such as "Well, I won't monopolize your whole night—I'm going to go grab another bite of guacamole. It was so great to meet you!"

GAINING MOMENTUM AND KEEPING IT GOING

No one's going to go out on a limb for someone they spoke to once at a networking event last year. Now that you made it through the event (whew!), you can begin the process of turning those one-time connections into real long-term relationships. To do this well, you should stay in touch like it's part of your job—in a way that's authentic to your personality, of course. Try blocking out time in your schedule each day or week to touch base with people, like during the 3 p.m. slump or on slow Friday afternoons. A few of our favorite ideas for keeping the momentum going:

- **After you first meet someone, send a friendly email within forty-eight hours,** while you're still top of mind. Mention something you discussed or joked about, or share an article they might find interesting. Express a desire to meet up again— either in general or with a specific date and time suggested. If you met at a recurring event, you can always ask if they're planning to attend the next one.

- **Follow new connections on Twitter** and make following *you* worth their while (if this is your thing, of course) by keeping your feed current, and full of thought-provoking tweets and posts.

- **Celebrate their accomplishments.** Follow them on LinkedIn and reach out to congratulate them when you see they've accomplished something, received a promotion, started a new job, or were featured in the news. We know someone who recently reached out to a former colleague whom she hadn't seen in almost a decade to congratulate her on her newly published book—they ended up getting together for coffee, and reigniting a relationship that's been fruitful (and enjoyable) for them both.

- **Keep them in the loop on what you're up to,** whether that's sharing a link to a company blog post you wrote or client work you were involved in. And don't be afraid to get creative! Some people take it up a notch and write email newsletters or digests of relevant industry information (with links to what they're working on as well) and send it out to their full network. It takes extra effort, but it's a powerful way to stay in touch.

Networking can sometimes feel all about you, but it's much more successful (and natural!) when it's a two-way street. If you're worried that sending people links to work that you've done or articles you've written is braggy or self-promotional, don't be (as long as you're doing it within reason—meaning not every week!). When you offer a piece of advice, expertise, or make an introduction between contacts who have opted in, most people are thrilled. Here are a few ways to make sure you're always giving back:

- Respond to requests for information on email or social media. For instance, if someone you know posted that they're looking for an intern, shoot over recommendations or offer tips that you've found useful.

- Make introductions you think might be worthwhile, but only after asking for permission from both parties. If someone's looking for a freelance writer and you know the perfect fit for his project, ask if you can connect the two of them. Just be sure to check with both sides before making the connection; no one likes to be blindsided by an out-of-the-blue "setup," and if one of the two parties is not particularly interested in getting to know the other and declines or doesn't reply, that's awkward for everyone (including you).

- Forward a link to an upcoming event to a few folks to see if they're going, or email an article that might help them with something you know they're working on.

All of these things will not only keep your network strong; they'll earn you a reputation as someone who is thoughtful and knowledgeable—giving your personal brand a boost as well.

THE WHO'S WHO OF YOUR NETWORK

Here's some good news: you don't need a huge network; you just need the *right* network. Just like the other relationships in your life, quality is better than quantity. We mean it: you're much better off with ten solid colleagues who know you well and will go to bat for you than five hundred LinkedIn connections who have no idea who you are. What this means is, as you're meeting and connecting with people and thinking about maintaining these relationships over the long term, you want to focus your time and energy on those with whom you can have the most meaningful and mutually beneficial relationships.

Most people think networking is all about making new connections. And while that's important, remember that it's equally important to invest in the connections you already have—whether it's the people you met at the last networking event or your current or former co-workers, clients, and friends. Don't neglect people in the latter category—your current team, boss, and clients are as much a part of your network as anyone you met at the last big industry conference! Yes, it can seem like there are a lot of relationships to juggle, so to be as strategic in your efforts as possible, we find it's helpful to think about everyone you know professionally in these buckets:

THE STUNT DOUBLE

WHO

People who are like you—job-wise, that is. In other words, people in your department, who do your job in other departments, and who do your job at other companies.

HOW THEY'RE HELPFUL

They're great for bouncing ideas off of, seeking advice for a specific problem, turning to when you're hiring someone, or simply having a buddy to hang out with at industry events.

HOW TO INVEST IN THE RELATIONSHIP

Chances are, these people are going to keep similar schedules, be interested in the same industry events, and face similar day-to-day challenges as you. This is great news—because it makes for an easy way to connect with them. Consider inviting someone in this category to attend a conference or event with you (bonus: you get to show up with a buddy!). If the person works at your company or is working on a project with you, you can also suggest going out to drinks to unwind after a significant company milestone (say, the product you've both been working on launches, or you hit a major deadline). Or, invite your conference buddy to meet up for coffee before the event so you can head over together. Finally, when spending time with people in this category, don't be afraid to open up a little—you'll never know that you might both be facing the exact same challenge, nor will you be able to help each other with it, if neither of you ever brings it up.

THE OUTSIDER

WHO

People who are in your industry but not your role, your role but not your industry, or your company but doing something totally different.

HOW THEY'RE HELPFUL

They can offer fresh approaches to solving problems and provide a broader perspective on your work, role, or industry. They can also be a good sounding board when you're thinking of making a career change.

HOW TO INVEST IN THE RELATIONSHIP

An easy way to start is by getting to know people in other departments at your company. Try getting involved in organization-wide events, whether that's a kickball league, a volunteer outing, or a casual happy hour, and connect with people you haven't spent a ton of time with before. Beyond your workplace, start spending time with friends or friends of friends whose jobs sound fascinating, even if it's something you might never have considered to be related to your work. And then continue connecting with them about everything from books you find interesting to recommendations for vendors. The best part about this group is, the sky really is the limit when it comes to how you can build the relationship.

THE HIGHER-UPS

WHO

People who have the jobs (or the jobs you're interested in) one, two, or more steps above you.

HOW THEY'RE HELPFUL

They're the ones with the power to hire and promote you (and/or give you the guidance that helps you get to the next level), mentor you by sharing advice and perspective that you might not otherwise have, and teach you more about your field.

HOW TO INVEST IN THE RELATIONSHIP

Make an effort to keep in contact with senior individuals whom you've worked with—even if just for the duration of a project—or whom you've connected with at an event. Check in with them on a regular basis (say, every six to twelve months) to share an update on where you're at, and don't be afraid to seek out their advice and input when appropriate. Sometimes asking for a quick piece of advice or bouncing an idea off someone is a great way to stay on his or her radar, provided you don't go overboard or demand too much time. Scheduling a lunch catch-up or coffee date is a good way to maintain the relationship, but also consider sending an email with your updates—for example, if you receive a promotion, change jobs, or win an award. Keeping these more senior individuals in the loop about your career will make it more natural for you to get in touch when you do want to ask for advice or for a favor.

THE NEWBIE

WHO

People with less experience: that is, junior employees or interns.

HOW THEY'RE HELPFUL

They can tell you a lot about team dynamics and morale that you might not be able to see on the surface and provide you with a chance to practice your leadership skills if you're not yet a manager. In the case of individuals newer to your function or industry, these relationships can give you a glimpse into a "beginner's mind-set" that may help you think about problems differently.

HOW TO INVEST IN THE RELATIONSHIP

People more junior than you may be afraid to strike up a conversation—so make it easy for them by being the one who initiates. Take the new intern out to coffee when he or she starts, and then check in every couple of months to see how things are going. Or round up the more junior people who sit near you for a midday coffee or ice cream break or a lunch out of the office, especially if their schedules are on the flexible side. Explicitly tell more junior members of the team that you are happy to help them, particularly if you can offer to share a specific expertise that is relevant to what they are working on. And when someone asks you for something, particularly something you offered, be prompt with your response—those more junior than you are the most likely to become intimidated by feeling blown off.

THE WORK MATCHMAKER

WHO

You know the type: these are the people who just seem to know everyone, and love connecting people and helping others out.

HOW THEY'RE HELPFUL

They can put you in touch with the right people, at the right time.

HOW TO INVEST IN THE RELATIONSHIP

Most "matchmakers" are great about reaching out from time to time; that's how they stay in touch with and connect others, after all! But make sure you're putting effort into the relationship, too. One great idea to pay it forward is to introduce *them* to other interesting folks (asking them, of course, if they'd like the intro before putting them in touch). Or, invite them to events, conferences, or parties—there's nothing they love more than new groups of people.

THE WINGMAN

WHO

Anyone you genuinely enjoy hanging out with, and would happily spend time with anyway, even if it weren't networking.

HOW THEY'RE HELPFUL

Everything's more fun—and less awkward—when you're interacting with people you actually like, right? That goes double for networking.

HOW TO INVEST IN THE RELATIONSHIP

This one's pretty easy—invest in the relationship the same way you would a new friend—over coffee or drinks! In all seriousness, though, many of our relationships blur the line between "work contact" and "friend," and we think that's a great thing.

———

Networking isn't something you "should probably do," it's something you *have* to do in order to move forward in your career. When you make it a priority, focus on building long-term relationships rather than "What's in it for me?" conversations, and use your network to its full potential, some truly remarkable things can happen—including being introduced to your dream companies, the subject of the next chapter. (And we promise: do it right, and it'll be way more fun than you think.)

SEVEN WAYS TO FIT NETWORKING
INTO YOUR REALLY BUSY SCHEDULE

Keeping relationships strong doesn't have to be an epic time commitment, or take over your life. Simply weave it into whatever you're already doing and most of the time it won't even feel like networking! Here's how:

1. If you're going to a meeting, walk over with a co-worker who's going, too, or linger five minutes afterward and chat with someone about what they're working on.
2. Talk to people in the elevator, instead of scrolling through your phone.
3. When you unglue yourself from your computer and get up to stretch your legs, walk around and chat with your cubicle or office neighbors. Or spend a few extra minutes in the cafeteria talking to people (hey, if you're going to wait in that long frozen yogurt line anyway, might as well use the time productively).
4. Instead of going on a coffee run with the same crew you always go with, ask someone new to join you.
5. Organize lunch with a few people in your department (and block time on the calendar so everyone actually goes).
6. Join a company sports team or volunteer with your co-workers.
7. Plan your own (low-key) networking group. Whether it's organizing a book club, gathering some friends (and their friends) for a weekly yoga class, or hosting a happy hour, every social get-together can boost your professional network—and may even be enjoyable to boot.

The New Rules of Finding Job Opportunities and Openings

THE OLD RULE: You'd comb through the big job boards (or, in the even more distant past, the classified sections of newspapers!) looking for any opening that was remotely related to what you wanted to do. If you found one, you'd proof-read your resume, switch out the company's name in your cover letter, and send off your application—fingers crossed! If not, you'd wait and try again tomorrow.

THE NEW RULE: People do still find their jobs through the big job boards, but success here is getting rarer and rarer. Nowadays, you have more resources than ever to help you find that position that will be the best match for you! Scouring the web for openings you can apply to blindly is hardly the best tool you have available.

In the new world of work, job postings are easier to find and access than ever. Great news, right? Well, not necessarily. Because today, more and more positions are also being filled without ever being posted. Which means that your job, O savvy job seeker, is a bit like that of a detective. You are going to have to find those job opportunities *before* most people know about them (read: before they get blasted everywhere online), and then smoothly and effectively utilize your company knowledge and your network to get in front of the right people—the people who are doing the hiring.

In this chapter, you will find out how to scope out opportunities through a variety of sleuthing methods—through uncovering inside information about your dream companies, through utilizing your network, through targeted industry organizations, and, yes, even through online job sites like The Muse. We'll also discuss how to make inroads into a company you really like, whether or not it's currently hiring for a position that is a fit for you. (Yes, you can sometimes even get a company to create an opening just for you!) Again, since the job search process is a human one, the relationship-building skills you learned in the last chapter are going to come in handy in this process.

KEEP YOUR CHIN UP!

The job search can be long, difficult, and even disheartening at times. If you're struggling to find jobs to apply to, if you haven't heard back from the companies you're really excited about, or if you've been rejected after an application you worked really hard on, it's easy to feel beaten down. But try to keep in mind that this is all (unfortunately) a normal part of the process—most job seekers feel this way at some point!—and trust us when we tell you that all of this hard work *will*, undoubtedly, pay off. Your job is to keep putting your best foot forward every day and to stay positive. Not only will you feel better; employers *will* take note of your fighting spirit and unwavering confidence.

WHERE ARE YOU IN THE PROCESS?

By now, you have filled out your Muse Grid and narrowed down your option set, determining which role or roles you are looking for. You've put together a list of dream companies that you've researched and are familiar with (and have networked with a few people who work there). You're working on actionable steps to get the training or experience you need to be a competitive candidate, and in the meantime you've put together your personal branding statement and know how to position yourself. By now you have a pretty good sense of where you want to go (even if you haven't homed in on one single thing), and of course, you've begun to build the kind of network that can help open those doors.

So what's next? You need to get cracking to see what jobs are actually available!

Essentially, you have four strategies for finding job openings that fit your criteria:

1. Keeping close tabs on your dream companies
2. Asking your network for introductions and referrals
3. Doing a job search online
4. Using social networks to identify openings

This may not seem like groundbreaking advice (we know you already know, for example, to use LinkedIn to find job openings!) but what most people don't realize is that you need to *strategically combine* all of these strategies to get the best look at the opportunities that are out there. But here's a very important caveat: you don't want to go crazy applying to anything that looks remotely interesting. Again, gone are the days when simply blasting the internet with your resume was the key to success. Today's job search is less a "numbers game" and all about hand-picking a few positions you really want to target—and then going above and beyond to tailor those applications and get noticed by the hiring managers. Just like your network, we're talking quality, not quantity!

Speaking of tailoring your application, we'll talk about the nuts and bolts of that—aka your resume and cover letter—in the next chapter. But in the meantime, let's walk through the above four strategies for finding the right openings in the first place.

STRATEGY 1: KEEP CLOSE TABS ON YOUR DREAM COMPANIES

You've been following a company, its leaders, its movers and shakers. You've become familiar with the culture of the place, the voices of its best people, the types of jobs that pop up. You're pretty sure this is a place where you'd fit in, a place you'd love to work. Then one morning, as you pop on the site to browse through the company's careers page, BOOM: You see that the team needs an account manager! Or a salesperson, a data manager, or a designer. Today is your lucky day!

So what's next? Well, you're going to throw your hat in the ring, of course! These days, pretty much any job opening requires an online application, but in today's world of work, where hiring managers are being more inundated with blind applications than ever, this is only step one. Yes, you should do it (and again, we'll get to how to craft an amazing resume and cover letter in more detail soon), but the New Rules of Work dictate a slightly more nuanced and time-intensive—though much more effective—approach.

Let's go back to your network. Do you know anyone at the company? Think through people you reached out to when building out your Muse Grid, folks you've met while networking, and former colleagues and classmates—these are your "first-degree connections." If you have one, reach out to that person directly and let him or her know you are interested in the role and, if appropriate, that you'd love a recommendation or an introduction to the hiring manager. If you don't know anyone who works at the company, don't give up hope yet, just hop over to LinkedIn and see if you have a second-degree connection (in other words, if someone you know has a contact at the company). If so, reach out and ask your contact if he or she would be up for making an introduction. One friend of ours used this approach during a recent job search for an editorial job, and got introductions to second-degree contacts at *Vanity Fair* and the *Huffington Post* in the same day!

Note: You want to treat this communication with people in your network just as professionally as you'd treat a hiring manager—it's another form of applying for jobs, after all! That means: attach your resume, describe why you'd be a great fit for the job, and show your gratitude by following up with a thank-you, no matter what happens.

Okay, so what if you've found your dream company and have been checking their job board compulsively for weeks or months, but they just don't seem to be hiring for a role that meets your skill set? Sure, you could wait and see if something opens up, but we recommend taking the proactive approach. If you have contacts at that company, send along your resume and ask to be kept in mind for future openings. Who knows, maybe HR was just about to post that coveted position! If not, at least they'll have your resume on file for when something does open up. And—potentially the best option of all—maybe they'll be so impressed by your background that they'll create a position for you.

We've actually done this, several times, at The Muse. For example, back in 2012, we weren't yet hiring for a head of marketing. Then one day, Kathryn received a message on LinkedIn from someone who had recently seen her speak. He told her he'd been blown away by her, her team, and most of all her company—and that he wanted to be a part of it. He then gave her a quick elevator pitch about his marketing background and experience in the start-up world and asked for the opportunity to tell her how his skill set could help The Muse reach and exceed its current growth goals.

Here's what that email actually said:

Hi Kathryn,

While slightly out of place, I attended the Women 2.0 conference yesterday with EatDrinkJobs and had the chance to see you pitch. I was blown away by you, your team, and most of all, your company.

I spent six years at Seamless.com, working closely with amazing leaders like Jason Finger (who you know well). I see such amazing potential in your company, and I would love to be a part of it in any way. My primary focus is marketing, with a lot of experience marketing to the same corporations and users you seem to be attracting. I'd love to tell you more about how my skill set could help you all reach and exceed your current growth goals.

*Congrats on all your current success. Again, I'd love to find a time to
chat more about the company and tell you how I could help.*

Best,

Elliott

The author of that message, Elliott Bell, was hired a few months later
and worked at The Muse for four years to build out our marketing team.

(As a side note, if you mention a mutual contact in your outreach,
there's a pretty good chance the recipient will ask that person what they
think of you. Make sure it's positive! In Elliott's email, he mentioned
a former colleague, Jason Finger, whom he knew that Kathryn knew
well; when she asked Jason about Elliott, his response included something to the effect of, I would work with him again in a second.)

No, happy endings like this don't happen all the time (this is a career
we're talking about, not a fairy tale), but sometimes these proactive out-
reaches *do* end in a job, especially in smaller or fast-moving companies.
To boost your chances of this approach working, you'll want to write a
killer cover letter or introductory email that captures who you are and
what you really admire about the company (we'll get to that shortly!).
Make your pitch concise, intelligent, and thoughtful. You can also ask
for an informational interview to learn more about the inner workings
of the departments that interest you, but in contrast to the information
interviews you set up during the research phase, the goal here is less to
learn about the company and more to get a foot in the door so you can
show them why you'd be a great fit and asset.

STRATEGY 2: LET YOUR NETWORK
KNOW YOU'RE LOOKING

We really can't stress it enough: your network is one of the most valuable assets you have in landing your dream job or role. So this step is
about how to let your community know that you are currently looking for a job. We get that asking for help can feel uncomfortable, but
look at it this way: you're just asking for intel about jobs people might

know of—not asking someone in your network to hire you. There's a big difference.

Remind yourself on a daily basis that you are a valuable asset and that most people want to help you; after all, if someone recommends you for a role in her company and it works out, *she* comes out looking good! Plus, most people have been in your shoes themselves at some point, so they know how you feel. Sometimes, people in your network are actively hiring themselves, so putting yourself out there benefits you both. For example, Alex's brother landed his first job out of college after connecting with an alum of his university who he didn't even know was hiring for a job that required his skill set.

The key to asking for help, in a job search or anything else, is to make helping you as easy as possible for the person you're asking. So how do you do it? Here's your action plan and sample email templates, adapted from one of the all-time most popular articles on The Muse, that'll help you get the most out of your outreach, while making helping you almost effortless.

HOW TO WRITE "HELP ME FIND A JOB" EMAILS

While it's tempting to write, "URGENT: Please find me a job!" in the subject line and blast your resume out to everyone you know, that is most definitely *not* the best course of action when you're emailing your network for a favor. What is? Crafting a detailed (but brief) message to the people in your network explaining that you're looking for a new gig in X (be specific) and that you're enlisting their help.

You can start with a bulk email that you send using bcc: to a large group of contacts you know well, either socially or professionally, but you'll also want to craft personalized messages for anyone who knows you very well, anyone who works for one of your dream companies, or anyone who could help you in a very specific way.

In all cases, your email should be easy to skim and very clear about what you need. In addition to your request, you'll want to attach your updated resume, as well as a short bulleted list in the body of the email of where you've been and where you're trying to go (especially if most people you know aren't totally familiar with your field). Even though you are attaching your resume, you should operate under the assumption that not everyone will open and read it, so you'll also want to remind people, in the text of your email, about your current position and company and the length of time you've been there. Even if your friends know this information, they may forward the email on to others who are starting from square one.

Here's how to put it all together:

EXAMPLE 1: MASS EMAIL TO YOUR NETWORK

Hi friends and colleagues,

I hope all is well! As many of you know, I have been an Account Executive at Weber Shandwick for the past three years. I'm looking to shift gears within the public relations field and am reaching out to ask for your help with any leads or contacts.

I am looking for a mid-level public relations position, with a focus on digital content strategy, in Washington, D.C., ideally in the hospitality or consumer products field. I am particularly interested in joining an agency, but would also consider interesting in-house work.

If you know of any job opportunities or leads, please send them my way. Below is a list summarizing my past experience, target positions, and dream companies. My resume is also attached for your reference, so please feel free to pass it along.

Thanks in advance for your help! I hope to catch up with you individually soon.

Work Experience
- *Account Executive, Weber Shandwick: Serve as main point of contact for consumer clients, including Unilever*
- *Account Coordinator, BCV: Assisted on digital strategy for a variety of luxury hospitality clients, including Starwood and Hyatt*

- PR Assistant, Siren PR: *Drafted press releases that resulted in media coverage in* Glamour

Positions Seeking
- *Senior Account Executive*
- *Account Supervisor*
- *Digital Content Producer*

Dream Companies
- *Edelman, Washington, D.C.*
- *Ogilvy, Washington, D.C.*
- *HUGE, Washington, D.C.*
- *Marriott, Bethesda, Maryland*

EXAMPLE 2: TARGETED EMAIL TO KEY CONTACTS

Hi Drew,

I hope all is well! I just read your recent blog post on how social media can impact hotel bookings—the data you included is so fascinating!

I'm reaching out because I'm currently seeking a new position. As you know, I have been at Weber Shandwick for three years, but I'm ready to take on new challenges in the PR world.

I know that you used to work at Edelman, which is on my short list of dream companies. Do you still have any contacts there, and if so, is there someone, specifically on their digital team, who might be willing to do an informational interview with me? Any introductions you could make would be greatly appreciated.

In addition, if you know of any job opportunities or leads at other companies that may be a good fit, please send them my way. I've attached my resume for your reference, and feel free to pass it along.

Thanks in advance for your help! Please keep me posted on how things are going and if there's anything I can do to return the favor.

End the email by including the same bullets as above (Work Experience, Positions Seeking, and Dream Companies) and, of course, attaching your resume.

The key difference between the targeted email and the general one you'll send everyone else is that you take a few extra minutes to personalize this one—both in the address (for example, complimenting Drew on his recent blog post) and in the ask (here, asking specifically for an introduction to anyone Drew might know at Edelman). The targeted email lets you make a specific request that may not be appropriate for your entire network, and is also an opportunity to invest some time into a handful of specific relationships.

Once you hit send, you may envision your inbox being flooded with instant job leads, but try to remember that this process takes time. If someone doesn't respond, it doesn't mean they deleted your email and forgot about it; more likely, they just can't help out right away, but even so, rest assured that you'll be on their radar—and they'll likely reach out if they hear of anything of note.

Another important note: Remember that people are usually happy to help, but you need to show that you appreciate their efforts. Thank everyone who responds to your email or offers to help you (even if it yields nothing). A little gratitude goes a long way. You never know where or how you will cross paths again down the road.

STRATEGY 3: OPTIMIZE YOUR INTERNET JOB SEARCH

Here's a story Kathryn often tells when she talks about why she started The Muse. Frustrated with the job at a consulting firm she had taken right out of college, she began scouring the big job boards for business-strategy jobs in New York. Then one day a search on one of those sites returned, right at the top of the page (among others that had no relevance to her experience or skill set), a job opening at a 7–Eleven convenience store—one that was located many miles away in another state! That's when Kathryn realized that the online job search tools most people used were due for an upgrade.

This, unfortunately, is an experience that too many job seekers have had. Online search engines are vast behemoths of data that spew out thousands of possible job openings for you, but unless you know exactly what type of job or role you're looking for, very few of the results are likely to really appeal to you. Which is why looking online shouldn't make up the bulk of your search strategy.

That said, even today, many job opportunities are posted online, so we don't recommend giving up on that approach entirely. But not all job search sites are created equal. The key is learning how to identify and best use the sites that meet your specific needs. First, make sure they cover jobs in your geographic region (unless you are open to moving). You might also want to see what other informational features they offer (The Muse, for example, creates an in-depth employer profile showcasing, with photo and video, what it's like to work at each company so you can get a feeling for the culture of a place before you apply) and what their search function/interface is like (the good search engines, ours included, let you save companies you love to your profile, so you can regularly check in on them to see if they have relevant openings).

Once you've settled on which job boards to use, here are a few tips on how to make the most of your search:

GO BEYOND THE BASICS

Many job sites let you search not only by job title and location, but also by experience level, expected salary, education requirements, and more. If you have set expectations in each of these areas, make use of the search filters so you'll only see positions that will align with your background.

MAKE SEARCH ALERTS YOUR FRIEND

Some sites let you set up search alerts based on your requirements (say, "HR Coordinator" and "Chicago") that'll automatically email you new postings when they're available. Read: less time scrolling, more time looking at opportunities that might be a real fit.

HEAD TO MORE NICHE SITES

These days almost every field or industry has a dedicated job search platform (or several): Think Sales Gravy for sales jobs, Mediabistro for editorial and media roles, Idealist for nonprofit gigs, and *Hacker News* and AngelList for positions at early-stage start-ups. If you've narrowed your search to a specific field, these specialized platforms can be much more useful (and much less headache-inducing) than trying to find a needle in the online job board haystack.

STRATEGY 4: KEEP AN EYE ON SOCIAL MEDIA

We know you're already on social media—and you're already also scrolling through Facebook, Twitter, and Instagram around the clock to check out what your friends and contacts are up to. But it's worth pointing out that social media can be a good resource for finding job openings, too!

We also know that you've refined your profiles on those sites you frequent most often to reflect your personal brand, and it should go without saying that before you go down this path you should triple-check to make sure your social profiles are polished and professional. (We've rejected more than one candidate for publicly sharing tweets or images that crossed professional boundaries.) But once you do that, here are a few ways you can uncover opportunities by scrolling through your social feeds and updates—that is, doing what you already do anyway, all the time:

FOLLOW THE COMPANIES YOU LOVE

"Liking" or following some of your dream companies on Facebook, Instagram, or Twitter has a dual benefit. One, you'll learn more about their culture, their traditions, and their working style. Two, social media is often the first place companies post about their latest open positions, so their followers have the inside scoop before the posting hits the rest of the web. Some employers even have dedicated jobs handles—for example, @NPRJobs or @PepsiCoJOBS—which makes it even easier to keep an eye on openings!

FOLLOW PEOPLE WHO WORK THERE

In addition to the companies themselves, don't be afraid to follow people who work there. And while it might be cool to see the ins and outs of the CEO's workday, it can be more effective to follow people who work in roles like the ones you want. You'll get a better idea of what their positions entail, and they're more likely to post about job openings on Twitter or LinkedIn than a higher-level executive is.

KEEP AN EYE ON KEY HASHTAGS

Companies that really want to get the word out about their open jobs will often tweet using relevant hashtags—which you, dear job seeker, can use to your advantage. Try searching by role (#writer, #sales) or by location (#nyc, #chicago), combining that with tags like "#jobs" or "#hiring" for the best results.

JOIN FACEBOOK GROUPS

Facebook groups probably aren't the first places you'd think to look for job postings, but many of our Musers report finding really engaged communities of people who regularly share the open positions they hear about on the social network. (For example, our editorial team loves Dreamers//Doers, NYC Tech Ladies, and Binders Full of Digital Journalists.) No matter what your field or interest, search for a group or two, and see what you find. You can check how often people post, if others comment and engage, and what type of content is shared to determine if it might be a helpful group for you.

GO WHERE YOUR PEOPLE ARE

In addition to the behemoths like Facebook and LinkedIn, there are lots of social networks out there that are more industry-specific—GitHub for developers, Medium for writers and bloggers, Behance for designers and artists, etc.—that can be a treasure trove of information and opportunities.

JOB TRACKING WORKSHEET

 As you start finding positions that are exciting to you, it can be helpful to set up a worksheet to keep track of them. An organized job search is not only a more efficient job search; it's more likely to be successful, since you'll be more on top of all your applications and remember to check in. As a bonus, this worksheet will also help you keep your spirits high by reminding you of all the progress you're making!

———

Finding a job is *not* an impossible task. The more you put yourself out there, the better you tap your network, and the better you master the tools of the search we described in this chapter, the better your chance of success. Will it happen overnight? Probably not. But trust us, the investment of time and effort will feel well worth it when you finally do land that amazing position. In the next section we'll give you the tools for doing exactly that.

JOB TRACKING WORKSHEET

NAME OF COMPANY	POSITION	CONTACT	DETAILS ABOUT THE COMPANY, POSITION	APPLICATION AND RESUME NOTES	MY CONTACTS AT THE COMPANY	INTEREST LEVEL (1 TO 5)	STATUS / NEXT STEPS

CHAPTER SEVEN

The New Rules of Crafting Your Application

THE OLD RULE: Way back when, the application process looked entirely different. You've likely heard stories of people mailing hard copies of their resumes to office addresses (yes, really, that happened) or even waiting for hours in the office lobby in the hopes that someone would agree to sit down and chat with them about job opportunities. In some ways, the job hunt was more challenging back then. But in many ways, it was also more personal.

THE NEW RULE: Today, hopeful candidates submit their materials online—into what often feels like a black hole. You're left feeling like a faceless data point, trying to make it through companies' applicant tracking systems, to stand out among a sea of competition and demonstrate that you're a perfect fit for the position—likely without ever actually directly speaking with, let alone meeting with, anyone at the company. These features of the age of technology present a unique challenge to job seekers. But they are nothing you can't conquer!

You did it. You pulled on your detective hat, dug into some research, and found several positions that sound like they could be a perfect fit for you. So now what? Cross your fingers, close your eyes, and click your heels together three times? Not quite. By now, you know better. The job hunt is exciting, but at the same time, landing the right gig involves quite a bit of—you guessed it—work.

Once you've identified some opportunities and you're feeling eager to throw your hat into the ring, it's time to pull together materials that are sure to impress that hiring manager and get your foot in the door (literally) for one of those coveted few interview spots. We'll start with the two crucial documents you'll need—your resume and cover letter— and then we'll talk about how to go above and beyond those documents to really make a memorable impression.

WAIT, DO I REALLY STILL NEED A RESUME AND COVER LETTER?

Even though we're playing by the New Rules of Work, that doesn't mean all past traditions and expectations should be completely tossed out the window. In fact, there are still quite a few long-standing elements of the traditional job search that you're going to need to honor and incorporate into your modern one. And, as you might already suspect, your resume and cover letter are two of these.

"But, wait!" you're likely thinking. "My LinkedIn profile has everything any potential employer would need to know. Wouldn't listing that information in a formal document just be repetitive—or even archaic?"

Believe us, we've heard that question many times before. But heed our advice when we say that nothing replaces your formal resume and cover letter. Not your LinkedIn profile. Not your impressive personal website. Not your articulate expression of your skills and talents in your informational interview, or your well-written email to the hiring manager. These are all important, of course. However, you absolutely still need to have a polished resume and cover letter prepared. Because all those extra trappings won't matter if you don't have the right packaging to catch the eye of your target audience—the hiring managers.

WRITING YOUR RESUME

Since you absolutely need a resume in your job hunt arsenal, now it's time to actually write one (or pull out that old document you haven't looked at in years and get it updated!). We know that can be intimidating—

fitting your professional history, your skills, your accomplishments, and what makes you an all-around excellent candidate all into one concise and well-presented document isn't easy. But, luckily, much of the work you've done up to this point in the book will give you a huge head start. Let's walk through the steps for pulling together a resume that's bound to impress.

STEP ONE: LAY THE GROUNDWORK

We've already talked in detail about research you'll need to conduct before you can even start your job hunt. You learned how to identify your values and interests, how functions and industries you may or may not have previously known about come into play, and how to dig in and find companies and positions that fit the bill for what you're looking for. But that doesn't mean the information-gathering stage is over. Now it's time to dive in even further and collect the information that will be especially helpful in putting together a resume that's tailored specifically to that position you are gunning for.

ANALYZE THE JOB DESCRIPTION

First, take a fine-tooth comb to the job description and ask yourself two key questions:

1. AM I QUALIFIED FOR THIS?

Being ambitious is a good thing, but applying for jobs that you're nowhere near qualified for will only set you up for disappointment. So it's important to be honest about your skills and qualifications. If you can check at least three-quarters of the boxes, then it's generally worth a shot. However, if they're seeking ten to fifteen years of experience—and you only have three? You're better off setting your sights a little lower.

2. WHAT EXACTLY ARE THEY LOOKING FOR?

Now is also a good time to begin pulling out key characteristics from the job description, which will be useful when you fill in the blanks on your resume. We recommend printing out the job description and tackling it with a highlighter to make everything super clear. What words do you see popping up over and over again? Maybe you've seen "skilled communicator" in a few different places. Or perhaps there's a lot of emphasis on project management. The important thing is to make note of exactly what skills and qualities they're seeking, so that you can work to make sure your resume fits that mold (while still remaining honest, of course!).

Once you've answered these two questions (and determined you want to move forward with applying), open up a Word doc or turn a new page in your Muse Notebook. It's time to switch the focus from the job description to yourself. Take a few minutes to list out some of your greatest skills and accomplishments, and take a look at how they match up compared to what the employer is looking for. This might be a good time to turn back to your old performance reviews, project wrap-ups, or past client feedback emails you've received. In particular, look for tangible accomplishments or quantifiable results—for example, that you planned a forty-person event that came in 10 percent under budget or hit your sales targets six quarters in a row. Having a roster of your strong points at the ready will make the resume-writing process that much easier. So once you've created this list, keep it nearby! You'll need it shortly.

IS IT A GOOD CULTURAL FIT?

You might *seem* like the perfect fit for the position—on paper, at least. But if you don't think you can gel with the company's culture, you'll find yourself with an entirely different set of problems on your hands.

It's for this very reason that it's important to take more time to learn more about that culture before ever pressing Send on that perfectly polished application of yours. Yes, we know you spent a good deal of time researching companies in putting together your Muse Grid, but now that you've identified a specific position you think would be the right fit, it's time to dig a bit deeper. If you did your research in the last stage, you probably uncovered a lot of important facts about leading players in your industry: what they do, who their competitors are, how well they pay. But now that you're getting serious about making one of these companies a workplace you'll *want* to get up and go to every day, it pays to spend a little more time looking more closely at what that day-to-day will look like. That includes questions like: Is the atmosphere fast-paced and high energy, or more laid-back and low tempo? Is it a highly social, collaborative workplace, or do people tend to keep to themselves? Is the vibe jokey and casual (that is, the kind of place where people prank each other on April Fool's Day), or is it more buttoned up and formal? Does management sit in an ivory tower, or do people feel comfortable stepping into their boss's office unannounced? Not only will you get a feel for whether or not you'd be happy there, but you'll also get your hands on some valuable information to differentiate yourself from the competition by presenting yourself as the very best cultural fit to fill that open role.

Here are a few places you can check for some helpful insights to get the lowdown on the culture of a particular organization:

Social Media: Oftentimes, companies will develop much more of a "personality" on their social media accounts than they do on their website or elsewhere. This can give you a good sense for whether they're more laid-back and friendly, or fairly rigid and corporate. Plus, combing through their actual social content can be revealing, too. Are employees in jeans and enjoying a company-wide guacamole contest? Or are they in suits attending an industry seminar? Of course, social media won't give you the whole picture, but it can definitely clue you in.

Industry Experts: The world is surprisingly small. So if you know someone who already works at another company in the industry, set up time to chat. Have they heard tons of positive things about the company culture—or has this organization fostered somewhat of a bad reputation?

Reviews: A quick Google search can unearth all kinds of useful and often uncensored information—including reviews from present and former employees and clients, and others who have interacted with the company previously. Just remember that while these can be informative, they can also be somewhat misleading—particularly those from former employees with an ax to grind. Remember to take them with a grain of salt.

Image and Video Search: We founded The Muse, in part, to help people see inside offices and gain a sense of company culture, so you can use TheMuse.com/companies to explore particular companies and get a sense for a variety of work environments—think of it as your own behind-the-scenes peek! If a company isn't on The Muse, a quick Google image or video search should uncover some interesting media that can be a helpful company culture primer as well.

STEP TWO: STRUCTURE YOUR DOCUMENT

So now you're armed and ready with all the skills and accomplishments you want to list on your resume. But, for so many people, this is where things really get tricky. You have so much information you feel is important to share, drawing it into a polished, one-page document seems next to impossible. (And yes, it should be one page, until you have ten or so years of experience under your belt.)

Before getting started, take some time to map out or outline the overall structure of your document—a framework that will help to keep you focused and organized. Now, we should note that there isn't a "one size fits all" resume structure that works for everyone. In fact, you should think less about fitting your resume into a traditional template, and more about how to immediately highlight the information that's most relevant to the hiring manager front and center.

Basically, you'll want to make sure that the top third of your document contains the most important facts you'll want someone to know.

For example, if you're a recent grad without much work history, high-lighting your educational background is key, so it should be right up top. But once you have even a few years of experience, you'll want to reserve that real estate for your key skills or current position. Or, if you're some-one with limited work history or your experiences don't quite align with the job you're applying for, you might opt for a nonchronological resume that brings your most relevant experiences to the top.

Let's walk through the elements that you might include on your re-sume, and then we'll give you a few options for exactly how to structure everything, based on your specific situation.

NAME AND CONTACT INFORMATION

We know it sounds obvious, but some people actually forget this crucial piece—we've seen it. Suffice it to say here that you'll have a tough time getting hired if people can't tell who you are, or how to get in touch with you! The basics include your name, phone number, and email ad-dress. You can also include a link to your LinkedIn profile, to make it easy for hiring managers to find you, as well as to professional social media handles.

SUMMARY STATEMENT

This is a short, one- to three-sentence statement summarizing your skills and experience. It's very common for senior-level candidates who want to sum up their decades of experience into a single blurb, but it can also be a useful way to highlight your transferable skills if you're chang-ing careers or want to weave a common theme through a wide variety of experiences.

WORK EXPERIENCE

An outline of your previous work experiences will likely make up the bulk of your resume. For each role, you'll want to include your title, the company name, location, and dates of employment, followed by pow-erful bullet points about your responsibilities and accomplishments at each job (more on that in a bit). This should typically be listed in reverse chronological order with the most recent first, unless your most relevant experience isn't your most recent—in which case, you can break your work experience section into two: "Relevant Experience" and "Other Work Experience," for example, and then list your experiences in reverse chronological order within each.

EDUCATION

Here's where you'll list your education (everything from college on—most employers for roles requiring a four-year degree don't care about high school education). You'll want to include the institution and the degree you've earned, but you can leave out your graduation year (especially if you're worried someone will think you're too young or too old) and GPA (unless it's highly valued in your field, such as consulting). However, if you received a special honor or cum laude status, don't be afraid to throw that in!

SKILLS

This is a section we see many people leave off their resumes. We get why: space is limited. However, including a few simple bullet points about your top skills is a great way not only to bring your expertise to the forefront, but also to naturally incorporate some of those keywords you identified in your research phase. See? We told you that legwork would come in handy.

AWARDS, ASSOCIATIONS, OR VOLUNTEER INVOLVEMENT

If you've won awards or have significant involvement in professional associations or volunteer organizations, you can add a short section to that effect as well—especially if it's relevant to the positions you're applying for.

———

Now, how do you pull it all together? Here are some templates for how to structure your resume based on where you are in your career, inspired by Muse career expert Lily Zhang:

RESUME STRUCTURE 101

FOR MOST PEOPLE

This is the traditional format, and the one you'll see most often if you use an online resume template.

1. Contact information
2. Work experience
3. Awards/associations/volunteer involvement (optional)
4. Education
5. Skills

FOR RECENT GRADS

If you've done a few internships or jobs during college, you can follow the structure above. Otherwise, if your education is more relevant to the jobs you're applying for, use the following:

1. Contact information
2. Education
3. Work/internship experience
4. Extracurricular activities
5. Skills

FOR CAREER CHANGERS

If you're switching to a whole new field, you'll want a summary section that'll help get the right message across to employers (since your work experience might not do the trick on its own). Then remember to split your experience section into two—either "Relevant experience" and "Other work experience," or something more specific to the jobs you're applying for; for example, "Sales experience."

1. Contact information
2. Summary
3. Relevant experience

4. Other work experience
5. Awards/associations/volunteer involvement (optional)
6. Education
7. Skills

FOR SENIOR-LEVEL CANDIDATES

Executives should use the standard structure, adding a summary section that serves as a highlight reel for your career front and center:

1. Contact information
2. Summary
3. Work experience
4. Awards/associations/volunteer involvement (optional)
5. Education
6. Skills

By the way, you've probably seen resume templates and examples online, and they can definitely be a helpful way to get yours looking sharp (and not spend hours in Microsoft Word trying to get it to look *just right*). (You can check out some of our favorites by searching for "resume templates" at TheMuse.com.) Just remember, you may have to rename or rearrange the sections in the template to suit your own needs. A structure that works for you is more important than a traditionally designed template any day!

STEP THREE: SHOW, DON'T TELL

When you've done your research, mapped out a structure, and filled in the blanks with your own skills and experiences, chances are things still aren't looking *quite* as impressive as you hoped. Don't worry—this is totally normal! And it's exactly why this step of the process exists. Those previous steps were more about getting everything out of your brain and down on paper. But this is when you'll comb through everything you have down so far and transform it from standard to super impressive.

RESUME VS. CV?

You might have heard the term *curriculum vitae* (CV) tossed around here and there. And, if you're like most people, you just nodded and pretended to know what on earth that meant.

Stacey Lastoe, a senior writer/editor for The Muse, breaks things down pretty simply: "Unlike the resume, which lists work history and experiences, along with a brief summary of your skills and education, the CV is a far more comprehensive document. It goes above and beyond a mention of education and work experience and often lists—in thoughtful detail—your achievements, awards, honors, and publications, things universities care about when they're hiring teaching staff. Unlike a resume, which is rarely longer than a one-sided single page, the CV can be two, six, or twelve pages—depending on your professional achievements."

Most people who need CVs are either academics or researchers, or are applying to work abroad. So if you don't fall into one of those categories, we recommend keeping your focus on the tried-and-true resume.

Pay attention to these two key things and you're sure to wind up with a resume that packs a punch.

INCLUDE QUANTIFIABLE ACHIEVEMENTS

There's a certain trap that's all too easy to fall into when you're working on your resume: you list your previous employment experiences, and they read exactly like job descriptions. Remember, the goal of your resume is to highlight what you specifically accomplished and what you excel at—not necessarily every day-to-day responsibility of a job.

A great way to show instead of tell is by making sure to include those *quantifiable* achievements that you jotted down in Step 1. There are numerous buzzwords you'll come across again and again in resumes:

Pretty much anyone can describe himself or herself as a "skilled communicator" or "motivating leader." But if you don't have any real-world examples to back that claim up, these words (even if they are true) are virtually meaningless.

So you're much better off placing your emphasis on what you do—not just saying it. Say you want to communicate that you're a self-starter, based on what you've learned from a job description. Here's what not to say: "I'm a self-starter." Here's an example of what you might say:

> *Independently launched company's first-ever intern training program, which streamlined onboarding process and required 50% fewer manager hours spent on training.*

In another example, let's say you were previously an event coordinator for a marketing company. Perhaps one of your existing resume bullets says something like:

> *Planned, coordinated, and executed events to grow brand awareness.*

Sounds like something you'd read in a standard job description, doesn't it? Instead, a concise bullet like this is much more impactful:

> *Executed 15+ events each quarter to grow brand awareness, resulting in a 12% increase in new client signups.*

By including those hard numbers, you display what you *actually* accomplished and worked on—and not just what you *should've* been doing. So work in specific details like these wherever you can. They make a big difference!

USE ACTION WORDS

Speaking of words that frequently appear in resumes, you'll often find yourself getting tripped up when choosing your verbs. You don't want every single bullet point to start with the same word—but you're having a hard time thinking of enough synonyms for "managed" or "led."

It seems like a minor detail, but making sure to use powerful verbs in your resume can make a world of difference. Hiring managers have become so used to seeing those same old words, they practically tune them out at this point. So go through your resume and see what verbs you can switch out for something that's more compelling and specific. For example, try using "chaired" or "oversaw" in place of "led," or "redesigned" or "streamlined" in place of "improved." (For more of our favorite resume-appropriate action verbs, check out themuse.com/thenewrules!)

REFERENCES AVAILABLE UPON REQUEST?

You may have seen this on resume templates. In fact, you may have it on your own resume—and if that's the case, you can delete it right now! The line takes up valuable space on your resume, it looks a bit presumptuous, and at the end of the day, it's really not needed. You can rest assured that if a hiring manager wants a list of your references, he or she will ask!

STEP FOUR: POLISH IT UP

You did it. You have a resume pulled together. And even better? It's one you're finally proud of. But wait! Before sending your hard work off into the world and waiting for the interview offers to roll in, there's one final step you want to make sure you don't skip: polishing.

You've already taken care of sprucing up the content in the previous step. But polishing is all about those things that your eye can easily skip over, like typos, grammatical errors, and weird formatting issues. Trust us, it doesn't matter how impressive your accomplishments are—if your resume is riddled with careless mistakes, you'll have a hard time convincing any hiring manager that you won't be just as careless in the job.

First, you'll want to dedicate some serious time to proofreading to make sure you catch every last blunder. (Don't think that quickly skimming over your entire document is enough to do the trick!) Try reading the document from the bottom to the top so that you truly need to focus on what's actually written on the page—rather than what your brain *thinks* it's seeing. Or read it aloud to force yourself to consider every last word. When in doubt, pass your resume along to a friend or family member so that he or she can pick up on anything you might've missed.

Another thing you'll want to ensure is easy skimmability of your document. The average hiring manager spends only six seconds reviewing a particular candidate's resume. *Six* seconds! So your document needs to be formatted neatly so that the hiring manager can immediately spot the information she needs to determine whether you're headed to the "yes" or "no" pile. If *you're* having trouble quickly finding the highlights, you can bet the hiring manager will as well.

Here are a few ways to make sure your document is skimmable:

- **Keep it to one page** (unless, again, you have ten-plus years of experience). If it's falling over to a second page, you can play with the formatting and font size a bit, but it's better to trim down a bullet point or two—you don't want people having to squint to read it!

- **Make sure there's white space:** No one likes looking at a big block of text. Make sure you leave at least an inch of margin on each side of the page, as well as a bit of space between each line and section.

- **Use bold and italics (selectively):** A bit of bold or italic text can help key elements, like your companies or job titles, stand out. Just don't go overboard, or you won't be emphasizing anything.

YOUR RESUME EDITING CHECKLIST

Are you ready to send your resume out into the world? Our editor in chief, Adrian Granzella Larssen, put together a resume-editing checklist to make sure:

LOOK AT THE BIG PICTURE

- Does this sell you as the perfect candidate for the types of roles you're seeking?
- Are there any gaps between the experience on the page and the experience required for the job?
- If so, are there ways in which you could bridge those gaps?
- What makes your experience stand out among other, similar candidates?
- Does the top third of your resume serve as a hook to get the hiring manager to read more?
- Is there anything on your resume that doesn't need to be?

SCRUTINIZE THE BULLETS AND DETAILS

- Is this the strongest possible language you could use?
- Can anything be said more clearly? Or in fewer words?
- Is there any language or acronyms that someone outside your company or industry wouldn't understand?
- Could anything benefit from examples?
- Can anything be quantified? Can you show a benefit?
- Are any words used over and over? Can they be replaced with more creative language?

FACT-CHECK

- Are the companies you worked for still named the same thing? Still located in the same city?
- Are your position titles accurate?
- Are your employment dates correct?

- Are all of the numbers and percentages you use to describe increases, quotas, budgets, savings, and achievements (reasonably) accurate?

PROOFREAD
- Are there any typos? Wrong word usage?
- Does each bullet point end with a period (or not)? Either is fine; just be consistent.
- Are you using the serial comma (or not) throughout?

MAKE SURE IT LOOKS NICE
- Does the page look visually appealing?
- Is the page overly cluttered?
- Is the font size too small? Is it difficult to read?
- Are the font size and format for each section consistent?
- Does the layout make sense?
- Is your contact information easily findable?

Finally, look back to the application instructions. Did you include everything that was requested? Failing to follow the instructions is a huge red flag to hiring managers—after all, if you can't follow instructions now, how can they trust that you'll do so once you're on the job?

Once your resume is finished, save it as a PDF. Unlike a Word document, the PDF format will maintain the exact layout and style that you selected, so what you see is what the hiring manager will see.

SAMPLE RESUME

Want a look at how it's done? We worked with Muse career coach Jena Viviano, who transformed this Muser's resume into a polished new version.

Melissa Warren
Salt Lake City, Utah 801.555.7428 missymelissy000@yahoo.com

Education

Skillcrush
- Currently enrolled in three-month Web Designer certification program

Utah State University
- Participated in classes for online program in Communication and Leadership

NRCSA Immersion Program – Lisbon, Portugal
- Traveled throughout Portugal and lived with a family in Lisbon studying the Portuguese language.

Experience

Lincoln Musical Leadership School (LMLS), Salt Lake City   2001–PRESENT

Development Officer
- Cultivate, solicit, and steward a portfolio of major gift prospects with the ability to secure significant gifts in support of LMLS' mission to be the leading source and teacher of musical skills and leadership.
- Assist with the implementation of a comprehensive strategy for the appropriate acknowledgment of donors and steward-ship of gifts and reviewing foundation and personal proposals connected to major donors.
- Create, Organize, and implement regional donor events and oversee two Event Steering Committees
- Part of fundraising team that successfully raised over $25 million for Campaign LMLS
- Assisted in putting together LMLS 50th Anniversary events
- Assisted in a silent auction
- Worked with donors to create scholarships focused on diversity and financial need.
- Build relationships with schools and community organizations within my region

Marketing Projects Liaison
- Networking and researching to allow the local community to be introduced, on diverse levels, to the LMLS mission. This Project was focused on building professional relationships in the Salt Lake City community with a focus on educational systems, police/fire departments, government agencies, and local non-profits.

Marketing Project Coordinator
- Planned a statewide event called Singing for the Nation. Responsibilities included talking with local schools and after-school programs to do development outreach, scheduling speakers, creating a budget, overseeing interns, reserving facilities, planning student projects with teachers, and planning media and advertisement.

Event Coordinator
- LMLS Summer program. During this time I was responsible for driving a twenty-four-passenger school bus from Salt Lake City to Portland OR alone for LMLS. Wrote the initial proposal for a LMLS program in Ecuador.

Field Instructor
- Instructor for LMLS, managed up to thirty-five students for four-week programs. Teaching leadership, communication, judgment, and decision-making, conflict resolution, along with singing skills.

Bravo Communications, Washington DC   2009

MusicNOW Film Project Intern
- Responsible for the research of future directors and films for the festival, reviewed seed grant applications for photographers and documentary film directors, assisted in preparation and management of events and film screenings, and collaborated with other departments to develop avenues to bring the MusicNOW Film Project mission to new audiences.

Caremore Inc., Salt Lake City, UT   2008–2009

Consultant
- Provide health screenings, review screening results with employers, and assist in tailoring a next step wellness plan to be reviewed by the corporation as part of the organization's health and wellness consulting service to provide

Referrals
- Provided upon request

MELISSA WARREN

Salt Lake City, UT | 801.555.7428 | melissa.sophia.warren@gmail.com

---

PROFESSIONAL EXPERIENCE

Lincoln Musical Leadership School (LMLS), *Salt Lake City, UT (2001–Present)*
Development Officer

- Cultivate and steward a portfolio of 250+ major gift prospects ($20k and above) in 21 states, helping LMLS remain the leading source and teacher in musical skills and leadership
- Implement a comprehensive strategy to appropriately acknowledge donors and keep them engaged
- Contributed to fundraising team that raised over $25M for Campaign LMLS from 2010–2014
- Assisted in creating, organizing, and implementing events across the country, including LMLS 50th Anniversary, raising over $26k in one weekend
- Built relationships with schools and community organizations to facilitate interest and access to LMLS in underserved communities; created various scholarships with cooperation and support of donors

Marketing Projects Liaison

- Broadened awareness of the LMLS mission to the Salt Lake City community via networking
- Built professional relationships in the Salt Lake City community, focused on educational systems, police and fire departments, government agencies, and local non-profits

Marketing Project Coordinator

- Planned a 400-person statewide "Singing for the Nation" event, overseeing 20 volunteers
- Coordinated with 40 local schools and after-school programs in an effort to complete development outreach; would schedule speakers, oversee up to 3 interns, manage budget, and partner with teachers to spread awareness
- Planned and coordinated the LMLS program in Ecuador; established the partnership between the National Singing Foundation and LMLS

Bravo Communications, *Washington, DC (2009)*
MusicNOW Film Project Intern

- Researched directors and films for the festival, reviewed 300+ seed grant applications for photographers and documentary film directors, and assisted in preparation of 13 events and film screenings
- Collaborated cross-functionally to develop awareness program, bringing the MusicNOW Film Project mission to 10,000 new viewers

Caremore, Inc., *Salt Lake City, UT (2008–2009)*
Consultant

- Provided health screenings as well as actionable plans for employers to create wellness plans in their businesses

EDUCATION

Utah State University – *Communication and Leadership; Remote*
NRCSA Immersion Program; *Lisbon, Portugal*
Skillcrush; *Web Designer Certification; Remote*

SKILLS + INTERESTS

Microsoft Office, fundraising, travel planning, entrepreneurial spirit, volunteerism, singing

WRITING YOUR COVER LETTER

Few people enjoy writing resumes. But say the words "cover letter" and the trembling really starts! Just the phrase is usually enough to conjure deep-rooted dread that sends a shiver right down your spine.

We get it: cover letters can be intimidating. After all, in the new world of work this is probably your first opportunity to show a future employer who you are as a real living, breathing person—rather than as a number spit out by the screening software or a faceless name on an application form. It's incredibly difficult to know what exactly you should be saying in that all-important introductory message. But there's no need to panic! We have what you need to know to craft the perfect cover letter that demonstrates just how amazing you are.

> BUT REALLY . . .
>
> DOES ANYBODY EVEN READ COVER LETTERS?
>
> It's a complaint we've heard time and time again: "Why would I spend so much time working on a cover letter when I *know* that nobody actually reads them?" We can understand where you're coming from with this. In fact, a September 2015 Jobvite survey found that 55 percent of hiring managers actually don't read cover letters at all.
>
> That's discouraging, yes. But instead of obsessing over that fact, think about it this way: that means 45 percent of hiring managers actually do. And you don't want to be that person who doesn't get the job because they failed to include that crucial piece. At The Muse, we read cover letters religiously—and they can make all the difference.

So let's get into it. Here's what you need to know to craft a cover letter that not only stands out, but stands out in a way that is all but sure to inspire that hiring manager to reach out for an interview.

STEP ONE: REMEMBER YOUR RESEARCH

Remember that research you did about the company culture when you were working on your resume? Well, that wasn't *just* for your resume. You can also use elements of what you found out when crafting your cover letter.

The great thing about cover letters is that you're free to show a little more personality and your understanding of the company culture— outside of the constraints and confines of formal resume structures and bullet points. So take advantage of that opportunity any way you can! One way to do this is to attempt to write your letter using the company's "voice"—mirroring the tone, language, and general attitude is a surefire way to subconsciously show you'd fit right in.

Another key thing you'll want to learn during your research is to whom you should be sending your cover letter. Seeing a letter addressed to a generic "To Whom It May Concern" or "Dear Sir or Madam" isn't exactly inspiring to a hiring manager, and certainly doesn't do much to forge that personal connection you are aiming for! So do some digging to find the hiring manager's name. If you really can't find that information anywhere, resort to addressing the head of the department; for example, "Dear Sales Director" or even the specific group (if there is one) doing the hiring, like "Dear Marketing Analyst Search Committee." The more personal and less generic, the better, as it'll show that you wrote your letter with a very specific audience in mind.

STEP TWO: RESIST THE TEMPTATION TO COPY AND PASTE YOUR RESUME

All too often, people feel that they've already mentioned everything worthy of note in their resume, and, unfortunately, their cover letters just become shortened, regurgitated versions of that same information.

This isn't something you want to do. Instead of a mirror image of your resume, think of the cover letter as your opportunity to *expand* on some of the key points that were included there (while also showcasing a bit of your personality). As our editors at The Muse have frequently noted, "A cover letter gives you the freedom to use full sentences—instead of bullet points—so use them to expand upon your resume points and tell the story of why you're the perfect fit for the company."

For example, instead of saying, "I was in charge of assigning quarterly budgets," you're much better off using that space to elaborate into, "Through the process of establishing and assigning quarterly budgets, I gained a deep knowledge of AcmeCorp's internal financial systems—and I also became adept at negotiating between multiple stakeholders across the business to come to consensus."

STEP THREE: HIGHLIGHT KEY SKILLS

First, it's important to note that while you don't want to copy and paste the contents of your resume into a new document, slap a "Dear Mr. Smith" on it, and then simply call it a day, there are a few things on your resume that are worthy of some repetition here.

Your key skills are one of them: you don't want to take a chance of anyone missing the things you truly excel at. Try pulling out two or three key skills you want to be sure to emphasize (by looking at both the job description and your resume). Then, for each of the skills you choose, think back on some specific projects, achievements, or assignments that directly relate to your expertise in that specific area.

Next, explain those skills in your cover letter. An effective way to do this is by including a sentence like "As a candidate, here's what I bring to the table:" after your introduction. You can follow that up by breaking down your two or three key skills, with an expanded explanation of how you've used them in previous employment experiences—as well as how you'll use them to benefit this particular company.

A common mistake people make when doing this is placing the majority of their emphasis on why they want that particular job. But it's important that you remember that the hiring manager already knows you want the job—he or she is looking out for the best fit for the role, not necessarily the person who wants it most. So make sure to highlight the value you're offering, and resist the temptation to go on and on about how much you'd love to land the position.

STEP FOUR: TELL YOUR STORY

Again, this is your chance to go beyond bullet points and share a little more of both your story and your personality. Remember, hiring managers hire *people*—not robots.

Kicking off your cover letter with a brief but attention-grabbing anecdote will demonstrate a little more about who you are personally. And you can bet it'll stand out a lot more than a standard "I'm writing to express my interest in the Sales Coordinator position" line. The more you grab their attention, the better your chances are at actually having your letter read.

Of course, any anecdote you tell should be related to the position you are hoping to fill. Perhaps, for example, you first discovered your passion for sales while working at your childhood lemonade stand. Or maybe a recent volunteer opportunity ignited your interest in the new career field of educational consulting. Whatever it is, craft a narrative about how your experiences led you to this very job.

Here are a few more examples:

> *When I was growing up, all I wanted to be was one of those people who pretend to be statues on the street. Thankfully, my career goals have become a little more practical over the years, but I still love to draw a crowd and entertain the masses—passions that make me the perfect Trade Show Coordinator.*

> *My last boss once told me that my phone manner could probably defuse an international hostage situation. I've always had a knack for communicating with people—the easygoing and the difficult alike—and I'd love to bring that skill to your Office Manager position.*

> *Last December, I ousted our company's top salesperson from his spot at the top of the sales leaderboard—and I've been there ever since. Now I'm ready for my next big challenge, and the Sales Manager role at the X company just might be it.*

While you won't find the title "Community Manager" listed on my resume, I've actually been bringing people together online and off for three years while running my own blog and series of meetups.

The Perfect Cover Letter Template

By Lily Zhang

So what does the perfect cover letter look like? Here's a helpful template showing how to structure a letter that includes all the elements we mentioned above:

Dear [name],

[Anecdote that talks about why you're applying to the position.] Which is why I would like to express my interest in the [position title] position at [company]. My interest in [field] has taken me from [experience] to [experience]. I believe that my passion for [aspect of your field or background], strong commitment to [aspect of your field or background], and interest in [aspect of your field or background] make me an ideal candidate to join the [department] staff at [company].

As a candidate, here's what I could immediately bring to the table:

An effective [descriptor that reflects transferable skill #1]: In my role at [previous job], I [action or accomplishment]. I was also able to showcase my [skill] abilities as a [role] in [project name] project by [what you did].

A disciplined [descriptor that reflects transferable skill #2]: I have always displayed my careful approach to [job duty] by [action]. At [previous company], I frequently [action]. In addition, I had the opportunity to [action or accomplishment], which further shows my dedication to [aspect of your field].

A passionate [descriptor that reflects transferable skill #3]:

Everything I have engaged in so far has all been driven by my keen interest in [aspect of your field]. Even as a [previous role], I made sure to dedicate some part of my day to [action]. It is this passion that has driven every one of my career decisions thus far.

I look forward to contributing my skills and experiences to the [position title] position at [company] and hope to have the opportunity to speak with you further about how I can be an asset to your team.

Sincerely,

[Your name]

Of course, you can (and should!) insert your personality, creativity, and knowledge of the company into your letter, Zhang says, but this framework is a helpful way to convey your most relevant transferable skills to the recruiter (making his or her job a whole lot easier). Don't bother walking through your entire career path and justifying every professional decision you made. Do the hiring manager (and yourself) a favor, and let your skills speak for themselves.

TAILORING YOUR DOCUMENTS

As you may have guessed from reading the examples above, it's pretty important to tailor your resume and cover letter for every single position you apply to. In fact, it's crucial! Remember: your goal when applying is to show why you're the perfect fit for *that particular job*. So, needless to say, there isn't a "one size fits all" resume or cover letter that will accomplish that for every single position you apply to. All jobs are different, all requirements are different, all companies are different—you need to be able to capture those nuances and differences in your own documents.

We know that this can be a challenge, and a good deal of extra work. So here are a few innovative ways you can make it clear that your documents are exclusively targeted to the specific job you're applying for, without having to reinvent the wheel each time.

KEEP A RUNNING MASTER RESUME

So you're not creating a resume from scratch each and every time, have one long document that contains all of your bullet points, project descriptions, accomplishments, and skills in one place, so you can easily mix and match for the right resume for each position.

PULL YOUR MOST RELEVANT EXPERIENCE TO THE TOP

Make sure that you've highlighted the experience that is most relevant and compelling for *that particular job*. Whether it's a previous position or a freelance project you worked on, you need to position the information that this specific hiring manager would be most excited about front and center, where he or she will definitely spot it.

REVAMP IRRELEVANT BULLETS

Even though you're tailoring for relevancy, there's not much you can do about the fact that there are things you need to include on your cover letter and resume (such as past work experience or even your degree) that might not be 100 percent in sync with the job you're applying for. Your best bet there is to try to rework how you describe them to be as relevant as possible. In most cases, that will mean emphasizing more of the transferable skills—think communication or even organization—that are of value in every job or position. For example, a background in international relations may have built up your ability to break down complex problems into individual pieces and solve them; a degree in mathematics might have honed your analytical skills; a position in media may have helped you become a stronger writer, and so on. Framing that experience in this way is a good opportunity to show the hiring manager what broader abilities you bring to the table, even if the experience itself isn't related to this specific job.

DO THE QUICK SCAN TEST

To put your tailoring to the test, give this a try. First, read through the description of the specific job you're applying for. Then read through the resume and cover letter you've written. Do the same key skills and requirements jump out to you in all three? If not, rework to make things clearer. Remember, hiring managers won't spend a long time reviewing your documents. So you want to make it as readily apparent as possible that you're a perfect fit.

PHONE A FRIEND

This is another effective way to test things out. Pass your resume and cover letter along for a friend's review—without telling him anything about the job you're applying for. When he's done reviewing your documents, ask: What skills and accomplishments stood out the most? What sort of job does he think you're applying for? The answers you'll get can reveal a lot about some areas where you still need to improve your wording and relevancy.

RESUME AND COVER LETTER DOS AND DON'TS

RESUME DOS

- Tailor your information
- Include quantifiable achievements
- Show, don't tell
- Make contact information easy to find
- Stick to one page (two at most!)
- Check for skimmability
- Include keywords from job description
- Use powerful and unique verbs
- Proofread
- Save as a PDF

RESUME DON'TS

- Make bullets read like job descriptions
- Include confidential information about a previous employer
- List "references available upon request"
- Neglect application instructions

- Squish it all to one page (you're better off cutting out some content than using six-point font)
- Lie—seriously, never do this (we hope that one's obvious!)

COVER LETTER DOS

- Share your personality
- Tell a relevant story about what brought you to the job
- Expand on your resume
- Highlight key transferable skills
- Use the company's "voice"
- Address the letter to someone specific

COVER LETTER DON'TS

- Fail to write one
- Regurgitate your resume
- Use stiff, formal language
- Address to "To Whom It May Concern"
- Include a desired salary (unless you're asked)

THINKING OUTSIDE THE BOX

Pulling together an impressive resume and cover letter is definitely crucial for landing an interview—and eventually a job. But, guess what? Plenty of other applicants will submit quality materials as well. As you already know, there's a lot of competition in the job hunt. So, in addition to your impressive documents, you might want to find some additional ways to stand out and separate yourself from the sea of other candidates.

No, we aren't talking about juggling flaming batons or sending a singing telegram to the hiring manager's office. But there are a few innovative (and more professional) things you can do to make a memorable impression.

GET CREATIVE WITH FORMAT

This tactic works well if you work in a creative industry. Most standard resumes are your traditional twelve-point Times New Roman black font on a white sheet of paper. While this might be perfectly fine, and even more appropriate, for more traditional jobs, don't be afraid to get creative with your own documents if you want to show off your design chops or marketing know-how.

We had one prospective Muse employee transform her resume into something that looked just like a Muse company profile. Similarly, we've seen a BuzzFeed applicant turn her cover letter into a classic, BuzzFeed-style article. We had another potential Muse employee go as far as to include a hilarious GIF in her cover letter. While this isn't appropriate for every job or every company (remember, every employer is different!), this particular example showed that the applicant really understood the Muse culture and the fact that we're passionate and serious about what we do, yet also love to have fun while doing it. Though we wouldn't advise doing something quite so "out of the box" unless you're fairly certain of how it will go over, using your cover letter to show that you not only understand, but will also really mesh with the company culture, can be crucial to landing an interview.

THE COVER LETTER THAT WON ABBY WOLFE THE JOB

Dear Muse Team:

It only seems fitting that I am writing this cover letter on October 21st, 2015—the day Marty McFly traveled to in the future to save his unborn children in *Back to the Future Part II*. Both *Back to the Future* movies communicate a very important point: one moment, one decision, one action can change your entire future. I am hoping this moment—11:26am on the actual October 21st, 2015—is the moment that changes my entire future and shifts my life path in a new, more desirable direction.

I hesitate to bore you with a traditional cover letter, so below I will outline my whys—why I want the position of "Editorial Intern" and why I think I would be a good fit for The Daily Muse and this position.

Why I Want the Position

1. I currently work as a health and wellness professional at an employee wellness firm and, to be frank, I am having a hard time. I am good at what I do and serve as an unofficial leader on my team, but I am finding myself unfulfilled and struggling to stay engaged. As someone who settles for nothing less than my absolute best, this is an uncomfortable and frustrating place to be in life. Over the past several months I have realized the following: maybe the reason I am not completely happy in my current position is because it is not providing me with the opportunity to do one of the only things I really want to do—write.

2. A firm belief of mine is people should be working at a job they love. I thoroughly enjoy having conversations with friends and co-workers about how they can apply their dreams, strengths, and goals to a real-life job. This position would allow me to combine two things I enjoy—writing and guiding people to where they should be in life and how to get there.

3. I had dreams of being Jennifer Garner from *13 Going on 30* when I was growing up—big time editor at a magazine? I'm in! But I didn't believe in myself, so I chose a different major in school and a different path in life.

Why I Think I Would Be a Good Fit

1. Because my jobs have not provided me with many opportunities to write, I have pursued it on my own. As an intern for Infinity Wellness Foundation in 2011, I was published as a co-author of two children's health e-books. Since January 2013, I have had my own healthy lifestyle blog; and in August 2013, I became an article contributor to Active Life DC, an online re-

source that shares everything health and fitness-related with the District of Columbia community. Most recently, I have taken on being a blog contributor, editor, and manager for my gym, MINT Club Spa Retreat.

2. Appropriate meme-finding is a strength of mine. Co-workers frequently ask me how I find such perfect memes. It's a natural talent.

3. My mom is a Reading Specialist, which means I grew up a grammar nerd. There were times she would stop a song in the middle and ask me "what is wrong with that lyric?" (Hint: it's usu-ally that a songwriter referred to a person as a "that" instead of a "who.")

4. I want this. I really want this. I am bouncing with excitement in my chair as we speak (erm, as you read this). I thought my days of internships were over, but this seems like the perfect way to break into a field I have subconsciously (and now consciously) wanted to be in since I could hold a pencil.

I think all of us want to feel something that we've forgotten or turned our backs on.

I would love to hear from you. I am available via e-mail, cell phone, and can make an in-person interview work as well. Ad-ditional information and writing samples are available upon re-quest.

Sincerely,
Abby Wolfe

[Note from the authors: This cover letter caught our editorial team's attention immediately, and bumped Abby to the top of the interview pile—and later on, was a key ingredient in the decision to offer her the job.]

Of course, it's important that you understand your audience before straying too far from traditions—not every place will be receptive to a unique and inventive application. But if you've done your research and think a creative cover letter or resume would be just the ticket to set you apart, go ahead and color outside the lines! It's just another way you can share your talents, while also demonstrating that you understand the company's culture.

UH, HOW DO I SUBMIT A COVER LETTER?

In some cases, you'll upload your resume and cover letter into an applicant tracking system, but in others, you'll apply via an email address. And in those cases, one of the most common questions we get is: Should I submit my cover letter as an attachment or in the body of an email? The truth is, it doesn't really matter (unless the job posting specifies one way or another), but the advice we give is: both! That way, you have the opportunity to catch the hiring manager's eye with your cover letter right in the body of the email, but you also make it easy for the recipient to save your resume and cover letter files. Done and done!

COMPLETE A SAMPLE PROJECT

Allowing a hiring manager to actually experience and witness your skills and qualifications will always be more effective than forcing him or her to simply read about them, right? While we don't recommend this approach for every role you apply for (and it may not be feasible for some), for certain types of roles, completing a sample project for an employer is an awesome way to stand out. Even if an application doesn't specifically request that you complete an assignment, taking the initiative to do so yourself will undoubtedly set you apart from your competition.

Let's say you're applying for a role as a social media manager—why not pull together a few ideas for an Instagram campaign to grow the company's brand? If you're a writer, you could submit a sample article. We've even seen sales candidates send over PowerPoint decks they've created just for the role! No, your work doesn't need to be so flawless that the team would implement it exactly as is. Simply showing that you're brimming with brilliant ideas—and willing to roll your sleeves up and bring them to fruition—will put you a step ahead of everyone else.

Again, the "know your audience" caveat exists here as well. But if your research tells you that this employer would admire and appreciate your go-getter attitude and readiness to take charge, it's well worth the extra effort to create a sample project that will knock them back in their seats! This can also be particularly helpful if your experience doesn't obviously tie to the role, but you know you have the skills to do it.

GET REFERRED

As you learned in the last chapter, having a solid referral can work wonders for hearing about job openings. But even if you didn't originally learn about the position from someone in your network, you can still find ways to get a good word put in for you. Before you send in your application, browse LinkedIn to see if you have any first- or second-degree connections at the company (ideally, in the department you're applying to). If you do, send a gracious message letting this person know you're applying and asking, if he or she is comfortable, to pass along your resume and a good word.

Here you'll want to ensure that you're including all necessary information this person would need in order to pass along a quality referral. Attach your resume as a PDF to the email, and craft a short blurb about yourself that can be easily copied and pasted into a message.

Do whatever you need to do to make the process as streamlined and simple for your referrer as possible. The easier you can make it, the more likely he or she is to actually do it.

FOLLOWING UP

In a perfect world, you'd hit Submit on a job application and get a response immediately. And that response would look a lot more like an invite to interview, rather than the "We've received your application and will be in touch if we're interested in moving forward" canned response.

But as you likely already know, hiring managers don't always share your same sense of urgency. In fact, more times than not, you'll need to follow up in order to get any sort of response or update. But when it comes to circling back and keeping your name on the radar, there's a fine line to walk. You want to make sure to stay top of mind, but you also don't want to cross over into pest territory. As a general rule of thumb, you should plan to wait about a week before checking in—if you check in with the hiring manager a mere twenty-four hours after submitting your materials you're likely going to come off as pushy, but wait much longer than a week and you'll run the risk of falling off the radar completely.

If you don't hear anything back after following up the first time? Try again a week or two later. However, if you've sent two messages and still have yet to receive a response, it's best to cut your losses and move on. Believe us, continuing to pester the hiring manager won't do anything to get your resume pushed to the top of the pile (and may even serve to take you out of the running for future positions)—and, at this point, they've likely already gone in a different direction.

THE NEW RULES OF FOLLOWING UP

1. BE POLITE

This should go without saying, but you absolutely always need to be polite when following up with someone—especially a hiring manager.

This means you shouldn't start your email with an accusatory "I applied for this job two weeks ago and have only heard crickets since then!" Remember, you want this person to see just how polite and professional you are—and just how fantastic you'd be to work with.

A TEMPLATE FOR POLITELY FOLLOWING UP
ON A JOB APPLICATION

Not sure what to say? Use this template to take all of the pain out of the process.

Subject: Following up on [position title] application

Body:

Hi [hiring manager name],

I hope all is well. I know you must be busy, but I recently applied to the [position title] position, and wanted to check in on your decision timeline. Upon seeing/hearing about [new development or news at the company] I am that much more excited about the opportunity to join [company name] and help [bring in new clients/develop world-class content/anything else awesome you would be doing] with your team.

Please let me know if it would be helpful for me to provide any additional information as you move on to the next stage in the hiring process.

I look forward to hearing from you,

[Your name]

2. STAND OUT

Remember when we talked about separating yourself from the competition? You likely won't be the only one following up about a job application. So find some way that you can stand out and make yourself memorable.

Showing that you're keeping tabs on what's happening with the company (even though you don't currently work there) can be a great way to do this. For example, perhaps the team just launched a brand-new website or won an award. At the bottom of your follow-up, you could include a brief note that says something along the lines of "By the way, I saw the new website design, and it looks phenomenal." Or perhaps "And congratulations on making this year's list of most innovative companies. What an honor!"

Not only will you demonstrate that you're actively engaged in what's happening; you'll also bring another element into the conversation (other than *just* following up), making the recipient that much more likely to respond.

Another tactic could be to provide an update on you—and something new you've achieved or accomplished since you originally applied. For example, maybe you've gotten an article published since applying to the job, or landed a big new client, or received analytics data pointing to the success of a marketing campaign you've just run. Whatever it is, include any new information that will not only bring you back on the hiring manager's radar, but also offer another impressive data point to bolster your application.

3. SWITCH YOUR TACTIC

They say that doing something over and over again while expecting a different outcome is the definition of insanity—whether you agree with this cliché or not, it's definitely not the smartest way to go about following up on a job. So, if you haven't experienced success with your first follow-up email, try a different approach.

No, this doesn't mean stalking the hiring manager at her favorite coffee shop or sending a fruit basket to her home. Instead, try emailing on a different day at a different time. Sometimes people are simply more attentive at certain points in the week and in the workday, and getting someone to respond comes down to just having the right timing.

Another thing you could switch up is your subject line. Instead of "Following up on my application for the Sales Coordinator position" try something like "Update on (your name)" and lead off the email by briefly describing your recent accomplishment, as we suggested above.

———

So there you have it: everything you need to know about crafting a compelling resume and cover letter and giving them that extra-special touch that will make them stand out. Of course, you won't be successful every time; no one is. But when you are, you'll want to be fully equipped and ready to move on to the next stage of the process: the interview.

Dun-dun-DUN . . .

Just kidding, you got this! Let's move forward.

The New Rules of Acing the Interview (or Interviews . . .)

THE OLD RULE: Interviews were formulaic meet-and-greets, where the interviewer was in a position of power and the interviewee was in a more passive role. Interviews were also generally restricted to one-on-one conversations, either in person or by phone. Often you were given a set of prepared questions or the interviewer would simply speak to you about your resume.

THE NEW RULE: Interviews come in all shapes and sizes, demand different preparation, and assume that interviewer and interviewee are both active participants. Interviews can be conducted in person, on the phone, or over video using platforms such as Skype, and can involve different, and sometimes more challenging, methods of assessing how candidates would actually perform on the job. Moreover, candidates are expected to show up with questions of their own, taking responsibility to make sure the fit is right for both interviewer and interviewee.

The mere thought of an interview can make our hearts pump a little faster, sometimes in abject fear, sometimes in enthusiasm—and sometimes in a mixture of both. Regardless of which camp you fall into, or even if you waver between the two, know this: being asked for an interview is a big milestone in your job search quest, so congrats!

In all the excitement (or nervousness), however, it's important to remember that interviews require a lot of preparation. After all the work you've done to get here, it's tempting to cut corners at this stage of the process, but think of it this way: with that possible job offer that much closer within your grasp, it's all the *more* important to take the time to set yourself up for success.

In this chapter, we'll walk through the most frequently asked interview questions and how to think about answering them according to the specific type of job and depending on exactly who in the company you're interviewing with (yes, that matters—a lot). We'll also get into the specifics of how to ace different interview formats (e.g., Skype vs. in person) and what sort of prep you should be doing ahead of the big day. Wherever you are in the process, from the first interview to the fifteenth (ouch!), these tips are designed to help you nail it—and hopefully get that offer!

HOW TO PREPARE

The first thing you should do when you've landed an interview (besides giving yourself a pat on the back and sending a few happy texts to your friends)? Research. We know: you've done this at several steps along the way, including unearthing lots of details about the company and the role when you applied for the job in the first place. But before you meet the hiring manager face-to-face, you'll want to go even deeper in learning about the company, position, and even the specific people you'd be working with if you got the job. You'll want to use those same tools of online immersion and mining the field you've used before, only here you'll be narrowing your focus even further.

Specifically, you want to have a good understanding of:

- **The company:** What are its strong suits? Who are its competitors? Has it won any recent awards, accolades, or honors?
- **The people you'll be meeting with:** At this point you'll likely have been given the names of the person or people who will be interviewing you, so dig up as much on them as you can

(if not, it's okay to ask!). What are their positions and what exactly do they do? How senior are they, and how long have they been at the company? What are their backgrounds? Do you have anything in common with them, like a shared alma mater or even overlapping LinkedIn connections?

- **The role:** What do the day-to-day responsibilities look like, and what key skills and strengths are needed to accomplish them? What would success in this role look like, and what are the metrics used to assess it? And most important, what questions do you need answered? Remember that while yes, technically, they are interviewing you, this is also your chance to interview them.

- **Finally (and this is the easy one, since it's about you), be prepared with specifics on _your_ background:** What are your key strengths that you bring to the position? What sets you ahead of other candidates? What specific projects and achievements relate to this role and highlight your skills? What questions or concerns might the interviewer have about your background, and how can you address them?

Having done this legwork ahead of time will give you a good grasp not only of what the role entails, but also of what you want to communicate as a candidate. This in turn will help you answer questions more thoughtfully and effectively, connect with the interviewer on a deeper level, and follow up in a more meaningful and personal way.

Now, let's get to the nuts and bolts!

COMMON INTERVIEW QUESTIONS YOU SHOULD BE READY FOR

Many interview questions sound so simple, but can be _so_ hard to answer if you're not prepared. But the good news is, many hiring managers ask the same things. So, armed with that knowledge and your pre-interview research, you can prepare ahead of time for most of what you'll be asked.

Now, note that this isn't about rehearsing your answers so you have them memorized word for word. That's no way to connect with someone! We'll give you some more tips on that in a minute, but for now know that your goal with each of these questions is to have thought about the main points you want to communicate to show that you're a fit.

So here are a few questions that you should be prepared to answer. Though the way they are phrased might differ from company to company and position to position, in general these are things that you're likely to be asked in just about every interview situation.

1. "CAN YOU TELL ME A LITTLE ABOUT YOURSELF?"

And . . . cue the deer-in-headlights look. Open-ended questions like these can be the toughest to answer. After all, you could talk about anything, from your family history to your favorite hobbies to a play-by-play account of your work history. We don't recommend any of these approaches. But don't worry, here's what to do instead.

Remember that elevator pitch you created a few chapters back? You'll want to use the same formula here, just tailoring your background and top accomplishments to the role at hand. There's no need to rattle off your full employment or personal history—just give a quick highlight reel of what you have to offer to the company. If it's been a while since you looked at your elevator pitch, go back to Chapter 5 and read it again. Could it be updated or tweaked according to the position for which you are now interviewing? If so, get out your pen and write your new and improved elevator pitch here:

_____

_____

_____

2. "WHY DO YOU WANT THIS JOB?"

Nope, this isn't the time to joke about getting away from your miserable co-workers or making more money to cover your expensive rent. Instead, draw on your research to show that you know what the company wants and how eager you are to deliver just that. For example, for a consulting job: "I'm innately a problem solver. So, having the chance to interact directly with clients and help them sort out their issues and improve their strategy is what gets me excited about coming to work each day." Also, most companies really want to know that you care about their mission, so be sure to explain why you're drawn to the team's vision and core values. For example, a job at a nonprofit: "I've always been passionate about animal rights and I volunteer on weekends at a shelter, so the opportunity to raise awareness of these issues is close to my heart."

3. "WHY SHOULD WE HIRE YOU?"

This one sounds pretty intimidating, but you'll nail it if your answer conveys that you (1) can do the work while delivering great results and (2) fit in with the team and culture. For example, if we were hiring a salesperson at The Muse, we might want to hear something like:

> I've spent the past five years hitting aggressive sales targets in a fast-paced start-up environment, so I know I have what it takes to succeed in this role. But why you should really hire me is this: I've been a passive job seeker and have seen firsthand the power The Muse has to recruit people to amazing companies. I'd be able to bring that passion and firsthand experience to every sales call I joined. Plus, I think I'd fit in great with the team—I even hear the softball team needs a new first baseman, and that's what I played in college!

4. "WHAT ARE YOUR GREATEST STRENGTHS?"

As cheesy as it might sound, the key to answering this question is simply to be yourself. By that we mean what are *true* strengths that are relevant to the position, not what you assume the interviewer wants to hear (trust us, they'll see right through it in an instant). And be specific! Instead of saying that "writing" is your strength, say something like "writing punchy website copy for consumer brands," "translating complex jargon into easily understandable language," or "telling stories in a way that makes them come to life." Then follow it up with examples of times you've put that strength to use in your work.

5. "WHAT ARE YOUR WEAKNESSES?"

We know—this one is tough. But before you pull the all-too-common (to the point of being clichéd) "I'm too much of a perfectionist!" line, know that in asking this question, the interviewer is trying to gauge your self-awareness and honesty (and, well, your ability to answer a tough question gracefully!). So ditch the cute or trying-too-hard-to-be-clever weaknesses that aren't really weaknesses, and be open about something that you struggle with, whether that's presenting to large groups, speaking up in meetings, delegating to others, or incorporating multiple points of view when you have a strong feeling on something. Most important, be sure to address how you're working on improving it. Try: "When I first became a manager, it was tough for me to let go of some of my old responsibilities. But I've been working on it with a career coach, and I've found ways to delegate that make me feel much more comfortable—not to mention improve the efficiency of the whole team."

6. "WHAT IS YOUR GREATEST PROFESSIONAL ACHIEVEMENT?"

We get that bragging can feel awkward, but if there was ever a time to sell yourself, this is it. Remind yourself that the interviewer is literally asking you to tell them the reasons why they should hire you, and nothing says "hire me" quite like a solid track record of achievements and results. So don't be afraid to share—with confidence—how you drove up impressive numbers, spearheaded a successful project, or solved a pressing problem. If you do it in a way that feels natural to your personality, it won't come off as bragging; it will simply come off as impressive—and honest.

7. "WHERE DO YOU SEE YOURSELF IN FIVE YEARS?"

Here's another scary one, especially if you don't know where you'll be! But don't worry, the hiring manager isn't looking for your life plan, she is just trying to gauge whether you have realistic expectations about where this position could take you. So good answers could include "in five years I'd love to have advanced to a management role" or "in five years I envision myself working with a diverse group of international clients." If you really have no idea, it's fine to say that you're not quite sure what the future holds, but that this job will play an important role in helping you shape that five-year plan.

What *not* to say here? We'd steer clear of anything too cheeky ("on a beach sipping margaritas!") or the not-so-classic "In your job!"

8. "WHAT OTHER COMPANIES ARE YOU INTERVIEWING WITH?"

So far we've been advising you to be as specific as possible, but here's an instance in which you might want to be a bit more vague, especially if you're interviewing with competitors. If that's the case, simply say you are exploring several options within the industry and then redirect the focus to how excited you are to apply your skills to this particular position.

9. "WHY ARE YOU LEAVING YOUR CURRENT JOB?"

This one can be a mine field if you don't come prepared. First, you'll want to refrain from saying, "Uh, because my boss is a psychopath." You have nothing to gain by being negative about your past employers, so keep things professional and positive. Show that you're eager to take on a new opportunity and that this role is a better fit than your current or last position, saying something like, "I've learned so much at my current company, but I'm really looking for the opportunity to work in a start-up environment like this one." If you were let go, keep it simple and say, "Unfortunately, I was let go."

10. "WHY WERE YOU FIRED?"

On that note . . . it's a small world, so be truthful. If the company had a round of layoffs, it's okay to say that. And if you were fired outright? In our experience, that's not always a deal-breaker, as long as you show what you've learned and how you've grown from the experience.

11. "HOW WOULD YOUR BOSS AND CO-WORKERS DESCRIBE YOU?"

This question is a great opportunity to discuss traits that haven't been covered in other questions, like your strong work ethic or sense of humor that makes late nights at the office more fun. And again, be truthful, because if your boss or colleagues are called as references, your answers need to be on the same page!

12. "WHY IS THERE A GAP IN YOUR EMPLOYMENT?"

If you were unemployed, be honest about how you filled the time (hopefully with some volunteer and professional development activities included). Then shift gears and talk about how you can use what you learned during that period to contribute to their company. No need to overexplain; keep this answer short and sweet.

13. "WHAT WOULD YOUR FIRST THIRTY, SIXTY, OR NINETY DAYS LOOK LIKE IN THIS ROLE?"

This is where the research we had you do earlier in the chapter comes in handy. No matter what the role, come prepared with some thoughts and ideas on how you'd hit the ground running. This shows that you've already begun envisioning yourself making an immediate impact—and that you're pumped to dive right in.

14. "WHAT ARE YOUR SALARY REQUIREMENTS?"

Do your research on sites like PayScale to determine a range based on your experience, education, and skills. You don't have to name a number (we'll talk all about that in the next chapter!), but if you do, start with the highest number you can justify to convey you know you're valuable, but be clear that you're willing to negotiate.

15. "WHAT DO YOU THINK WE COULD DO BETTER OR DIFFERENTLY?"

This isn't a trick question. Companies (especially start-ups) appreciate when a candidate keeps tabs on them and comes to the table with fresh ideas. So don't be afraid to share your thoughts and how your expertise could bring those ideas to life. But keep it positive and constructive! This is probably not the time to dump on the "terrible newsletter design"— you might be sitting across from the very person who created it! For example, in this case, you might say: "I've been a subscriber of your newsletter for two years, and I've noticed that the design hasn't changed. I like it, but at my current company, we've redesigned the newsletter twice, and each time seen higher click-through rates. It might be something to consider here."

ALL ABOUT BEHAVIORAL QUESTIONS

In addition to these common questions, there's another type that will inevitably come up in an interview: "behavioral questions," or those that ask you to talk about a specific situation and how you dealt with it. For example:

- How have you dealt with a challenge or conflict at work?
- What's a time you exercised leadership?
- Tell me about a mistake you made and how you handled it.

Hiring managers ask these questions because they don't just want you to tell them about your skills, they want real-life examples of how you've handled challenges on the job. So you'll want to prepare an arsenal of several stories ahead of time that showcase your strengths and allow you to elaborate on why you're perfect for the position. Preparing several options gives you flexibility, depending on the question asked, and makes sure you don't give the same example to all of your interviewers (since, you know, they talk afterward).

Here's how to turn a typical answer into a memorable story:

1. SET IT UP WITH A SUCCINCT ONE-LINER

"A mistake that I learned from was when I was giving a client presentation over a web conferencing system, and just as everyone dialed in, the site crashed."

2. PROVIDE THE BACKGROUND INFORMATION

"We use this web conferencing system regularly, so I wasn't expecting any issues. But this was our campaign wrap report, and we only had a one-hour meeting with lots of information to cover. And as the account lead, I was in charge of presenting the results."

3. EXPLAIN YOUR SOLUTION

"Although I have a great, comfortable relationship with the client, I didn't want them to be frustrated that we were losing valuable time. So I quickly saved the PowerPoint as a lower-resolution PDF and emailed it to everyone."

4. SHARE THE RESULTS

"Although emailing the report wasn't ideal, the client was thrilled with the presentation and the results generated for the campaign."

5. EXPLAIN THE LESSON LEARNED

"It was a good reminder to always test the technology at least a half hour before the meeting so I can troubleshoot any web conferencing issues and ensure everything runs smoothly."

See? A story about a technical glitch became one that showed you have a good relationship with your clients, they're pleased with your team's work, and you know how to think quickly to avert a crisis. No matter what example you use, though, be sure to connect the dots on how this past experience will help you in the new role.

CONNECTING WITH THE INTERVIEWER

So, you've practiced your elevator pitch, you've written talking points for the trickiest questions, and you've rehearsed a few key stories that showcase your strengths and accomplishments. In other words, you've covered the aspects of the interview that will be focused on you. But it's equally important to be prepared to focus on your interviewer—particularly if you are being interviewed by the person you'll be working for or reporting to. So the goal here is to build a strong rapport and to show that you'd be a great co-worker. Here are a few tips.

DON'T SKIP THE SMALL TALK

This might seem odd in an interview, but a little banter can make your personality shine and help the interviewer envision you interacting with clients or other team members. Plus, you might uncover some common interests that foster an even better connection!

BE YOURSELF (THE PROFESSIONAL, CHARMING, GRACIOUS VERSION)

Don't try to fit into a perfect candidate mold or sound so rehearsed that you're coming across like a robot. And you don't want to be so overconfident that you sound condescending.

For example, if an interviewer explains that the company offers training workshops to employees, don't say:

> *"Oh, I already taught myself how to edit videos without any training."*

Try:

"That's great to hear. One of my biggest strengths is that I'm always expanding my skill set. I recently taught myself how to edit videos on [X software], and I'd love to keep learning and perfecting it."

MIRROR THE INTERVIEWER

You should always be authentic to who you are, but try adapting to your interviewer's demeanor and style of communicating. This will make the interviewer feel more comfortable (yes, they might be feeling awkward, too), and that in turn makes *you* more comfortable.

FOCUS ON THE CONVERSATION, NOT A RAPID-FIRE Q&A

Don't just answer the interviewer's questions like you're on a timed game show; weave in some of your own questions throughout the interview. Getting a back and forth going will let you show you're thoughtful, passionate, and engaged in the conversation.

MAKE SURE YOU'D PASS THE "AIRPORT TEST"

In addition to having the qualifications and skills to do the job, would a manager want to be stuck in an airport with you? It seems silly, but interviewers often use this as a gauge of whether or not they could see themselves getting along with you, especially if you'll be spending a lot of time together. Be pleasant, polite, interesting (and interested), and you should pass this with "flying" colors.

WHAT TO WEAR

Even if you say all the right things to convince the interviewer that you're a good fit for the job, you also have to *look* like a good fit. Like it or not, you will be judged, to some extent, on your appearance, so it's important to bring your A-game when it comes to appearing polished, professional, and on par with the company dress code.

THE NEW RULES OF WORK

But this is a little tricky, because in the new world of work, there's no "interview uniform." When we graduated from college, it was pretty much the norm to wear a suit, but today there are many more accepted options, depending on the company you're meeting with. (In fact, rarely do people wear suits to interviews at The Muse!)

Your best bet is to scope out the company's social media profiles, its Google image search results, or its profile on The Muse to see day-in-the-life photos of employees at the office. Of course, just because you see someone wearing a hoodie doesn't mean you should be that casual—you still want to be appropriately professional, but you probably don't want to be overly formal, either. A good rule of thumb is to dress one to two steps above what you see online.

Here are some loose guidelines:

Corporate Classic: For more traditional or corporate cultures, keep your look basic and conservative. For the first interview, women should wear a jacket with tailored pants, a knee-length pencil skirt, or a dress; guys should go with a suit and tie. If the people you interview with aren't wearing jackets, you can probably skip it for the second interview (or wear a more casual one).

Business Casual: This is a good bet for most companies that aren't overly corporate or buttoned-up. For ladies, this could mean a professional sheath or wrap dress or well-tailored pants and a simple top. Guys could wear a button-down shirt tucked into dark pants, a belt, and loafers or leather dress shoes.

Edgy, Start-up, or Creative Environments: If this team looks like they strolled into work straight from the runway, don't show up in a suit. They're most likely seeking someone who fits into a creative environment where personal style reigns free. Women can keep the look low-key with straight-leg pants, flats, a stylish top, and jacket, and men can try dark denim with a blazer or casual pants with a button-down top.

The Best Rule of Thumb: Target your look to the job you want—just as you would your resume and your answers to the interview questions.

CALMING YOUR NERVES

When you get the invite for an interview, you're pumped, elated, and ready to take on the world. Then pre-interview panic sets in. This physiological response to risk gets your heart thumping, palms sweating, and thoughts racing. Don't worry: this response is completely natural. All you need are some strategies to keep your anxiety from crushing your confidence when you need to put your best (calmest) self forward:

JUST BREATHE

Shifting your focus to your breath—and noticing the sensations you feel as you inhale and exhale—halts anxiety in its tracks and brings a sense of calm in the moment. Simply taking a few minutes before walking into the interview to mindfully focus on your breath can work wonders for slowing that racing heart rate and ramping down those overactive thoughts. As a side bonus, science shows that taking just ten minutes a day to practice mindful meditation can help with long-term stress management—which every job seeker could benefit from. (There are even apps for that—we love one called Headspace!)

WORK OUT BEFORE YOUR INTERVIEW

Whether you go to yoga or for a jog, exercise gets your endorphins running, clears your head, and eases nerves. (And while not scientifically proven, we personally believe that listening to "Eye of the Tiger" to pump you up couldn't hurt!) Just make sure you leave time to shower afterward!

DON'T BE YOUR OWN WORST ENEMY

In stressful times, our subconscious minds tend to go straight to the negative; it's our brains' way of protecting us from danger and disappointment when we're faced with an unknown outcome. Yet listening to these negative voices can undermine our confidence and sabotage our efforts to present our best selves. So, next time your thoughts veer into "I'm definitely going to screw this up" or "I'll never get this job" territory, step back and recognize that your fears are not your reality. Visualize success, instead.

RETHINK THE EXPERIENCE

Repeat after us: the person on the other side of the table doesn't want you to fail. Truly. She wants you to nail the interview—because your resume already showed you have real value to bring to her company. It will help keep intimidation at bay if you humanize the interviewer by thinking of you two being on the same team with a common goal.

ALL THE OTHER TYPES OF INTERVIEWS

So far, we've talked a lot about the most common form of interviews: when you sit down with the hiring manager face-to-face. But in the new world of work, this may not be the only type of interview you do—you may be asked to do a phone or Skype interview before you come in, make a presentation to your potential future co-workers, or come in for multiple rounds. Each interview format comes with its own set of benefits and challenges, but no matter the method, the better prepared you are, the better your chances of making a great impression and standing out from the crowd.

Let's walk through how to prepare for a few of our "favorite" (and not-so-favorite!) interview types.

YOU HAD ME AT HELLO: SIX TIPS FOR MASTERING A PHONE INTERVIEW

Employers often screen candidates over the phone before moving forward with an on-site meeting. Without any visual cues, making a connection can be tricky, so follow these six tips to start on the right foot:

1. GET THE LOGISTICS RIGHT

It seems obvious, but it's critical to confirm you have the right date, phone number, and time (especially if you're not in the same time zone), as well as clarity on who will be calling whom. Nothing sinks an interview faster than calling in three hours late (or early), or failing to follow the dial-in instructions. It should go without saying that you should make sure your phone is fully charged and you have good reception. Or go old-school and use a landline.

2. SKIP THE PJS

Just because you *can* wear yoga pants and do the phone interview while lounging in bed doesn't mean you should. With no visual cues, interviewers are paying extra attention to your voice—and being cozily tucked under the covers may lower your energy level and make you sound tired or bored. Plus, getting dressed as if you were going in for a face-to-face interview will help get you into "professional mode," and in turn make you *sound* more professional in your demeanor and tone. Kathryn likes to walk around and gesture during phone interviews—it helps keep up her excitement level and communicate her passion for the topic. (Just one word of caution: don't walk so much that you get winded!)

3. GET PUMPED WITH POWER POSES

Harvard Business School professor Amy Cuddy's research has demonstrated that standing in a two-minute "power pose"—think Wonder Woman's bold stance with legs shoulder width apart, hands on hips, chest out, and chin lifted—immediately changes your body chemistry to make you sound and feel more confident by raising testosterone levels and lowering cortisol. Though you can do this right before going in for an in-person interview, too, one of the best parts of doing a phone interview from home is that no one will see you "strike a pose" in the middle of the interview.

4. STAND TALL

You can collapse onto the couch with a sigh of relief *after* you hang up. But during the call, if you position yourself as if you're giving a speech, either standing or sitting up straight, you'll sound stronger and more engaged—and your interviewer will hear it in your voice. You might even watch yourself in a mirror to make sure you have as much energy as you would if you were interacting with a human face-to-face.

5. USE A CHEAT SHEET—IF YOU NEED IT

Another advantage to the phone interview is that you can have your prep materials on a table in front of you for reference as you would while giving a talk or presentation—just don't read anything verbatim; if it doesn't sound natural, they'll notice.

6. SMILE!

Without verbal cues, it's easy to sound dull or disengaged while on the phone. One tip for transmitting enthusiasm when you're not in person is to smile while you're speaking.

———

Above all, be friendly, laugh, and don't psych yourself out too much. The rules from the last section about staying positive and reminding yourself that the interviewer *wants* you to succeed still apply.

VIDEO OR SKYPE INTERVIEWS

Whether you're meeting through Skype or recording a video assessment to send to a hiring manager, video is becoming another common screening tool. Similar to a first-round, in-person interview, you'll get traditional questions like "Why do you think you'd be a good fit?" or "Why do you want to work for us?" But answering these questions into a computer instead of talking to a live person can pose some hurdles.

Here are a few tips for managing those hurdles and keeping your video presence impressive and polished:

- Always make sure your lighting and camera angles are flattering and the setting is uncluttered. (Yes, the interviewer wants to get to know you, but they don't need to know what the inside of your closet looks like.)

- Test your tech setup beforehand so you know everything works. Make sure the volume is at the right level and the Wi-Fi connection is strong enough that you don't have to worry about freezing up—or worse, getting disconnected. Even better, plug into a wired connection instead of using Wi-Fi.

- Make sure your Skype username and photo are work-appropriate (you'd be surprised by some of the doozies we've seen!).

- If the sound quality isn't great, use a headset or earphones to avoid an echo.

- Wear business-casual attire. (And yes, not just the part of you they can see—are you really going to feel professional and confident sitting there in a button-down shirt and pajama bottoms? As a side note: we've caught someone doing a video interview in boxers when an unexpected knock meant they had to get up to get the door. Don't make this mistake!) On a slightly less comical note, avoid busy patterns and bright colors that don't play well on camera, and keep jewelry minimal.

- Look straight ahead at the camera on your computer, not down at your screen or at the little window with the interviewer. If you need a cheat sheet, try putting a few sticky notes with key points in large handwriting on the perimeter of your screen. You don't want your eyes darting all over the place (and they'll see you looking at a stack of papers, even if it's off to the side!).

- Don't open any other windows on your computer (the ping of a new Gchat coming in will be disruptive).

- Smile and use natural (not excessive) body language. If you're totally frozen, your interviewer might think it's a bad Wi-Fi connection!

THE **411** ON VIDEO ASSESSMENTS

A video assessment is essentially a prerecorded interview, in which you record a view of yourself responding to a set of questions, and then send that in to your potential employer. Typically used as a prescreen to get a sense of your skills before you're invited in to interview, a one-sided conversation (on camera, with a timer going!) can feel pretty awkward. But if you pass the assessment with flying colors, chances are you'll get the opportunity to meet the hiring manager in person soon.

- **How it works:** You'll get a series of questions ahead of time (sometimes a couple of days before, sometimes just a few minutes), then you'll record your answers on camera.
- **How to prepare:** In addition to checking all your technical equipment like you would for a Skype interview, do a quick dry run and record it. You'll have a chance to see how you look and sound on the other side of the screen and course-correct if you need to.
- **What's really important:** Conveying your excitement about the role (instead of just answering the given questions like a robot), communicating succinctly, and selling your skills.
- **Pro tip:** Practice your answers out loud with a timer so you know you're covering all the bases within the time limit, and that you're comfortable seeing yourself on camera while concentrating on the task.

GIVING A FLAWLESS PRESENTATION

As if interviewing weren't stressful enough, some companies request that you give a presentation, especially if you are interviewing for an executive-level role or if part of your job will involve presenting to groups. Scary as it is, a well-developed presentation gives you a unique chance to impress the powers that be with your public speaking prowess, knowledge of a subject matter, and ability to stay calm under pressure. For tips on this type of interview, head to themuse .com/thenewrules.

CONQUERING THE SECOND, THIRD, AND FINAL INTERVIEWS

Whether you had an awesome Skype interview or won over the hiring manager in person, you'll have to continue the good-impression streak in rounds two, three, and beyond. And this means—you guessed it— more prep work, because when you're a top contender for the role, you can't go on autopilot and say the same thing to everyone you meet (or worse, say the same thing to people you've already met with!).

Speaking of which, whom might you meet with in these follow up rounds? At The Muse, candidates meet with the hiring manager, the department head, and then depending on the role, two or three other key members of the department they'd be working in, one to two people from other departments, and one or both of us, the founders. That's a lot, but at other companies you can expect to meet with a minimum of one or two people from your team and a senior leader.

The key here is to repackage old stories with a new spin while also sharing new information. You *do* want to reiterate your relevant skills, since you'll probably be meeting with new people (and the person you've already met with probably doesn't remember everything). If you're meeting with the same person, summarize what you've already said while adding in something new. If you're asked (yet again), "Why are you drawn to this role?" you can say, "When we met last time, we discussed the opportunity to lead a group of sales associates, which is still something I'm very enthusiastic about. Additionally, the information you shared about how the team collaborates is very appealing to me, since I worked on a very collaborative team in my last position, and saw first-hand how many creative ideas can come out of successful teamwork."

OH NO YOU DIDN'T . . .

INTERVIEW MISTAKES TO AVOID

Your resume is typo-free, your outfit is crisp, and you have solid references lined up to help you land this dream job. Unfortunately, there are still lots of little blunders to avoid (from tiny nuances to big red flags) that can make you appear unprofessional or off-putting in an interview. Here are a few things to look out for:

Appearing desperate: Being enthusiastic is good, but being *too eager* or effusive makes you less desirable (kind of like dating).

Being too aggressive: If you've ever ended an email or cover letter with "I will call you next week to set up time when I can come in for an interview," you're probably being a bit too forward. Same goes for sending follow-ups; avoid aggressive wording that assumes you got the job, and as noted in the last chapter, if you send more than two and don't hear back, move on.

Using industry jargon and acronyms: You won't impress people with big words that say very little about what you actually do. For example, don't say something like "I leveraged our synergistic network of influencers for the DOC brief . . ." Know the industry lingo, but be straightforward enough that a layperson can understand you.

Showing up too early or too late: Aim to arrive five to ten minutes ahead of your meeting time. Being too early puts pressure on the interviewer to start sooner than they anticipated, and being late is just rude! Here at The Muse, we've occasionally had people show up more than thirty minutes early for the interview—we definitely do *not* recommend doing this! It can be awkward if the reception area is small or has few chairs, and puts extra pressure on the receptionist and hiring managers. For everyone's sake, just go to a nearby coffee shop instead.

Having a terrible handshake: Like the tale of Goldilocks and the Three Bears, there's a way to do the handshake that's just right. You don't want to overzealously crush someone's fingers or be remembered as having limp-noodle hands. (Practice with a friend if this isn't something you're used to!)

Talking too much: Don't ramble on, overshare personal things that have nothing to do with the job (e.g., "I'm going through a tough breakup right now"), or speak negatively about a previous employer.

Getting too comfortable: Yes, you want to be relaxed enough to let your personality shine through, but no, it's not a good idea to ask to charge your phone, drop the f-bomb, or discuss the details of your hangover.

Asking "What's in it for me?": Remember that interviewers want to know what you can do for *them*. Stay away from questions that make you look arrogant or entitled like "How much vacation time do I get?" "What are your promotion cycles like?" or "Will my office have a window?"

Bringing up salary: Typically, the recruiter or hiring manager will bring up the topic of salary at some point in the interview process. But if not? Don't be the first one to raise it. Unless you do it very well, you may look presumptuous. In this case, unless you have hard-and-fast requirements and are willing to risk it, better safe than sorry.

Lying: Just don't do it. Honesty is always the best policy. You *will* get caught if you lie about a previous role or being proficient in a skill that you're unequipped to pull off. The vast majority of skills—whether it's Photoshop or coding or a language proficiency—can't be faked. Why risk your professional credibility?

Okay—you've gotten through the hard stuff. Now stick with us for the final section of the interview—where the tables turn.

YOUR TURN: QUESTIONS TO ASK

You already know interviewing is a two-way street, so chiming in with good questions helps determine if it's the right gig for you. Moreover, if you don't have any, you risk looking unprepared or disinterested. On the flip side of that coin, you'll want to stay away from asking any questions that you could have answered yourself through a simple Google search (e.g., "So what exactly is it that you do around here?"). The goal is to express curiosity and thoughtfulness, without looking like you failed to do your homework.

Here are some questions to weave into your conversation that are sure to impress the interviewer:

- What does a typical day look like?
- Can you share examples of projects similar to what I'll be working on?
- What would make someone really successful in this role?
- What type of skills is the team missing that you're looking to fill?
- What training programs and professional development opportunities are available?
- Where have successful employees previously in this position progressed to?
- What accomplishments would you like to see in the first thirty, sixty, and ninety days I'd be on the job?
- What gets you most excited about the company's future?
- What are the company's current goals? And how does this team work to support hitting those goals?
- Whom will I work with most closely?
- How does your team typically resolve conflicts?
- How would you describe the work environment? Is it collaborative or more independent?

THE NEW RULES OF ACING THE INTERVIEW (OR INTERVIEWS . . .)

- Do you have a favorite office tradition?
- What are the next steps in the interview process?

As the interview winds down, you will inevitably be asked, "Is there anything else I can answer for you?" Rather than shrugging off the last call for questions with a "nope, I think you covered it," wrap things up on a high note with this one:

- What's your favorite part about working here, or an experience that's made the biggest impact on you?

Not only does this question tap into their emotions as they recall something they really love about their job, but it will provide you with great insight into the company's core values and opportunities for employees, while also ending the interview on a positive note.

WRITING A GREAT THANK-YOU NOTE

After you walk out the door, you can let out a sigh of relief, because the next (and hopefully final!) interview-related task won't be nearly as stressful—but it is equally important.

It's true: crafting the *right* thank-you note (that subliminally says "hire me!" without being pushy or presumptuous) is more than a formality and can make all the difference in whether or not you get the job. In fact, since you've gotten this far along in the process, that means you're probably a top contender and a really thoughtful, prompt follow-up could give you an edge over the competition (especially if they wrote a generic one-liner, or came across as too aggressive). When it really comes down to it, the hiring manager may just like your tone better.

Your thank-you note should include:

- A professional greeting ("Dear Sofia,")
- An introductory thank-you and compliment (think genuine, not brownnosy!)

- Brief recap of what you discussed (including how you can help the company achieve its goals)
- Personal reference so the interviewer recalls who you are
- Closing summary with a confirmation of the time frame for filling the position

Let's put it all together:

Dear Ms. Davis,

Thank you again for your time today. After hearing you speak at the recent Communications Summit, it was wonderful to meet you in person. The Account Supervisor position sounds like an excellent fit, due to my experience in managing consumer-facing healthcare initiatives.

It was very helpful to learn more about how your teams are structured. In my current job, I handle project management and frequently collaborate with designers on content development. I'm thrilled to know that your staff wears many hats, too! I was particularly interested in the workflow issues we discussed—between my project management experience and a penchant for loving to organize things, I would be well positioned to help the team develop a more streamlined workflow, and I hope we have a chance to work on that together.

Being new to Chicago, the chance to build my career at such a highly regarded agency—whose mission I admire—is very exciting.

Again, I appreciate your time, insight, and the opportunity to interview with Agency X. You mentioned you hoped to fill the position in the next two weeks. In the meantime, if there is anything else I can provide as you make your decision, please let me know. I look forward to hearing from you.

Sincerely,
Jane Smith

In addition to showing that you are polite, courteous, and appreciative of the time the interviewer took to meet with you, the thank-you note can serve one other useful purpose. Let's say that although you were superprepared and practiced all your talking points there was that *one* question you wish you'd answered differently or a key skill you forgot to mention. Use the thank-you note to subtly revisit that topic and say what you wish you said in person. Tie it into the overarching theme of the note—like your desire to work at the company or how you can add value to the team. That said, this isn't your second shot at an interview, so keep this part short and sweet.

No matter what, triple-check for typos, send it within a few hours of your interview, and make it specific (a generic thank-you is almost worse than not sending one at all). Oh, and email is definitely the norm these days, but if you think the hiring manager is the type of person who'd appreciate a handwritten note, go ahead and send that as well. Just make sure it gets there quick, as some employers move quickly, and you don't want to risk their not getting your note right away. Either drop it off with the receptionist later that day or send an email the same day as the interview, with the letter following a few days later.

THE REJECTION RUT AND HOW TO DEAL

After hitting Send on that thank-you note, there is nothing to do now but wait (and refresh your inbox approximately one million times throughout the week). But you're feeling good. You nailed the tough questions, clicked with the team, and all the logistics went smoothly. This job is so yours, until it . . . isn't.

Rejection is never easy, and can really throw you for a loop if it happens when the interview seemed to go perfectly. You start questioning everything. Was your handshake sweaty? Should you have focused more on management skills and less on teamwork? What if there was something stuck in your teeth that was distracting and that's what caused them not to hire you?

This kind of reaction is normal, but plunging headfirst into a downward spiral of self-doubt makes it much harder to rally and move forward in your job search. It's not always something you did; sometimes another candidate was just a better fit for the company. When negative thoughts take over, take action instead. You may not have gotten the job, but you can still use the experience to learn something useful. Here are some things you can do:

- Follow up with the hiring manager to gather feedback on improving your interviewing skills. Just remember not to get defensive or act incredulous that you didn't get the job. Instead, politely ask if she has any comments on what you could do better in the future. If you ask the right way, she'll be impressed by your initiative; plus, you never know, another job that's a better fit could pop up and she'll be more likely to remember you.

- Take a closer look at what you could have done better and work on it. Could you have spent more time researching the company to learn their pain points? Could your answers have been more tailored to the position? Write these down in your notebook to come back to next time (and we promise, there will be a next time!) you land an interview. If you're not sure what you could have done better, consider working with a coach, who can run through practice interviews with you and give you candid feedback about how you might improve in the future.

- Instead of moping (for *too* long), remind yourself that rejection is a normal part of the process. No one lands every single job they apply for. Plus, you never know: something much better for you could be just around the corner.

Rejection isn't always easy to shake off, especially when it feels so personal. But it's an opportunity to learn, improve, and become a much stronger candidate. And if you follow these New Rules, you *will* land the right offer before you know it. And in the next chapter, we'll talk about how to nail the negotiation to get the most out of that offer once it's yours!

INTERVIEW CHEAT SHEET

We know we covered a lot in this chapter. So here's a cheat sheet summing up all the things you need to prepare before you go in and nail those interviews! (For a printable version visit themuse.com/thenewrules.)

Company: _____

Position: _____

Date: _____

Time: _____

Place: _____

Who I'm meeting with: _____

WHAT I LOVE ABOUT THE POSITION

The (specific) things about this company and position that make it a great fit for me

1. _____
_____
_____
_____
_____

2. _____
_____
_____
_____

3. _____
_____
_____
_____
_____

WHAT SKILLS I BRING TO THE POSITION

The key skills and experiences that make me perfect for this job

1. _____
_____
_____
_____
_____

2. _____
_____
_____
_____

3. _____
_____
_____
_____
_____

CHALLENGES TO ADDRESS

Questions the interviewer might have about my background, and how
I'm going to tackle them

1. _____
_____
_____
_____

2. _____
_____
_____
_____

3. _____
_____
_____
_____

ACCOMPLISHMENTS TO HIGHLIGHT

My specific projects and achievements that relate to this job and highlight my skills

1. _____

_____

_____

_____

_____

2. _____

_____

_____

_____

3. _____

_____

_____

_____

_____

QUESTIONS TO ASK

Things I don't know about the job or company, but want to ask during
the interview

1. _____

_____

_____

_____

_____

2. _____

_____

_____

_____

3. _____

_____

_____

NOT TO FORGET

Contacts I have at the company, fun facts about my background, or anything else to mention!

1. _____
_____
_____
_____
_____

2. _____
_____
_____
_____

3. _____
_____
_____
_____

POST-INTERVIEW NOTES

_____
_____
_____
_____

FOLLOW-UP NEEDED

1. _____
_____
_____

2. _____
_____
_____

3. _____
_____
_____

SEND THANK-YOU NOTES TO

1. _____

2. _____

3. _____

WHAT I LOVED

1. _____

_____

_____

_____

_____

2. _____

_____

_____

_____

3. _____

_____

_____

_____

WHAT I DIDN'T LOVE/POTENTIAL RED FLAGS

1. _____

_____

_____

_____

_____

2. _____

_____

_____

_____

3. _____

_____

_____

IN-PERSON INTERVIEW CHECKLIST

- ☐ Directions to where I'm going (*don't always count on GPS*)
- ☐ Cash (*for parking, gas, transportation, emergencies*)
- ☐ Three or more copies of my resume
- ☐ Work samples or portfolio
- ☐ A notepad and pen
- ☐ A list of references
- ☐ My Interview Cheat Sheet (*duh*)
- ☐ Business cards (*if you have them*)
- ☐ My phone (*charged and turned off*)
- ☐ A granola bar or other snack (*to avoid getting hangry right before game time*)

PHONE OR SKYPE INTERVIEW CHECKLIST

- ☐ Time has been verified (taking into account time zones) as well as phone number, and who will call whom
- ☐ Equipment is working properly and ready to go (including a fully charged phone)
- ☐ Desktop (both literal and virtual) is cleared of mess and distractions, and notes are on hand (but out of sight in the case of a Skype interview)
- ☐ An appropriate professional outfit is selected and crisply ironed

EMERGENCY KIT (BECAUSE, HEY, YOU JUST NEVER KNOW)

- ☐ Tissues
- ☐ Brush or comb
- ☐ Umbrella
- ☐ Phone charger
- ☐ Stain remover
- ☐ Advil
- ☐ Band-Aids

CHAPTER **NINE**

The New Rules of Nailing Your Negotiation

THE OLD RULE: When you got a job offer, you accepted it gratefully, no questions asked. Negotiating was reserved for senior hires and executives, and even then, the only element of the job offer up for discussion was salary. At any level lower than that, trying to negotiate a job offer could come across as greedy, ungrateful, or entitled. So in most cases, if you got an offer, you took it. End of story.

THE NEW RULE: Companies make offers with the expectation that you'll negotiate—so in many situations, if you don't haggle a little, you'll end up with less than you're worth. You also have more to work with in today's marketplace; these days companies are often willing to consider factors beyond salary, so you can negotiate for other benefits, such as vacation time, a flexible schedule, moving expenses, and more.

Congratulations! You made it through the job search process—and now you have an offer in hand. You're probably already envisioning that first day, imagining what it's going to be like stepping through that door, picturing your office with the downtown view, and preparing to ask your new co-workers to lunch.

While it's great to be excited about a prospective new job (otherwise, why would you be considering it?), there's one more vital step you need to take before you sign on the dotted line: negotiating the details of the offer.

We consider negotiation an essential part of the job search process, as it affects factors that could keep you fulfilled in your new position—or cause you to rethink your agreement just a few months down the road.

As important as it is, though, we know that negotiating doesn't feel natural for everyone; in fact, the process makes a lot of people feel downright uncomfortable. You might get worried that you'll be perceived as ungrateful or greedy. You might even fear that by trying to negotiate, your potential employer will revoke the offer entirely. But trust us: that isn't the case. Negotiation is an expected part of the job search process and, done right, can be extremely beneficial to you and the trajectory of your career.

And we don't expect you to do it on your own. In this chapter, we'll give you the tools you need to move from job offer to signed deal. We'll discuss how to evaluate your current offer, determine what you're worth, and create your ideal compensation package. We'll even show you how to negotiate beyond the obvious (in other words, salary) and ask for the perks and benefits that will make the job offer completely irresistible.

Before you can adjust your demands, however, you have to *understand* the initial offer. So that's exactly where we'll start.

EVALUATING THE OFFER

One of the most exciting calls you'll ever get—at least, while you're in the depths of your job search—is the one from the HR department extending you an offer of employment. Of course, you'll be tempted to jump at the offer immediately, saying that you thought it felt like a great fit, too, and eagerly asking when you can start.

But as powerful as this temptation can be, it's best to postpone your answer until you've completed a few final steps to fully evaluate the offer and make sure you're happy with it. Essentially, you have to objectively evaluate what the company offered in relation to your value in the market, as well as weigh the other benefits that will impact your overall satisfaction.

We recommend going through the five steps below to get the best understanding of the offer, compare it to what you want (and what you are worth), and decide how to move forward.

STEP ONE: GET THE OFFER IN WRITING

When you get that exciting phone call, the recruiter will probably briefly run down the basics of the offer: the salary and the benefits that are included, like the number of days of vacation you'll receive. While that's a solid place to start, it leaves out important details that you'll want to consider before accepting the job, like your official title and job description, how fast you'll accumulate vacation days, how much you'll pay per paycheck for healthcare coverage, how long it'll take for the 401(k) employer match to kick in, and more.

You should also be aware that a job offer is a contract. Up until this point, everything you've heard or read about is a good indicator of what the job will involve, but certainly isn't binding. Since you'll be putting your signature on this document, you should be comfortable with every part of the contract before agreeing to the terms.

So, as excited as you may be when you receive that call, don't blurt out an answer right away. Instead you might say, "I'm thrilled to hear back from you, and I'm delighted to hear that you think I'm a good fit for the position. I'm excited to look over the details in the written offer."

In most cases, employers will expect this and won't hesitate to send you the written offer. However, it's also not uncommon for them to push to get a better sense of which way you're leaning, so they can anticipate your ultimate decision. "What are your initial feelings on the offer?" they might ask. "Is there anything that's making you hesitate?" Don't let this pressure you into blurting out "Okay, I'll take it!" Stay calm and noncommittal, providing a response like "From what you've told me, the offer sounds promising ['exciting,' if you must], but I'd like to review the details in the written offer before moving forward."

Once you receive the written offer, read it carefully, looking for the following:

- **Job title and description:** Make sure these elements align with your understanding of the role. If, for example, the written offer includes a responsibility you never talked about during your interview, you should bring it up during the negotiation process. Same goes for your proposed title—if you assumed you were interviewing for an associate position, but the offer specifies your title as "assistant," you'll want to clarify before signing.

- **Details of the benefits:** Make sure you understand the details of your benefits, such as whether the company offers paid parental leave or whether it would be classified as short-term disability. Some companies provide two weeks of vacation up front; in other organizations, employees accumulate a certain number of hours during each pay period. You may not be able to negotiate every element of your benefits (for example, insurance isn't usually up for debate), but understanding the details of each will help you evaluate the offer as a whole.

- **Base salary and details of any additional incentives:** You'll clearly see your base salary, but make sure you also understand any additional incentives—such as performance bonuses and a promotion schedule, if there is one.

With a better understanding of what the offer does and does not include, it'll become increasingly clear if there's anything missing that's important to you. For example, maybe you have big plans to travel in the next few years, but the company doesn't offer many vacation days. Or perhaps you're thinking about starting a family soon, and the parental leave is unpaid. Keep all this in mind—we'll come back to it in Step 5.

STEP TWO: DIG IN A LITTLE FURTHER

If you did your homework during the interview process, you found out a lot about your potential new work environment, such as the culture of the team you'd be working with, whether the role requires more collaboration or independent work, what kind of personality is most likely to succeed there, and how often employees get promoted. All those factors should play into your decision about whether the company—and job—is right for you.

But now that you're considering an offer, you might have a few lingering unanswered questions. To make the most informed decision possible, you may need to do a little more detective work before you can commit to the position.

Start by reading up on the recent news within the industry. Is there anything happening in the market right now that might affect the company? If, for example, a couple of the largest competitors in your space have been acquiring small firms, the small business that just offered you a job might be facing some difficulties in the near future. It's not realistic to think that you can anticipate every move a company will make, but you may spot a couple of red flags (like declining profits or news of recent lawsuits)—which can influence your decision.

You'll also want to get a read on employee turnover, and the potential and timeline for advancement. Besides Google, a great source for this information is LinkedIn. Look at the employment timelines of people who currently work at the company, which can yield valuable information about your long-term potential with the business. Have most of the current employees been there less than a year? For some industries, like management consulting, that may be standard—but for others, it could be a sign that turnover is high. Next, look at employees' career timelines. If you see that most people tend to move up to a new position every couple of years, you can probably assume that there's opportunity for advancement and that the company values promoting from within.

If you're still not feeling confident, or your research hasn't painted a clear picture, try reaching out to a few of the people you find on LinkedIn who have worked at the company—if possible, in the department you'd be working in—and request a phone call or coffee meeting. This is a great way to gain some valuable intelligence on what it's like to work there. Like your other informational interviews, though, make sure to have questions prepared ahead of time, so you don't take up too much of the person's time.

Here are a few ideas for questions to get your conversation started:

- Can you tell me about the management style of my potential boss?

- What were the biggest challenges you faced in the role?

- What did you enjoy about the company culture? Was there any part of the culture you didn't like?

- Does the company respect its employees and support their advancement?

- What do you think is in store for the company in the next few years?

With this knowledge, you should have a pretty solid assessment of whether you'd fit in with the team, have the room to grow and advance, and gain the type of experience you're looking for.

STEP THREE: ASK *YOURSELF* THE TOUGH QUESTIONS

Now that you've gathered the information necessary to make a decision, it's time to put your excitement for the job aside and be honest with yourself: Is this opportunity a good fit? Remember that for this job to truly satisfy you and put you on the road to future success, it must align with the things that you value most. For a refresher, go back to the Muse Grid you created in Chapter 2 and ask yourself the following questions:

DOES THIS JOB ALIGN WITH MY VALUES?

In your Muse Grid, you identified the values of a job that were most important to you. For example, maybe you wanted a deadline-driven role that heavily relied on team collaboration and creativity. For each value that you identified as essential, how does this job rank? It's okay if it doesn't rank high in every category, but if it doesn't satisfy several key values, it may be a sign that your excitement is more about simply getting *a* job offer—but not necessarily *this* job offer.

IS THE POSITION INTERESTING AND CHALLENGING?

It's not unusual to feel a little nervous when taking a new job, as each new role you take in your career journey will challenge and stretch you in new ways. And that's a great thing; it's what's going to help you stay engaged and motivated! Otherwise, you may find yourself bored (and job hunting) by the time you get through orientation.

WILL I LIKE MY BOSS AND CO-WORKERS?

Again, think back to the interactions you experienced during your interview process. In addition to your future boss, you may have met some would-be direct reports, other employees in the department, and senior leaders. Can you see yourself working with these people on a daily basis? Sure, you only got a quick first impression—but what was your gut feeling?

CAN I BE PRODUCTIVE IN THE WORK ENVIRONMENT?

It may seem like a minor detail, but considering you'll be spending forty hours a week (or more) in your work environment, it should be one that's conducive to your productivity. When you were interviewing, did you see that the entire floor is an open workspace that encourages collaboration? If you know you need a quiet, solitary space to do your best work, that's a sign it may not be the best fit. Keep in mind that there may be something you can do to make the environment work for you (e.g., invest in noise-canceling headphones)—but it's something you should weigh carefully and discuss with your potential employer before committing to the position.

DOES THIS JOB ALLOW FOR THE LIFESTYLE I WANT?

Does the role require travel for weeks at a time? For some, that might be exactly what you want—a way to see the world while still advancing your career. Others, however, might rather spend that time with local friends and family, and taking that travel-oriented role might not allow them to have the home life they want. Similarly, what are the company's policies on flexibility? Is the occasional work-from-home day okay? Is it accepted for parents with small children to adjust their hours in accordance with school schedules? However amazing the role is, consider if it also provides the means for you to fully live your life *outside* of work.

WILL I FEEL PROFESSIONALLY SATISFIED?

Will you feel like you're doing something valuable and important, or will you feel like your work doesn't really matter? Will you be constantly learning and doing new things, or will every day look more or less the same? Will you be proud to explain your new role to your friends and family? If you can't see this job as satisfying to you now, when it's new and exciting, it likely won't fulfill you in the long run.

DOES THIS JOB FIT INTO MY CAREER NARRATIVE?

It may be a big promotion on paper (or, at least, a quick escape from your current role)—but does it move you closer to *your* long-term career goals? If you want to be a writer, but take a role as a business analyst, you probably won't be gaining any skills or experience that will get you closer to your dream career. And in that case, no matter how great the salary or benefits are, it's not necessarily a smart move.

STEP FOUR: KNOW YOUR VALUE

Before you can even think about starting a conversation about your salary, you have to have a good idea of what you're worth in the industry. This is known as your market value, and it's a number (or, more likely, a range) based on your role, location, field, and years of experience. Knowing this information will help you quickly determine if what the company is offering is aligned with what you deserve and (hopefully) help you negotiate a fair salary.

It used to be that the only way to figure out your market value was to be lucky enough to know people in similar roles or positions who were willing to open up to you about their salary. But today there are multiple websites that can help you determine your number. On PayScale, for example, if you answer a series of questions about your potential company, role, qualifications, experience, education, and more, you'll see a range of salaries for that type of role. Similarly, Indeed can help you determine average salaries for a specific job title in your location.

You can also talk to your peers in the industry. It may seem like an off-limits subject, but with the right phrasing, the question doesn't have to put them on the spot. Instead of asking them point-blank what they make, simply say something like, "I'm considering an associate marketing role with a healthcare technology company. From my research, it looks like I should be looking at a salary of $55,000 to $60,000. Since you work in that industry, does that range sound reasonable?"

Whether that person comes out and reveals his or her salary or not, the answer should give you a good idea if the proposed salary you've been offered reflects your market value—or if the company is lowballing you.

WHAT YOUR MARKET VALUE IS *NOT*

Keep in mind, your market value does *not*, as many people incorrectly assume, depend on what you're currently making or what you made in your last job. Recruiters will often ask for your salary history so they can base your job offer on it. But you're not asking for a raise from your current position; you're being considered for an entirely new role, which likely carries different responsibilities and tasks than your previous job—and, as a result, should carry a completely unrelated salary.

If a recruiter asks what you're making now, you don't have to immediately offer it up. You can respond to a question about what your current salary is simply by answering with the question "What's the salary that accompanies this position?" Another option is to answer with what you're looking to make, according to what you've learned from your research on the industry standard. For example, you might say, "For this position, I'm looking for a salary range of $70,000 to $75,000." Set the low end of the range you share in the middle of your actual range (so in this case, maybe you were hoping to make $65,000 to $75,000) so that you're aiming high and in a better position for the negotiation. If pressed for what you're currently making, you *can* share it—but make sure to clarify that it shouldn't influence your offer for this role: "At my current company, I'm making $55,000, but I'm looking to bring my position up to market value, which I've determined to be right around $70,000."

If the employer shares a number first and it's significantly higher than what you're looking for, that's great— but it doesn't mean you shouldn't still negotiate. In the case that it's lower than you expected, you might respond with "Based on market value, I was under the impression this position would be closer to $75,000."

Oh, and note that your market value also is *not* the salary you need to make to fulfill your personal financial responsibilities. Your rent may have increased and you may need to budget for daycare, but, sorry to say, those don't have any impact on your market value. That's determined solely by the demand for your role and your experience and skills—not what you simply want your salary to be.

STEP FIVE: PREPARE TO NEGOTIATE

Before the negotiation begins, it's important to remember it's not all about salary. In the new world of work, compensation also includes everything from vacation days to flextime to benefits. With a complete picture of what's included in the offer, take a moment to step back and see how it compares to the factors that you value most, from your ideal benefits to goal salary. Do they match up? Where would you like to see some adjustment? At this point, it can be helpful to rank the factors of the offer by how important they are to you. Maybe salary is first, followed by paid vacation time and a flexible schedule. Or maybe you'd be willing to accept a slightly lower salary knowing that there is the option to work remotely twice a week, or that you get a month of vacation. If you're looking at start-ups, look into equity as part of your total compensation. There's no right or wrong answer here; it's all about what matters most to you.

With these five steps out of the way, the real fun begins. Schedule a phone call or in-person meeting with the HR representative you've been in touch with to go over the offer. And then what? Don't worry, we wouldn't leave you hanging at this all-important juncture. The next section will cover exactly how to ask for—and get—what you want.

NEGOTIATE LIKE A PRO

Plenty of doubts may enter your mind as you approach your negotiation conversation: Will the hiring manager get angry? Does bargaining make you seem ungrateful? Will he or she assume you don't want the job? Are you too low on the totem pole to negotiate?

Those worries are completely normal—but don't let them get in the way of your asking for what you deserve. Remember: companies *expect* candidates at every level to negotiate (this doesn't mean that they always do; according to Salary.com, only 37 percent of people always negotiate their salaries, while 18 percent *never* do). We know it can be intimidating, but think about it this way: do you realize how much you could be giving up if you don't have that tough conversation? In fact, a study by George Mason University and Temple University found that, by failing to negotiate your first salary from $50,000 to $55,000, you could miss out on $600,000 over a forty-year career. That's a tough number to stomach.

That said, you do have to approach the conversation with realistic expectations, which also means taking into account a few factors that impact your bargaining power. Large companies, for instance, tend to have more resources, so they may have more leeway to adjust your salary.

Smaller companies, on the other hand, might not have as much financial flexibility, but could make up for that by adjusting your nonmonetary benefits, like a flexible schedule, a more impressive-sounding title, or more vacation time.

And while in the new world of work all candidates have the power to negotiate, those getting recruited for senior positions will have significantly more ability to tailor their compensation package.

We don't say this to discourage you (the whole point of this chapter is to encourage you to ask for what you deserve!); we just want you to be realistic in what you ask for. If you are early in your career, you're probably not going to negotiate doubling your salary or getting three months of paid vacation. Now that we've issued that caveat, you're ready to get into the meat of the negotiation—starting with what most candidates rank as their top priority: salary.

SHOW ME THE MONEY

You've already done your research and come up with a number for what the market says you are worth. But before going any further, you need to come up with yet another figure. Let's call this one your walk-away number—that is, the point at which you would turn down the job. We know, it's tough to picture walking away from an offer—especially one that we know you worked so hard to land in the first place. And if you decide that the job has enough other great attributes—whether it's a foot in the door to the industry you want, opportunities for learning, or a great work environment—that are worth the lower salary, that's completely fine. But you still have to decide how low you are willing to go, and what wouldn't be worth your time. With that in the back of your mind, you can move on to asking for what you really want.

At this point, the employer has thrown out one number, while you have determined another: your market value. Ideally, they're not that far apart. But even if they are, you may still be able to come to a compromise that suits you both. To start, counter the employer's offer with a number toward the top of your range. It's important to start high because your employer will likely negotiate down, so to land on your ideal number, you need a little wiggle room. Try phrasing it like this: "I'm excited about the position and think I would be a great fit. I've researched the market and, considering my experience and the value I could bring to the role, I was hoping for a salary closer to $70,000."

You'll likely go through a little back-and-forth at this point. That's why you determined a walk-away number—if the company doesn't at least hit that figure, you know that you'll decline.

That said, if you can't agree on a base salary number that satisfies you, consider asking for the potential to earn more through bonuses, or after a predetermined period of time at the company (for example, your midyear review). Still can't reach a satisfactory compromise? Don't give up hope yet, because while salary and financial incentives are typically the focus of negotiation, they aren't the only elements of the contract that can be adjusted. A company may offer a lower salary than you were hoping for, but the addition of other intangible benefits and perks can sweeten the overall compensation package. So before you make the decision to walk away, see what else you can negotiate—which includes:

FLEXIBLE SCHEDULE

You might ask that your contract specify that you can work from home one day per week, or that you're free to work any eight hours during the workday, whether you choose to come in at 6 a.m. or 10 a.m.

The great thing about flexible hours is that they generally cost your employer absolutely nothing—but can significantly increase your job satisfaction and make it worthwhile to accept a slightly lower salary than you'd otherwise agree to.

JOB TITLE

Even if a new job title doesn't come with a bump in pay, it can add value to your resume—which can help you in the long run. For example, maybe the company offered you the position of "HR assistant," but you know that in your field, that title conveys a lower level of experience. So in your negotiations, you might ask for your title to be changed to "HR generalist."

Again, this doesn't cost the company anything, but it can position you for faster career growth when you decide it's time for your next step.

CONTINUING EDUCATION

You may be focused on this job in the moment, but your short-term success shouldn't be the only thing on your radar. You should also be starting to think about what it takes to move your career to the next level—and for many people, that will require some professional development, whether it's in the form of an advanced degree, a certification, or just a few online courses here and there. The good news is that it's in the company's interests to support your continuing education, because the more skills you gain, the more you can offer the company.

With that in mind, consider asking your potential employer to include some continuing education allowance within your contract. Some companies will offer a dollar amount toward tuition reimbursement; others may agree to cover a certain number of courses. Just make sure to read the fine print: at some organizations, if you don't remain with the company for a certain period of time after you redeem the benefit, you'll have to pay all or part of it back.

VACATION TIME

Your job offer almost certainly includes some vacation time—that should be a given. But of course, some will be more generous than others, so if yours seems on the low end of the spectrum, it certainly doesn't hurt to try to negotiate for more. But first, you have to be aware of exactly how the company designates the vacation time. For example, some companies offer generic paid time off (PTO), without separating it into sick time and vacation days; you're simply allotted a number of days, and you get to use them however you choose. Other companies divide them up, so you get a certain number of days for sick time and a certain number for vacation.

The way you earn those days may also differ—some organizations give you the total number of days up front; others require that you accrue them over time (e.g., for each pay period, you might accrue four hours of PTO).

Once you know the details, consider your "ask." Do you want five extra days of PTO? Can you swap four of your sick days for four additional days of vacation? If your company typically uses an accrual method for PTO, can you ask to start with five days available to you, rather than starting from zero?

If the company offers unlimited vacation, well, consider yourself lucky. But before you accept, it's a good idea to ask how many days employees *typically* take off. After all, you wouldn't want to accept a job based on the expectation that you'll take five weeks off, when the average employee takes only one.

LIFESTYLE PERKS

These are the kinds of benefits that almost sound too good to be true. Free dry cleaning, subsidized gym membership or an on-site gym, a fully stocked snack room—you get the picture.

In many cases, these are already part of company culture—or not—so if no one is getting free dry cleaning, the recruiter may give you a strange look if you try to add it to your contract.

However, you may have *some* leeway, and this is where it pays to be creative. For example, you may be able to ask the employer to reimburse you for commuting or parking costs. Or, if you determine that the company doesn't offer the software you prefer to use (e.g., as a designer, you prefer to work on a Mac, but the company only offers PCs), you may be able to get them to agree to purchase new equipment for you.

MOVING EXPENSES

Are you relocating for the job? Moving can rack up more expenses than you might expect—and quickly.

The most obvious benefit to ask for is for the company to cover the expenses of physically moving your belongings to your new place. The company may agree to pay you a lump sum (so you can decide whom to hire and for which services), or it may coordinate with a moving company to set you up with a comprehensive package.

But that's not the only expense you have to worry about, especially if you're relocating from someplace far. For example, you may have to make an advance trip or two to your new location to secure a house or apartment—and if that involves plane tickets, you could be looking at a couple of thousand dollars. Or, if you can't find a place before your start date, you may have to pay for temporary housing while looking for a more permanent place in your free time. And don't forget about all those other moving-related expenses—like storing your belongings for a few months or renting a car before you can arrange to get yours to your new location.

Your company may be able to reimburse you for some of these fees—so if they apply to you, make sure to ask for the added benefit.

––––––

Whatever it is you choose to negotiate, remember this: you never get what you don't ask for. And sometimes it pays to think big. Recently, a friend of ours—we'll call him Justin—was offered a position as a designer at a smaller company that couldn't match his salary requirements. Instead, he came up with a bold proposal: that he be allowed to work remotely in Europe for six weeks the following summer, with no change or reduction in salary, since it was a bucket list item he was planning with his girlfriend. After a few internal conversations, the hiring manager came back with a "Yes," and Justin signed his dream job—and gave himself the travel opportunity of a lifetime.

WHAT IF THE ANSWER IS "NO"?

The hiring manager may agree to some of the things you ask for—but at some point, there's a good chance you'll receive a flat-out "no." Don't panic! Hearing "no" doesn't mean the discussion is over. It's simply another chance for you to voice your value and ask questions that will help you come to an agreement.

For example, you might say:

> *I'm excited for this opportunity and think I'd be able to im-*
> *mediately jump in and begin bringing in new clients. However,*
> *I'm surprised to see that the position doesn't pay market rate/*
> *that there is no flexibility on hours/that you can't increase my*
> *number of vacation days—do you know why that is?*

If there truly are circumstances that are preventing the company from granting your requests (for example, if it's a cash- or manpower-strapped start-up that's just getting off the ground, or maybe the HR rep simply isn't authorized to offer the things you want for this position), well, then it's time to do some real soul-searching about whether or not this is the dream job you thought it was.

WHAT IF YOUR ANSWER IS "NO"?

In the job search process, it can seem like employers have all the decision-making power. They decide when to set the interviews, whether you're qualified for the position, whether or not they make you an offer—and what that offer entails.

But there is one thing that *is* up to you—whether or not to take the job. You might realize that what the company is offering—even after negotiating—simply isn't enough. Or maybe you find out from a former or current employee that the work-life balance is awful or that even with an unlimited vacation benefit, most employees don't take more than two or three days off each year.

Or maybe some other element of the role just doesn't feel right. Once, Kathryn interviewed for a position that sounded fantastic on paper—but when she met the team she'd be working with, she quickly realized her would-be future colleagues were the complete *opposite* of inspiring. Not to mention, the office environment had about as much energy as a wet sock.

In the excitement of the moment, it can be hard to imagine turning down a job. But think about the long term: Will you be happy in this role? Does it help you move forward on your path to your career goals? Will you look forward to coming to work (at least, on most days)?

THE NEW RULES OF WORK

Remember that jumping into a job that isn't right for you can have long-lasting effects on your happiness and professional growth. Take your time, and make the best decision for *you*—and if that decision is to turn it down, well, we can help you with that, too.

TURNING DOWN A JOB WITH GRACE

By this point, you've invested significant time and effort in the interview and negotiation process—but don't forget: so has the company. Whether you're turning down this offer because you have a better option lined up, because the offer wasn't enough, or because something just didn't feel right about the position or the company culture, we recommend responding with as much integrity and graciousness as possible. You never know whom you might come across (or even work with) later in your career, and burning bridges now can only work against you.

Start by offering your sincere gratitude to the hiring manager. (After all, he or she did spend a considerable amount of time vetting you for the position.) Then offer a specific reason for why you're turning down the offer. For example:

> *Thank you so much for considering me for the social media*
> *coordinator role. I enjoyed learning more about the company and*
> *team, and I appreciate the generous offer. After much consider-*
> *ation, however, I've decided to pursue a role with a smaller com-*
> *pany where I'll have the opportunity to take on a wider range*
> *of projects and have more influence on the organization's overall*
> *social media strategy. Thank you again for your time.*

Or, if you don't have another opportunity in the works, you can write something like:

> *Thank you so much for considering me for the social media*
> *coordinator role. I enjoyed learning more about the company and*
> *team, and I appreciate the generous offer. After much consid-*

eration, however, I've decided this is not the best move for my career at this time. Thank you again for the opportunity and your time.

You may feel uneasy after turning down a job, especially if you don't currently have anything else lined up. But trust us: it's worth waiting for the right opportunity. And when you do find that perfect role, you'll knock it out of the park. How do we know? Because in the next few chapters, we're giving you all the tools you need to thrive and advance in the job and career that are the right fit for you.

PART THREE

CHARTING YOUR COURSE THROUGH THE MODERN WORKPLACE

The New Rules of Communication

THE OLD RULE: With only so many ways to communicate, getting your point across was relatively straightforward. You had your choice between an in-person meeting, a phone call, or—believe it or not—a fax to share your message. Your options were limited, but for the most part, communication was clear and straightforward.

THE NEW RULE: Social media may have truncated some messages to 140 characters, but it's done nothing to reduce the importance of top-notch communication skills in the workplace. In fact, it's now more important than ever to communicate clearly and effectively—after all, your virtual communications can all be easily deprioritized, ignored, or completely deleted, and if you don't get to the point quickly, they likely will be. Yes, you may have become accustomed to a more casual online style, but you still need the know-how to communicate with everyone professionally in this twenty-first-century digital workplace.

It's entirely possible to find a job or career path that allows you to skate around or even avoid many of the things you aren't good at. In fact, throughout most of this book, you've been learning how to play to your strengths and do exactly that.

But communication? Well, that's one of those skills that is necessary in every single job you'll find. Because while the modes and mediums of communication have changed (and will continue to change) drastically, the importance of clear communication hasn't. In fact, whether it's by phone, by email, or in person, being a competent communicator in the workplace is more essential than ever. If you communicate effectively, you'll improve collaboration, work more efficiently, and be able to nip any potential interpersonal issues right in the bud. On the other hand, communicate poorly and you're looking at decreased productivity, strained relationships, and—to put it simply—a big ol' mess.

For some people, effective communication comes naturally. But for others, getting a point across in a way that's concise, clear, and efficient can seem like an uphill battle. Regardless of where you find yourself on the spectrum, we could all stand to brush up on some basics. Luckily, that's exactly what you'll learn in this chapter. From leading a productive meeting to writing a professional email to making the most of those dreaded conference calls, we'll touch on everything you need to know to be a top-notch communicator in the modern workplace.

Let's get started with some basic ground rules that always apply—no matter what method you're using to communicate.

COMMUNICATION: THE GROUND RULES

1. KNOW YOUR PURPOSE

Whether you're writing an email or speaking in front of a group of people, you need to have a clear-cut purpose. After all, why speak up in the first place if there's no point to what you're actually saying (and yes, it's okay not to talk at all if you have nothing to contribute!). So, before chiming in with your two cents, ensure that you're zoned in on the purpose of what you're expressing.

There's one key question that will make this easy for you: *What am I trying to achieve?* Perhaps you're attempting to gain clarity on a project or assignment. Or maybe you're trying to provide a suggestion for a way that a method could be improved. There are virtually limitless reasons for speaking up. But you still need to make sure you're clear on what yours is. If *you* don't understand your purpose, you can't expect anybody else to.

2. KNOW YOUR AUDIENCE

We're willing to bet that conversations between you and your grandparents don't take the same tone and style as the ones between you and your best friend. And you probably speak to your boss much differently than you speak to your co-workers or teammates. It's human nature—we adjust the way we're communicating based on who exactly we're talking to.

It should go without saying that the root of successful communication lies in knowing your audience. We all have different communication styles—for example, some of us are direct, while some of us tend to avoid conflict. Similarly, we all have different values and preferences—some of us prefer communicating face-to-face, for instance, while others feel more comfortable expressing themselves in writing. Being attuned to these nuances not only in yourself but also in others will allow you to appropriately target your message, timing, and format to the people you're talking to, making you that much more likely to not only be heard—but actually listened to. Alex learned this lesson early in her career when she worked with two managers who had very different styles. One was gregarious, quick on her feet, and liked to brainstorm; when Alex had a question, no matter how small, she could pop into her manager's office, get a helpful and fast answer, and get on with her work. Soon after, Alex switched to another team where her manager was very thoughtful, analytical, and valued focus, so it was more effective to bundle questions together to ask all at once, at a predetermined time. If Alex hadn't changed her approach, it would have been a huge hit to her productivity—not to mention very disruptive and frustrating for her new manager.

3. BE RESPECTFUL

This one should *really* go without saying (we hope so, at least): you absolutely need to be respectful in the way you communicate.

We get that, occasionally, things can get heated in the workplace. Whether it's a co-worker who doesn't pull his or her weight on a project, a client who is being unreasonable, or anything else, it can be tempting to respond in a less than professional way. But, even if someone says something that really gets under your skin, it's imperative that you keep your composure and always communicate in a respectful manner. After all, think of the last time you heard someone speak in a way that was rude, brash, or offensive. If you're like most people, you couldn't get past it and likely became so wrapped up in the way he or she was choosing to communicate that you were unable to actually listen and absorb his or her message. In the new world of work, relationships matter more than ever. Trust us when we say that flying off the handle or dishing out curse words really won't do you any favors.

But being respectful isn't just about keeping your cool; it also means not hogging the conversation, and making space for others to speak. If you tend to be one of the louder voices in the room, try keeping yourself in check and seeking out the thoughts of your quieter colleagues. They likely have a lot to contribute, but may feel they sometimes just can't get in a word edgewise.

4. LISTEN AS MUCH AS YOU SPEAK

Communication isn't just about the times when you get to open up your mouth and speak. Being an active listener is an equally important piece of communication—and respectful communication in particular. If you're naturally more introverted, this is likely already something you're good at, but for extroverts (like us), it's important to put in the effort to build a strong listening muscle.

Here's a secret about people who are really solid communicators: they listen just as much as (or maybe even more than) they speak. But note that listening isn't the same as hearing. Truly listening means that when others are talking to you, you are engaged in what they're saying. And no, your halfhearted focus with occasional glances over your screen doesn't fit the bill.

Why is paying attention so important? In addition to communicating respect, active listening allows you to actually follow the flow of the conversation, and then respond accordingly. This makes for a high-quality, productive, and balanced discussion—without all of those time-wasting (and frustrating to the other person) "I'm sorry, what was that?" questions littered throughout. Even more important, you'll reduce the potential for miscommunication—and make your conversation partner feel valued and heard.

5. REMEMBER YOUR NONVERBAL CUES

What you're saying is important. But sometimes what you're *not* saying—in the form of your nonverbal communication—carries even more weight.

Your nonverbal cues include everything from your body language and your tone of voice to your facial expressions and the way you present yourself. Think of it this way: if you gave your co-worker a hearty "Congratulations!" on her recent promotion, but did it all with your arms crossed and a look of disdain on your face, your message would undoubtedly lose some of its impact (and its sincerity). Similarly, if you approach your boss with good news to share, you might undermine your credibility with colleagues—and his or her appreciation of the message—if you can't restrain from bouncing up and down or waving enthusiastic jazz hands. (A good rule of thumb here is to take cues from those around you; like much of the advice in this book, norms around what behavior is appropriate do vary by workplace!)

That all goes to say, be conscious of not just your words, but also how you say them to ensure that you're sending a message that is clear and—perhaps more important—consistent. Of course, your nonverbal cues will need to be adjusted depending on the exact message you're sharing. When in doubt, remember to stand up straight and make eye contact. Those two small changes alone can make a world of difference in the way you're perceived.

THE TRICK TO COMMUNICATING HARD MESSAGES

One of the biggest mistakes people inadvertently make when communicating with others is passing off their feelings, perspectives, or observations as fact. This happens *especially* when sharing difficult messages, like critical feedback for a colleague or boss. Unsurprisingly, this often leads to conflict or frustration, instead of the resolution or change you were going for. In such situations, the key is to avoid passing off your feelings as objective statements, and in particular to avoid doing it in a way that could come off as judging. Take these two examples of giving a seemingly checked-out colleague feedback:

> *"You weren't interested with what I had to say at last week's meeting."*

> *"When I shared my ideas at last week's meeting, I noticed you didn't make eye contact or share your thoughts, and I felt like you weren't interested in what I had to say."*

The former states your feelings as fact, and it shuts down the conversation by giving your colleague the opportunity to deny or disagree—he might answer, "Well no, I was actually very interested." In the second example, however, your colleague can't argue with your feelings. You also make it harder to deny by giving specifics as to what made you perceive the situation the way you did. Even if he didn't mean to, you *felt* like he wasn't interested. The conversation can now focus on the effect, rather than the intention.

The trick is to use this simple formula: "When you did/said X, I felt Y." You can even add "Next time, it would be great if you could do Z" if there's an actionable change you think would help. With a little practice, this strategy can become second nature and make you a pro at handling challenging conversations.

ALL ABOUT MEETINGS

Mastering these basic ground rules of being a master communicator doesn't happen overnight. But luckily, there's going to be an opportunity to practice those skills regularly: meetings.

Whether you're leading a meeting, participating in one, or just sitting quietly and trying to make it through one of those "I have no idea why I'm even in here" meetings, these get-togethers are an unavoidable element of the workplace. But, if you've ever sat through a terrible meeting, you know that not all are created equal. Some are productive, inspiring, and send you out of that conference room with brilliant ideas and a skip in your step. Others? Well, let's just say you'd rather zip yourself into a sleeping bag filled with hungry mosquitoes than suffer through that again.

Despite what some people like to think (you know who you are), getting the most out of meetings requires more than a "just wing it" philosophy. It takes thought, consideration, and—believe it or not—some prior planning.

PREPARING FOR A MEETING

Whether you're spearheading the entire sit-down or are just filling a seat at the table, we have some tips on how to ensure you're getting your ducks in a row beforehand.

Let's say you're the one tasked with leading the charge and ensuring that the meeting is valuable and informative for everyone. It's quite a bit of pressure, we know. But it's nothing you can't handle. Here, Muse career coach Ashley Cobert outlines a few key things you'll need to do to make sure your meeting is a success:

1. START WITH A PLAN

Remember when we said you wouldn't want to walk into a meeting and wing it? We meant it. Any great meeting starts with a clear plan—aka an agenda—in place. Think of this as the outline of your meeting. It will list out all of the key points you hope to touch on and discuss with the participants.

An agenda pays off most if you're able to share it beforehand with the other people who are attending the meeting. That way, everyone is on the same page (quite literally) right from the get-go. But, whether you share your outline or not, the important thing is to have some sort of structure and road map in place before ever waltzing into that room. That way, you'll keep the entire group focused and you'll be more likely to walk out having accomplished what you set out to do.

2. FACILITATE FOR FOCUS

We know that there are endless distractions in the workplace that can quickly derail even the best-planned meeting. So, in order to keep everyone focused on the discussion at hand, you'll want to find someplace where you can all have a productive conversation without constantly being interrupted or pulled off course. Find a quiet room away from the hustle and bustle of the rest of the office where you can shut the door and have some space for valuable discussion. It seems like a minor detail, but it makes all the difference.

Another way to set your team up for intense focus is by restating your goals as you're welcoming everyone to the meeting. Saying something like "Thanks for being here, everyone! As a reminder, we're here to iron out the remaining details for our upcoming marketing initiative," makes it clear that there's a distinct purpose to your sit-down—and that you're ready to roll up your sleeves and get to work. This would also be a good time to pass out the agenda and any other meeting materials your group will need to stay on course.

3. BRINGING THE GROUP BACK

You've done your best to prime the situation for laser-like focus. But things happen—it's natural for your team to go off on a tangent at some point. When that happens, you don't need to throw up your hands and call the whole meeting a wash. Instead, there are a few actionable strategies you can use to bring your group back and regain control of your meeting.

THE BOUNCE-BACK

If someone in your group moves on to a completely different topic, acknowledge that's something you need to discuss (assuming that it actually is), but bring the attention back to the current discussion. Something like "Yes, that's an important aspect we need to talk over. But let's tie up the loose ends on our conversation about the launch schedule" should suffice.

THE PARKING LOT

Ideas are bound to come up in your meeting that are worthy of extended conversation—just not at that time. Bring a notepad in with you and jot down anything that should be brought up at a later meeting. That way, you can reassure your team that you'll come back to it and still stay focused on the topic at hand.

THE TIMEKEEPER

Let's be honest—no matter how hard you try to make your meeting engaging, you're likely to have at least some attendees who would like to escape that room as soon as humanly possible. But letting them know that the end is in sight can help. So if things start to head off the rails, remind everyone of the time that's left. Something simple like "That's a great point, but we only have about fifteen minutes left, so let's be sure to stick to our plan here" is sure to snap your group back into focus.

4. WRAP IT UP

Per rule number 1 above, there should be a clear, distinct purpose to every single meeting you host. And that means that people should be walking out with action items and deadlines for the things that they need to accomplish. Otherwise, there truly was no point to your meeting. Finish off your discussion with a brief summary of what was accomplished during your conversation, and any subsequent to-dos that your team members need to take care of. Finally, send those next steps out via email to serve as a reminder to your colleagues and keep everyone on track. Then you can rest assured that your time actually served

21 UNWRITTEN (NEW) RULES OF RUNNING A MEETING

1. Make sure you really need a meeting before scheduling it. Could this be resolved by ten minutes on the phone or via email instead?

2. Every meeting should have a purpose: you either need to make a decision or complete an action together. Giving an update can almost always happen by email.

3. Do not schedule more time than you need. Most meetings are scheduled for a full hour, when they should be 20 minutes, 30 minutes, or 45 minutes—*max*.

4. Start on time. Don't wait for stragglers—it only encourages them.

5. End on time. Not only does this show respect for people's time, but it will remind people that you want an efficient meeting just as much as they do.

6. Invite only the people who absolutely need to be there. In general, the more people in a meeting, the less that gets done.

7. Every meeting should have someone clearly assigned ahead of time to run it. If it's not you, name someone else (and make sure that person knows he or she's in charge, well in advance).

8. Bake in a few minutes for chitchat at the beginning of the meeting. We are people, not robots, and building rapport with colleagues helps business run more smoothly.

9. If you want people to read something ahead of time, sending it at least three hours ahead of time is the bare minimum, and the day before is better. Sending it twenty minutes before is useless.

10. Book your meeting space ahead of time, and if you need to, give yourself ten minutes before the meeting to figure out where exactly it is. Wandering the halls with everyone in tow is wasting everyone's time.

11. Set an agenda, and share it at the beginning of the meeting (or beforehand) to keep everyone on track.

12. If you want people to pay attention, don't give them several handouts at the beginning of the meeting. They'll start flipping through

them, and they'll be distracted. If there is written material to share, present it using a screen or projector instead.

13. Do not check your phone or email during the meeting. Everyone can tell what you're doing, and they'll start doing the same.

14. Keep track of next steps as the meeting goes on. Any action items should be sent around as a reminder after the meeting.

15. An action item without someone assigned to it is worthless. In most cases, a deadline is needed as well.

16. If someone is speaking too much, cut him or her off (nicely). Likewise, if someone is speaking too little, try to engage him or her.

17. If the conversation goes off topic, it is both acceptable and necessary for you to *rein it in*. A simple "Let's schedule time to discuss that later if it's helpful, since we only have ten minutes left" works perfectly.

18. If the meeting is more than an hour long, schedule time for breaks, and let attendees know about them ahead of time. Knowing they can check their email in forty-five minutes will help keep them focused now.

19. Watch body language. You can easily tell if people are bored, disengaged, or feel like their time is being wasted, so long as you look for it.

20. If needed, assign a note taker, so that you can focus on running the meeting.

21. Regularly assess if recurring meetings in your calendar are needed at all, and if so, if the format, length, and attendees are contributing to their effectiveness. If not? Change 'em up!

to push a project along—rather than wasted an hour of everyone's time on yet another brainstorming session with no concrete results.

Even if you're not the one leading the meeting, you should still do a little prep to ensure that you can make valuable contributions to the conversation. It won't be as complicated as planning to spearhead the entire meeting, but you should still take a few minutes to review the agenda and any necessary materials, generate any helpful ideas, and jot down any questions you have. Just that little bit of prior thought can lead to a much more productive discussion—and make a good impression on your team members. If no agenda was shared ahead of time, don't be afraid to ask the person who set up the meeting to send one out; at a minimum you'll be better prepared, and in some cases you may just find that you're not needed after all and can use the time for something more productive.

BEING HEARD IN MEETINGS

As with anything, in group conversations like meetings, there's a right way and a wrong way to go about making sure your thoughts are given serious consideration. This all comes down to the art of persuasion. First, you need to actively listen to the questions, objections, and suggestions that other people are presenting. And no, this isn't for the purpose of poking holes in their ideas or shooting them down. Instead, it's your chance to demonstrate that you're sincere about finding the best solution for everybody involved.

Then, emphasize results. It's far too easy to get wrapped up in the competition to be heard—after all, many people want *their own* method chosen and implemented, regardless of whether or not it's actually the best choice. So make sure that you emphasize to your team *why* you feel this way—not because it's your own suggestion and you're being stubborn, but because you truly believe that this will lead to a better outcome. It's hard to argue with results.

What if you're nervous about sharing your ideas and thoughts? We're here to tell you that it's totally normal, especially when you're in a new job, facing a new situation, or working with people who are much higher up than you are (in fact, there's a name for it: "imposter syndrome," or the fear of not being good or smart enough to be in the role or situation you're in). If you're feeling this way, try to remember that you've been invited to this meeting for a reason: the other people in this room want to hear your thoughts, so share them!

THE ART OF PUBLIC SPEAKING

You've likely already heard some of the stats and research findings that share just how much we all hate getting in front of a crowd. In fact, some studies even show that many people fear public speaking more than they fear death. That might seem a bit ridiculous, but if you've ever experienced butterflies in your stomach, dry mouth, or a lump in your throat before addressing an audience—be it an auditorium full of people or just a few co-workers—you can probably understand where these feelings are coming from. And the less accustomed we are to doing it, the more public speaking can be terrifying. Kathryn now speaks regularly on stages large and small, but earlier in her career, her hands used to shake uncontrollably before every speaking engagement.

Fortunately, there are a few things you can do to make the entire process a little easier on yourself—and we aren't talking about picturing the entire audience in their underwear (honestly, that's never worked for us). In fact, being an effective public speaker starts well before you ever step foot behind that podium. That's right, it all comes back to one of our favorite concepts: preparation.

PREPARING TO SPEAK

The single most important element to giving an effective presentation is self-assurance. Knowing you have a plan of attack will make it that much easier to tame those butterflies and stand up and address the room confidently.

Preparation all starts with your topic. You first need to be clear on why people should care about what you're saying. Why is this relevant? What impact will it have on their work? If you're drawing a blank on those answers, it really doesn't matter how phenomenal your presentation is.

Treat your speech exactly like you'd treat a term paper: sketch out an outline (with an attention-grabbing introduction, body, and conclusion), add supporting arguments (or dive into research), and start filling in the blanks with examples or specifics. Taking the time to lay this foundation will ensure that your talk hits on all of the major points, while also maintaining an easy-to-follow flow. Plus, having a solid framework for your speech makes it that much easier to move things around, cross things out, and pull in additional information.

Additionally, remember that simpler is always better. No, this doesn't mean you need to talk to your audience as if they are children. But simple, straightforward language will always have more of an impact (think: "I'm excited to share my experience with building communities on social media," not "Today I will brief your organization on augmenting social engagement among target demographics"). It will also help you improve your own mastery of the topic, because you need to understand something incredibly well in order to explain it in simple terms.

Finally, you'll want to rehearse your speech until you feel comfortable with it. Seriously, practice on someone and ask for constructive comments—we know your dad or best friend would love a chance to be brutally honest with you! Running through it with someone is bound to boost your confidence; plus the feedback of someone you trust can truly help you.

Of course, this doesn't mean that you need to have the whole thing committed to memory—that could make you look rigid and robotic. However, you should feel like you have a solid handle on the overall structure and your key points, without looking at your outline or notecards. We recommend writing down bullet points instead of what you would say word for word; it'll make for a much more natural, confident speech. And you'll feel much more at ease if you aren't white-knuckling those notecards. Remember, they're there to guide you—not hide you.

SPEAKING WITH CONFIDENCE

Adequate preparation is crucial, but it's still no guarantee that you'll be able to stand in front of a crowd feeling completely self-assured. Nerves have an obnoxious way of creeping in, regardless of how much you prepare beforehand. Still, that doesn't mean you need to let anxiety derail your entire speech. Instead there are a few things you can do to portray confidence—even if you're secretly terrified.

1. IT'S ALL ABOUT BODY LANGUAGE

We've touched on nonverbal cues a few times already. But when you're aiming to put on a brave face in front of a crowd, your body language becomes that much more important. Remember that power pose we talked about in Chapter 7 for interviewing? That tip works wonders for public speaking as well. Strike that pose and you'll instantly feel like you can take on anything. It seems ridiculous, but it actually causes hormonal changes in your body that boost your feelings of confidence and power. Awesome, right?

Another body language tip? Eye contact. Of course, you can't lock eyes with absolutely everybody in the room—particularly if you're speaking to a large group of people. And it can be a bit distracting and unsettling to the audience (not to mention come off a bit creepy) if you stare at a single person the entire time you are speaking. Instead, pick a few people in the audience you can make eye contact with throughout your speech. Being able to look into someone's eyes immediately sends a message of confidence and will make you that much more engaging.

2. SPEAK SLOWLY

When you're nervous, your pulse quickens and you can practically hear your heartbeat echoing around in your head. But that's not the only thing that hits the fast track when the pressure is on—many of us have the tendency to speed up our speaking pattern as well. So to ensure that your message doesn't get lost in your rapid-fire delivery, you need to make a conscious effort to slow down—*way* down.

During those times when you're rehearsing your speech, do so slowly. Get in the habit of talking much slower than you normally would, enunciating each syllable, and pausing between phrases. If you feel like you sound a little silly because you're going too slow, you're probably going at just the right speed. (You can even test your speed using an online calculator like the Speed of Speech.) Plus, that way, if your speed does kick into overdrive on the big day, you'll at least be talking at a normal rate.

YOU'VE GOT MAIL

All right, let's shift gears a bit. While public speaking may or may not be part of your everyday work life, there's another form of communication that most definitely is: email. Despite the central role it plays in our everyday communication, not everyone knows how to craft an effective email. If you've ever received a halfhearted, poorly thought-out email lacking in any kind of useful information—or, on the other end of the spectrum, a long-winded, convoluted one that takes paragraphs to get to the central issue or question—you know where we're coming from.

We're sure you don't need us to tell you that email has become one of, if not *the* primary tool of communication in the modern workplace. So if you want to be an all-around master communicator, crafting a great email definitely needs to be within your skill set.

THE BASICS

Let's start at step one. We live in a world where immediacy seems to trump all else. So it's understandable that we often feel tempted to fire off responses seconds after each message hits our inbox. However, in order to craft an email that serves a purpose, you're going to need to slow down. For certain purposes, shooting off a quick message is understandable (and even encouraged!)—for example, when your boss asks for a quick confirmation of a meeting start time or when someone asks for your help ASAP and you want to let them know you're not at your desk and will get back to them as soon as you can.

But, if you're really trying to get a point across or provide a detailed answer or explanation to specific questions, make sure you're taking your time. Getting that message off fast won't do you any favors if it's all wrong or impossible to understand.

To craft an email that is as clear and easy to follow as possible, you want to ensure it has some structure to it. Yes, that means a beginning, a middle, and an end. You'll always want to start with a greeting (we know it seems formal and old-school, but we believe it's important!) and a heads-up about what exactly you're reaching out about. Then get directly to any requests or action items—that is, *what do you want the recipient to do?*—or directly answer any questions that you have been asked. If your email needs details, data, or other context, add it to this middle section, and tie everything together with a conclusion briefly summing up the purpose of the communication (don't be afraid to reiterate the request or action items) and including any relevant deadlines by which you need those requests met or questions answered.

Think of emails like any other piece of writing: something that can (and should) be edited. Reread what you've written, check for typos, and cut down unnecessary detail. By taking thirty seconds to trim the fat and make sure your message comes across clearly, you're saving the person on the other end the time and headache of trying to decipher a jumbled message—and you're increasing the likelihood they'll reply in a timely and useful manner.

There's one other basic email element we need to touch on: the subject line. Writing a subject line might seem like the simplest thing in the world, but you'd be surprised by how many people do it poorly and derail their communications in the process. In an effort to keep things short and sweet, you may find colleagues sending emails with subjects like "Hi," or "thanks," or "tomorrow." The first problem is that these don't give the recipient any clue as to what the email is about— "tomorrow" could just as easily contain important details on the big project you're working on as it could a suggestion for where to go for lunch. Also, people with this habit tend to use that same subject for *every* single email—making those emails impossible to sort through. By the same token, you may often encounter the polar opposite—the person who uses the subject field to act as the entire first paragraph of the message. These subjects, which usually go something like "Just checking in on that sales report that's due at the end of the week because Dave is asking about it already . . ." are equally unhelpful, and miss the entire point of a subject line, which is to *briefly* preview the topic of the email.

Your subject line should be somewhat short, but also clearly communicate the main point of your message. So, sticking with the above example, something like "Sales Report Due Friday" would fit the bill.

Oh, and no need to put your name in the subject line (since it'll show up anyway!). The one exception to the no-name rule, though, is when you are introducing two people over email. Here you'll want to make sure the subject line specifically (but briefly) explains who exactly the two people are. "Intro" is not descriptive enough. "Intro: Alex (The Muse) // Jennifer (XYZ Co)" is better.

22 UNWRITTEN (NEW) RULES OF EMAIL

What are some other things you should be aware of when sending email? We've got your need-to-know tips right here.

1. Keep every email as concise as you can, while still containing the necessary information; it saves you time and, more important, respects the recipient's time.
2. The faster you respond, the shorter your response is allowed to be.
3. Always include one line of context if the recipient isn't expecting this email. This is as relevant for first-time emails ("We met at X conference last month") as it is for emails to someone you work with regularly ("This email is about the next phase of that project we're working on together").
4. Put your "ask" or "action items" first in the email, not last, and make them explicit. It should be immediately clear to the recipient what you want.
5. If there is a deadline, say so. If the request is not urgent, say so.
6. If you don't need a response and an email is FYI only, say so.
7. Make any questions as specific as possible. "What do you think about the proposal?" is not a good question. "Can we go ahead with the vendor's proposal of $20,000 by Friday?" is better.
8. Use bullets or numbered lists when possible. These are easier to skim than blocks of text.
9. When something is really important, bold it.
10. Do not *overuse* bold in your emails.

11. Use legible fonts. Comic Sans is not a legible font.

12. If you receive an ask from someone else but can't respond right away, reply (briefly!) letting him or her know when you'll get to it. But there is no need for a long-winded explanation about all the things on your plate that are preventing you from getting to his request. "Back to you on this Friday" is sufficient. This will save you from having to respond to check-in emails and help the other person plan.

13. Always cc the minimum number of people necessary to get the job done. The more people on the email chain, the lower the feeling of responsibility and the less likely you'll get the reply you need in a timely fashion. If you do include a number of people, make sure to direct questions to a specific person to mitigate this (e.g., "Sally, can you send the latest projects for Q4?").

14. Use "reply all" only when truly needed. Don't be that person who clogs the whole department's inbox.

15. If someone is on an email thread he or she no longer needs to be on, move that person to bcc in your next reply, and say so in the first line of the email. ("Sam, thanks for the introduction to Mary— I'll move you to bcc and take it from here.")

16. Always do double opt-in intros, that is, asking both sides before connecting them to ensure they are interested in the connection, comfortable with their contact information being shared, and that this is a good time for the introduction. If you don't, people eventually will start to dread hearing from you.

17. Don't hijack a thread on one topic to discuss another topic. Start a new email thread instead, with the relevant subject line and recipients.

18. Don't pile on. No one needs a twentieth "This looked great to me, too!" email.

19. Include your contact information and title in the footer. But (unless you use these mediums regularly) skip the mailing address and fax number.

20. If you are emailing a very busy person, it is acceptable and some-what expected to follow up. If you haven't heard back from the person in a week or two, forward the initial email back to him or her with a short follow-up message. Most busy people require at least one of these reminders. Don't send more than three.

21. It is not acceptable to follow up on an email within forty-eight hours unless it is truly urgent. Many people treat email as a form of correspondence and may simply have higher priorities than answering you right away.

22. If you receive a rude or angry email and feel tempted to reply in kind, wait before hitting reply. If it's urgent, get on the phone instead.

GETTING A RESPONSE

We've all been in a situation where we've put all sorts of thought and care into writing an email—only to never hear anything in return. That's frustrating, isn't it? Unfortunately, while you can (and should!) control the work that goes into crafting your message, there's no silver bullet to ensure that those people on the receiving end will actually read or respond to your thoughtful message. However, there are a few things you can do to increase the likelihood of your emails getting read, and not only getting a response—but getting the response you're looking for.

1. TIME IT RIGHT

A few of the basics we've already touched on (such as a compelling subject line) will help greatly with this. But timing is another important thing you need to consider when firing off messages. The best timing will vary depending on whom exactly you're emailing. For example, afternoon tends to be better for most people—most of us are already swamped digging out of our inbox in the early-morning hours. But for those in leadership roles, early morning or late in the day will be better timing-wise, as their days tend to quickly fill up with meetings and other commitments. If you're unsure of the best time, do an experiment and keep track of the results. That should help you figure out which times that person tends to be most responsive and avoid those that frequently result in radio silence.

2. KEEP IT SHORT

The length of your email can also greatly affect your response rate. We're all busy, and there's a seemingly endless barrage of messages rocketing into our inboxes. So, if someone clicks open your email and is greeted with a giant wall of text? Chances are, they're going to close out of that message as soon as possible.

To counter that, try to keep all of the most important information toward the top (after all, that's what's read first!) and use bulleted lists wherever you can. Those are much easier for recipients to skim through than long paragraphs.

3. BE CLEAR ABOUT WHAT YOU WANT

When you don't receive a response to your email, it's tempting to blame it on the inconsiderate, no-good, lazy recipient of your message. However, did you ever stop to think about whether or not you made it clear that you expected a response? Did your email read like a statement or fact sheet that didn't need continued discussion? When emailing, you need to be explicit about what exactly is expected from the recipient. Ending your message with a question—even as simple as "What are your thoughts on _____?" (e.g., the new budget; the launch timing)—makes it clear that you're waiting on a response. Avoid the all-too-common open-ended question like "thoughts?," which isn't specific enough and can be challenging for your recipient to reply to.

DOES YOUR OFFICE USE CHAT?

The increasingly popular internal messaging tools like Slack, HipChat, and Google Chat claim to increase collaboration and reduce email within offices. While this can be true, they can also be a hyperdistracting, inappropriate mode of communication when used improperly. Most of these issues are due to the fact that a new set of social norms has not yet been determined and internalized to get the most out of these awesome new tools. So what's the office chat etiquette you should be living by? Here are a few tips:

1. Chatting a question is easy—in fact, too easy. So before doing so, make sure you're not just being lazy and avoiding finding the answer for yourself. Next time you want to ask your colleague a "super quick question," ask yourself these two questions: Can I Google this? Can I find this in our internal drive or documents?

2. If someone's offline or using a "Do not disturb" status, consider it like a closed office door. Only message your colleagues if it's the sort of issue that you'd barge into their office for, because that's effectively what you're doing. With that said, when you don't want to be disturbed, make that clear as often as possible by signing off or enabling DND.

3. Don't need a response today? Then you should always send an email instead of a chat. A chat means "I need this now."

4. Even if you need the response today, if the answer would take more than five minutes for your colleague to figure out, you should still opt for email. This is giving that colleague the courtesy of deciding when to interrupt his or her work to deal with your issue.

5. Know that when you say "Got a minute?" (or any variation thereof), you're really saying, "I'm going to take up your time right now." Because the answer you'll almost always get is usually "Yes, what's up?" and the reality is that the person was likely

in the middle of something else. Instead, try "When you have a minute, I'd love to bounce something off you. No rush!" Or even better, "When you have a minute, I'd love to bounce something off you regarding [the thing you want to talk to them about] . . ." so they can decide how to prioritize it.

6. Assume good intentions. Similar to email and texts, tone can be hard to gauge via chat. So always give people the benefit of the doubt. Think they're being snippy or sarcastic? Reread the message to yourself with a pleasant tone and a smile as a gut check. On the other hand, if you're worried your message might be misinterpreted, consider adding a GIF or an emoji to make your intentions clear.

7. Just as reply all to the whole company is *the worst,* sending a chat that's only relevant to a handful of people to fifty co-workers is obnoxious. So, when you're debating whom to loop in, loop small at first.

8. If it's an announcement you want your team to be able to refer back to, use email. The exception here is if your company uses pinned chats regularly and everyone knows how to use that feature and where to look for key info.

9. Use tools and plug-ins to make chat smarter. Asking "Is everyone free for a team lunch on Thursday?" opens up a floodgate of replies and back-and-forths. A simple polling plug-in like Simple Poll takes care of this well and reduces all that noise to a single message.

10. Learn how to read between the lines in a conversation. Because chatting so casually does make it easy to get off topic, it happens a lot. (And it's okay! Breaks are good!) But if you notice you're dominating the conversation or supplying 75 percent of the GIF reactions, it probably means it's not the best time for the other person.

11. Don't ever assume someone saw your *important* message in a group chat. If it's something you 100 percent want someone (or everyone) to see, send an email instead.

12. If you chat a group and then it turns into a one-on-one conversation that the whole channel doesn't need to be privy to (or shouldn't have to be), relocate the discussion with a quick "Jose, I'll DM you the details." Even if it's not confidential, it's oftentimes best to have those talks away from the group.

13. Unless the office is currently on fire, try to take a minute to say "Hi, how are you?" to someone before launching into a chat storm. It'll start you off on a friendly note and make the conversation go a lot more smoothly.

14. If a conversation doesn't directly require your input, don't feel pressured to chime in if you're busy. And, on the same note, if you are busy, don't distract yourself by following every single conversation.

15. Finally, this last one isn't really a rule, just a reminder. Even if your boss doesn't participate in random, silly group chats, he or she could still be watching. And if you're struggling to get assignments completed on time, he or she won't be thrilled to see how active you are. So, have fun, be appreciative you work for a company that recognizes a good GIF, but also get your work done.

HOW TO CONDUCT AN EFFECTIVE CALL

With the development of so many other, faster methods of communication—email, interoffice chat, and even text messages—many of us are often hesitant to hop on the phone. And perhaps for that reason, even when we do make the dreaded phone call, we sometimes lack the skills or practice to effectively communicate our message.

But no matter how technologically advanced your workplace is, the occasional need for the good old-fashioned phone call is inevitable. There are some things that are just much more successfully and efficiently resolved when you can actually talk them out—as opposed to constantly emailing (or chatting!) back and forth. So, dread them or not, phone calls are something you're going to want to master. We'll dig into how to choose which communication is best for each intended conversation a little later. But for now, let's touch on some basic etiquette of phone conversations. Because, let's face it, we're all a little out of practice.

PHONE ETIQUETTE

Have you ever had to suffer through a phone call with someone who rambled on and on with little to no point? What about someone who called you from the car and kept getting cut off, or called from a loud and crowded place and seemed to be yelling into the speaker? Or— perhaps the worst—have you been in a meeting when someone rudely answered his or her phone smack in the middle of your conversation?

Yes, there are so many dos and don'ts involved in phone etiquette, we could likely write an entire chapter on that topic alone. But for now, let's just touch on the basics that everybody—and we mean *everybody*— should be sure to abide by at all times.

1. USE YOUR NAME WHEN YOU ANSWER THE PHONE

Let's say you dial someone you've never actually spoken with directly and are greeted with a short, swift "Hello?" and that's it. You're *pretty* sure you dialed the number correctly. But, since that person didn't use his or her name when answering, you can't be positive that you're actually connected with the person you want to speak to. So you have no choice to respond with a hesitant "Hi there, is this [name]?"

This short little anecdote alone should illustrate the importance of identifying yourself when you answer the phone. A short line like "Hello, this is Alex" is all it takes to immediately let the caller know that he or she has reached the right person (or not), and get the conversation started on the right foot.

2. FIND A QUIET PLACE

In today's work environments, with open-plan offices becoming increasingly common, there's no denying that phone calls can be a little distracting—for you and the people around you. Not only can it be challenging for you to focus on the person on the other end with all the hustle and bustle going on around you, but it's easy for your co-workers

to get wrapped up in your conversation, no matter how hard they're trying to avoid eavesdropping and stay focused on their own work. Moreover, the person on the phone might have difficulty hearing you over
the constant background drone of your office environment.

So, if you know when a phone call is coming (or even immediately after you've answered), find a quiet place to have the conversation.
You'll save everyone frustration, and ultimately have a more productive
discussion.

3. GIVE A HEADS-UP ABOUT SPEAKERPHONE

This might seem like a very minor detail. But failing to do it can easily put off or annoy the person you're on the phone with. Whenever
you put someone you're talking to on speakerphone with others in the
room, be sure to provide a heads-up that he or she is now addressing
multiple people—and not just you. As we've mentioned, a big part of
communicating is knowing your audience. Your conversational partner
deserves to know whom exactly she's speaking with.

4. BE PREPARED

One good thing about phone calls is that we often know when they'll be
coming in and can schedule them to happen at our convenience, rather
than having them come out of the blue. This advanced warning gives
you the opportunity to take a few minutes to prepare. Jot down the goal
of the conversation as well as any questions you want to make sure to
have answered. That way, you'll be able to get exactly what you require
out of the discussion—as quickly as possible.

5. KEEP IT SHORT

There are some phone calls that lend themselves to or require a longer
format—like a conference call (more on those in a bit!). However, you
don't want to be stuck on the phone for an hour discussing something
that could have been resolved in minutes. More often than not, you
want to keep your phone conversations as brief and concise as possible.

In those cases, challenge yourself to follow the nineteen-minute rule. Set a goal to get off the phone in nineteen minutes or less and you'll likely find yourself cutting out a lot of the irrelevant small talk and tangential paths and get more done in less time.

CONFERENCE CALLS

It's not too often you'll run into someone who raves about how much they adore these. If we're being perfectly honest, most of us dread them. Why? Well, meetings in and of themselves are stressful enough, but when you're also dealing with everything from technical difficulties and background noise to the lack of nonverbal cues and people constantly talking over each other, they can be that much more painful. But you will likely experience many throughout your career, so it's best to learn how to cope with them. A few of our favorite tips:

1. SET AN AGENDA

Remember when we talked about hosting effective meetings and the importance of having a solid structure in place? Well, a conference call is still a meeting—just over the phone. So, plan to have some sort of road map in place to guide the entire conversation and keep everyone on track. Share this (and any presentations) over email with the other conference call attendees in advance and you'll avoid many of those uncomfortable pauses that frequently crop up.

2. APPOINT A LEADER

People talking over each other is an issue you're going to run into frequently on the phone. However, assigning someone to lead the entire conversation will help things run much more smoothly. That point person can call on specific people to provide feedback, or even request that everyone saves questions until the end, allowing for a much more fluid and beneficial discussion.

3. TEST YOUR SYSTEM

Technical difficulties are one of the things that cause the most frustration when it comes to conference calls. And while there are some that will simply be out of your control, taking some time to test the system beforehand and work out any potential glitches will save tons of confusion when it's actually time for people to join the call.

4. ENCOURAGE USE OF THE MUTE BUTTON

When you have numerous people on the phone at one time, background noise can quickly escalate from a dull hum to a loud roar. At the beginning of the call, the leader should encourage all participants to have their phones on mute unless they're speaking. You'll be pleasantly surprised by how many distractions that one little button can eliminate! Now, if only there were a Mute button for in-person meetings . . .

COMMUNICATION 101: CHOOSING THE RIGHT METHOD TO CONVEY YOUR MESSAGE

When it comes to choosing what tools and methods you should use to communicate, you have tons of different options right at your fingertips. This can definitely make for increased convenience. But, at the same time, it can introduce a certain element of confusion. How can you know which communication method is best for your exact conversation? Should this be resolved via email? Or are you better off walking down the hall to talk to someone in person, or picking up the phone to sort it out? Here's a rundown on which situations lend themselves best to each method.

IN PERSON

- Brainstorming sessions
- Delicate or personal matters
- Performance issues
- Confidential conversations
- Relationship building

EMAIL

- Quick questions or FYIs
- When an attachment is necessary
- When time for consideration is required
- When you want documentation of the conversation

PHONE

- Urgent matters
- Requests for candid feedback
- When a quick response is needed
- When you need to give an extended explanation or elaboration

Whether you're the office social butterfly or someone who'd rather just keep your head down and focus on your work, there's really no way around it: you *need* strong communication skills to succeed in the modern workplace. Of course, there's no rule saying that you need to adore everybody you work with. But in the new world of work, where teamwork and collaboration are more important than ever, you have to know how to build positive professional relationships in order to be your most productive and effective self.

We don't deny that this can get complicated. The workplace can easily breed a sense of competitiveness. And when you stick a bunch of people with different personalities and communication styles between the four walls of one office, things aren't always going to be seamless. So in the next chapter we'll talk about how to avoid or minimize all these potential pitfalls and build the kind of interpersonal skills that will help you thrive and advance in your chosen career—including building relationships with your colleagues, navigating the boss/subordinate relationship, and resolving the inevitable conflicts that arise in even the most amicable office environments.

CHAPTER **ELEVEN**

The New Rules of Interpersonal Skills

THE OLD RULE: Interpersonal skills were considered personality traits—something you either had or you didn't. As a young or new employee, you weren't necessarily expected to know how to interact with managers and bosses, take the initiative to schedule one-on-one meetings to ask for feedback, speak up for yourself, or develop relationships across the company. However, it was considered possible that in time, you could eventually learn these "people skills" on the job.

THE NEW RULE: Today, if you want to succeed as a professional, you can't sit back passively and expect strong people skills to emerge over time. Instead, you must take responsibility for refining your interpersonal skills, which includes both building strong relationships with your colleagues and learning how to manage up (that is, proactively communicate with your boss to go above and beyond) early in and throughout your career. You can't depend upon your superiors to show you the way, take you by the hand, or challenge you to grow into a leadership role or mindset. It's up to you.

In today's workplace, you often have to juggle professional relationships with multiple groups of people: your colleagues and teammates, your manager, senior executives, clients, vendors, and, depending on the stage of your career, interns and direct reports. Making matters more complicated, none of these relationships will look exactly the same; after all, you wouldn't interact with a high-level manager the same way you would an intern. And the more you grow, the more people you'll work with—and the more these people will matter in the success of your career.

It used to be that the only relationships we had to worry about, at the early stages of our careers at least, were our direct bosses and maybe a handful of peers. But in the modern workplace, it's not unusual for young professionals to interact with people at every level within a business. As companies are moving away from strict hierarchical structures and becoming increasingly aware of the unique perspective that younger professionals have to offer, it might be that only a year out of college you'll find yourself in charge of part of a presentation for a senior client or asked to provide input to a C-level exec. Forget the "thirty seconds in the elevator with the CEO" situation (you know, when that was the only chance you'd ever get to interact with your company's leader). Today, no matter what position you hold, you're likely to have far greater opportunities.

But your work relationships are more than the sum of individual communications and interactions. And it's not enough to simply transmit information like we walked through in the last chapter. Instead, you need to forge authentic, meaningful relationships, which will help you gain professional allies and advance in your career. And that's where the skills you'll learn in this chapter come in.

Go back and look at any of the job descriptions you considered during your last job search, and you'll notice that employers tend to value several common qualities: communication, collaboration, and problem solving—just to name a few. The problem is that in today's work culture, these soft skills aren't explicitly taught. However, they *can* be learned.

But just as it takes time to learn hard skills (like coding a website or speaking a foreign language), you can't master soft skills overnight. If you aren't proactively and deliberately developing these skills, it's time to change your approach.

First, let's talk about what we mean by soft skills. Career coach Lei

Han breaks soft skills into two categories: self-management skills and people skills.

Self-management skills are those you use to manage your emotions, perceptions, and reactions—for example, the ability to stay calm in a stressful situation or bounce back after experiencing a setback in your career. People skills are exactly what they sound like—skills that enable you to effectively interact with other people, like being able to work with a wide range of team members regardless of their personalities or talents, building rapport with your superiors, and more.

Developing these soft skills will help you navigate office politics, collaborate with others, become an influencer in your organization, and manage up—an important strategy for developing your career (we'll cover this more in depth later in this chapter). Perhaps most important, these skills can set you apart as a prime candidate for leadership opportunities and help you move up to the next level.

Mastering a new set of skills may seem daunting, but just like so many other aspects of your career we've talked about, a few key strategies and a little practice will go a long way.

MASTER THE ART OF CONVERSATION

Gone are the days when junior-level employees were explicitly expected to be seen and not heard. In today's workplace, everyone from interns to executives has a voice, and learning the art of casual conversation will help you feel comfortable talking to anyone—and more important, help you build relationships that can open the door to opportunities and partnerships down the road.

It doesn't always come as second nature to strike up conversation with someone you don't know well—especially if they are at a more senior level—but a little preparation can take the awkward sting out of those interactions. We know what you're thinking: Won't planning my conversation ahead of time make me come across as scripted and forced? Actually, done right it can help your authentic, natural self shine through (which is the whole point).

CONVERSATION STARTERS 101

Stacey Lastoe, senior writer/editor at The Muse, developed an invaluable template of conversation starters for some of the most common workplace chatting situations. Here are a few to help you get those conversations off the ground.

1. WITH THE FOUNDER OR CEO

> You: "Hi! How's your week going?"
>
> CEO: "Not bad. Busy! How about yours?"
>
> You: "It's going well. I'm excited to be working on [whatever project feels most significant to you]."

A simple greeting and open-ended question gives your company's leader the chance to talk a lot (be sure to listen to what she says) or a little (be sure to have an answer to her query back to you). If you're not sure whether she knows you by name, introduce yourself: "I'm [your name]. It's a pleasure to meet you."

2. WITH THE NEWBIE

> You: "Hi. You started [this week, last Friday, "recently" if you're not exactly sure], right? My name is [your name] and I'm a part of the [X] team. Are you starting to feel settled? Have you been to [popular coffee shop in the area] yet?"

Your job here is to be welcoming and help to put your new co-worker at ease. Remember when you were brand-new? It's never easy. Extending yourself beyond a simple "hello" can make a real difference in your new colleague's day—and distinguish you in the process.

3. WITH THE (INTIMIDATING) COLLEAGUE WHO'S BEEN THERE FOREVER

> You: "Hey, I'm looking for recommendations for places to go for a lunch meeting this week. I haven't gotten to know the neighborhood well, but I thought, as someone who seems

*to know the ins and outs around here, you might have some
suggestions."*

Approaching the intimidating company veteran may not be the easiest conversation to have, but it can be an important one. You're doing two things at once here: tackling your own feelings of intimidation, while also giving this slightly scary co-worker a chance to show his friendly, helpful side. Giving him the chance to play advisor is a great way to break the ice.

4. WITH ANY VIP

*You: "Hi. My name is [your name]. I know you've probably
got to make the rounds, but I didn't want to regret not
coming over and introducing myself—and letting you know
that your app is genius."*

This is another conversation you could conceivably skip, but why would you? If you've got something genuinely complimentary to share about a VIP's work, or product, or idea, roll it out. You might only get a simple "thanks," and that's okay. But you might also engage this important person in a more substantial conversation. That's a chance for you to learn and to make an impression at the same time.

5. WITH YOUR FORMER BOSS

*You: "It's so good to see you! How is everything over at
[company name]? I read that they're expanding [department
or product]. You must be excited to be spearheading that."*

Maybe you parted on friendly terms, or maybe not so much. It doesn't matter. In this circumstance, professionalism and good manners rule the day. If nothing else, this is a chance to get some experience in conversing with people you're not thrilled to talk with. Trust us, that happens more than once in a career. Be pleasant and kind, and make eye contact. Extending yourself in this way may even smooth ruffled feathers and past hurt feelings, if there are any.

6. WITH THE PERSON FROM THE DEPARTMENT YOU KNOW NOTHING ABOUT

You: "How's your week going? Busy with projects?"

Person: "Busier than usual because we've got [major initiative the team is focused on]."

You: "Oh, interesting. I hadn't thought how that might affect your team. What are you working on specifically?"

This is part friendly chat, and part reconnaissance for future encounters. Rather than trying to front like you know more than you do about a person and their work, give them a chance to talk about what they're doing. The next time you share the elevator at the end of the day, you'll have more information to work with and inquire about.

7. WITH THE BOSS'S SIGNIFICANT OTHER

You: "It's so nice that you were able to make it tonight. It's always fun to meet the people we hear so much about. Susan has mentioned that you both like to cook together. Do you have a favorite dish?"

Remember that relationship building doesn't happen just within the confines of the office but at after-work social events as well. In fact, social gatherings with your colleagues—whether it's the annual office Christmas party, a birthday lunch, or a celebratory happy hour—are a great opportunity to build rapport with your superiors in a setting where they are more likely to be relaxed and approachable. And often, this will mean making small talk not just with them, but with their spouses or partners. The trick in this situation is to strike a balance. Too much familiarity is not appropriate—you're not friends or family, after all. But you don't want to risk offending by avoiding your manager's SO altogether, or miss a great opportunity to say hello. Take a deep breath to quell your nerves, and start with something that you know of the SO's interests. Keep it light and uncontroversial, some subject that your manager has shared with you and others (in other words, the personal tidbit that you accidentally overheard isn't the right place to start).

8. WITH ANYONE

You: "How was your weekend? Are you watching or reading anything really great at the moment?"

Talking television, films, and books is an almost surefire way to get conversation rolling, with anybody. Chatting about these cultural touchstones is fun, easy, and offers plenty of opportunities to connect. You don't have to like the same stuff to have an engaging conversation about these topics. The discovery—and the debate—can be part of the fun, as long as you stay good-natured. This conversation starter gives you much more interesting terrain to work with than the boilerplate "How's your week going?"

———

But while these scripts can help you launch a good conversation that will put everyone involved at ease, mastering the art of conversation isn't just about getting good at small talk. Real conversations are about more than (just) communicating; they're about building relationships. And often, that's done through the details. Just think: When you brought up the end of the fiscal year to the sales rep down the hall, did he tense up, cross his arms, and angle his body away from yours? Probably a topic to avoid. As you interact with others more frequently, you'll learn how to read body language (and adjust your own), so you can encourage productive conversations that deepen your relationships.

With practice, you'll also learn how to *listen*. In your first few conversations, you might be a little nervous, causing you to spend the majority of the conversation thinking about what question you're going to ask next, rather than listening to the other person's responses. But with time and practice, you'll master active listening—making a conscious effort to understand the message the other person is conveying. This will help you ask intelligent, relevant follow-up questions and let the person know you truly care about getting to know him or her. And that—much more than small talk about the weekend—will help you take a major step toward an authentic relationship.

BE A GOOD COLLABORATOR

Any effective organization relies on its employees to collaborate.

Working as a team cuts the time it takes to develop an idea, build a project, or move a product from concept to completion. It fosters innovation and varied ideas by bringing different perspectives together and, when done correctly, makes everyone on the team feel engaged and valuable—which boosts morale.

How can you become a good collaborator? First, don't be tempted to fall into the trap of looking at your co-workers as competition. These are your people, your team—and ideally, your allies. Treat them as such. For example, when you're working with a team on a project, balance speaking and listening. Good collaborators don't hog the conversation, but they don't clam up, either. The balance you strike will likely depend on the dynamics of your team, which can change over time as employees move in and out, projects progress, and relationships grow and change.

You should also strive to be concise in your communications. Everyone you interact with is busy and values their time—so you can't monopolize every interaction. You'll become known as a top-notch collaborator if people recognize that working with you doesn't dominate their time or interfere in the things they need to get done. Not to mention, your ideas stand a much greater chance of being heard (and implemented) if they're focused and concise.

As much as collaboration is important, healthy competition among colleagues isn't always negative, and in fact can sometimes fuel great work. Intense competition or rivalry, on the other hand, can be isolating and divisive. For example, do you feel jealous of others' success? Is it hard for you to overhear your co-workers being praised? These competitive feelings may reflect more on your own (lack of) confidence than on your true feelings about others' accomplishments.

It's easy to fall into the trap of thinking that another person's success is your failure—that because your co-worker was selected for a promotion over you, for example, you must not be cut out for a management role. This kind of binary thinking creates tension where it shouldn't exist. Team members who shine aren't casting a shadow over you; if anything, they're providing an example you can learn from. Focus on your own self-confidence and you'll likely see any unhealthy competition with your co-workers decline.

MIND YOUR COMPETITIVENESS

Paying obsessive attention to another person's accomplishments is a distraction that gets in the way of your own good work and impedes truly effective collaboration. So when you're feeling overly competitive or jealous, try a few of these mindfulness techniques to refocus your thoughts on the present—so you're no longer stuck being resentful and unproductive and can spend your time being the best version of *you*, instead.

- Mindful breathing: Breathe in and out slowly, focusing on letting go of any worries or resentment.
- Mindful listening: Put on your headphones and play a favorite song. For those few minutes, put everything else out of your mind. Soon you'll feel less stressed and be in a better mood.
- Mindful immersion: What's next on *your* to-do list? Rather than obsessing about what other people are doing, try immersing yourself fully in your next task, and focus on doing it to the very best of your ability.

LEARN TO IDENTIFY INFLUENCERS
AND CONNECTORS—AND EVENTUALLY
BECOME ONE OF THEM

If there are two must-know types of people in your company, it's influencers and connectors.

What makes someone an influencer? These are the people in your organization who get things done, effect change, and, as their name implies, have influence on others. You can often spot influencers in brainstorming meetings: They are the ones who voice their ideas with a high degree of confidence, but without being overly aggressive. They always listen to others, but aren't afraid to speak up and share why their strategies will produce the best results.

Connectors are people who bring together different networks and social groups. These are the people who seem to know everyone and are constantly looking for ways to connect those people for the benefit of those individuals, and of the company. How to spot a connector? Let's say you're preparing a presentation for a client, but you need some statistics about the company's growth over the last few years. Immediately, a connector might pipe up and say, "Oh, Kevin in the finance department can get you exactly what you need. I can introduce you to him after this meeting." No matter the situation, the connector knows someone who can help—and is happy to get the two of you in touch.

Both types of people are necessary to an effective team or organization—and both can be incredibly valuable to your career. Identify the influential and connected people in your organization or team, and position yourself both to get to know them, and to learn from them. Think about not only what they do, but also *how* they do their jobs. You might notice, for instance, that influencers consistently speak up but rarely openly argue with others. They believe in their ideas, but they aren't too stubborn or hardheaded to consider the opinions of others. Connectors, as you might expect, are typically social. You won't see them eating lunch with the same group of people every day, because they know and want to interact with people in nearly every department.

But critically, they're not known as schmoozers—they're genuinely well liked and respected.

Pro tip: Influencers and connectors exist at every level of your organization, not only the top. By the same token, a senior title or high pay grade doesn't make someone an influencer or connector by default. Don't miss out on the opportunity to learn from people just because they don't have a job title that sounds important.

Clearly, connectors and influencers are doing something that works. They've figured out how to expertly build relationships with people that matter, make their ideas heard, and gain respect from the people they work with. Ultimately, interacting with these people will help you navigate your company culture and build the same beneficial relationships yourself.

DEVELOP MENTORS—AND *BE* A MENTOR

Mentorship is a big buzzword these days, but what does it mean, exactly? A mentor is someone you trust, someone you can go to for advice and for objective feedback. In many cases, mentors are able to take a step back and see the bigger picture of you in your career, giving you insight into how others perceive you and how you can better yourself.

When Alex was in her first year at McKinsey, for example, she worked with a manager whose communication style she felt she wanted to—and could—emulate. Some of her previous managers had been very effective, but their leadership styles were sometimes too aggressive, too passive, too blunt, or too subtle. Alex wanted to develop a balanced style that was somewhere in the middle, and she found an incredible example in this woman. In consulting, you change managers frequently, but Alex sought out opportunities to work with her again, and to learn from her style. Over time, this manager became a mentor for Alex, giving her feedback, creating opportunities for her, and advocating for her advancement over the following years. It was during their time working together that Alex really started to hone her communication and management style.

A manager can seem like the obvious choice for a mentor, but really, there's no specific formula you have to follow. Someone you currently work with can help you navigate company-specific situations, for instance, but someone outside of your industry can offer an external perspective that you may not have otherwise considered. And don't think that a mentor needs to be someone highly experienced or senior. It's true that a mentor who's older than you can provide wisdom and advice on how to move up in your career, but a peer mentor can understand and appreciate where you are in your career *now*. Fortunately, you can have more than one mentor!

In certain cases—for example, roles or industries where things change very quickly—a peer or close-to-peer mentor can actually be ideal, because they've *lived* (very recently!) exactly what you're going through. In Kathryn's case, as The Muse was getting off the ground and she was beginning to reach out to investors, peer mentorship from other early-stage start-up founders was critical. Another friend of ours found that the best mentorship she received at her role (in consulting) was from another consultant just three years her senior.

As in Alex's case, most mentor-mentee relationships develop organically. Maybe you ask a senior employee about how to handle a specific situation, and that turns into a monthly coffee meeting to chat about any issues you're currently facing. He or she might begin to show interest in your professional development and start forwarding you opportunities that he or she thinks would be great ways to advance your career. Or perhaps you meet someone at a networking event, follow up with a quick question they answer willingly, and then establish a cadence of reaching out to them regularly with updates. There's no need to formally ask, "Will you be my mentor?" Kind of like with dating, when a mentor-mentee relationship is working, it'll be clear to both of you.

But like any type of relationship, mentoring goes both ways. Just as you have mentors in your life and career, you should also think about how to be a mentor to someone else. This isn't just about paying it forward. Guiding a mentee can actually benefit your own professional development, because it helps you reflect on where you are in your career and think critically about your most challenging and successful experiences—which can shine a light on where you should go next. Mentoring can also help build self-confidence. Sharing your knowledge and expertise with another person illuminates how much you know (which might surprise you!), and seeing someone use your guidance to succeed is a major confidence booster. And if you are worried that you don't have enough experience to be a mentor, think again. Even if you are just at the beginning stages of your career, trust us that you still have valuable wisdom to share, whether it's guiding a college student through the job search process or offering your fresh perspective to a seasoned leader.

Plus, your willingness to help others is, at the very core, an exercise in empathy: As a mentor, you're constantly thinking about another person's needs and putting yourself in his or her shoes—which is a key trait of successful leaders. Mentoring proves that you're willing to take the time to help others learn and grow. Those are all management qualities, and they won't go unnoticed.

CONFLICT RESOLUTION IN THE WORKPLACE

Even in the best of times, office and team dynamics are tricky to navigate, so it's no surprise that it takes finely tuned interpersonal skills to manage workplace conflicts. From open disagreements between colleagues to rivalries brewing beneath the surface to the new guy who just isn't fitting into the workplace culture, a leader-in-the-making must be prepared to confront these kinds of tensions, because they are a natural part of any workplace.

In general, we're big proponents of being as direct as possible in tough situations. In this section, we offer some specific problem-solving techniques that will help you tackle a range of interpersonal issues— which will not only make your day-to-day work life easier, but also show your employer that you possess the leadership traits necessary to advance to the next level.

OWN YOUR MISTAKES

Mistakes, errors, and slipups—they happen to all of us. They sting, they're embarrassing, and they can cause no small amount of anxiety and self-torment. So when you make a blunder, you might be tempted to hide and hope no one notices. There's a better way, though—one that will strengthen your credibility with your co-workers and superiors.

First, take responsibility immediately. As hard as it may be in the moment after you realize you made a mistake, the best thing you can do is come clean and let people know what's happened—quickly. Trust us, failing to immediately take responsibility will only cause more issues down the road.

Start by identifying the people who might be affected by your mistake, and get in touch with them right away. Be clear about what happened, how and why the error occurred, and what steps you're taking to correct the situation (and to make sure it won't happen again). If the people who might be affected are external, highly senior, or any other form of partner/client where managing the relationship may be key, you should likely go directly to your manager first with your mistake, to talk through your proposed communication.

One word of caution: keep the impact of your mistake in perspective. You haven't single-handedly tanked the company's future prospects. (Really, we promise, you haven't.) In the grand scheme of things, the ramifications of your slipup are probably quite minor—and definitely don't require a crying, groveling apology. So, look at the big picture. Stay calm and composed, and deliver your bad news in a simple, straightforward manner. And whatever you do, don't try to blame other people for your error—even partially. It will only stir up resentment, and earning the reputation of a finger-pointer will be far more damaging to your career than your original mistake.

OWN UP TO IT

Just as important as admitting to a mistake is appropriately *wording* that admission. So here are a few dos and don'ts to help you own up to your screwup with professionalism and grace.

Let's say you're organizing an important sales event, but because you didn't sign a contract in time, you lost the venue.

DON'T GO OVERBOARD

> "I absolutely ruined everything! There's no way the event can happen now! I'm so, so sorry. I can't believe I let this happen. You must hate me!"

DON'T DEFLECT THE BLAME

> "It really came down to the legal department. They never got back to me with their approval, so there was no way I could have signed the contract."

DON'T OFFER A NON-APOLOGY

> "It probably wasn't the best venue for the event anyway."

DON'T BE PASSIVE-AGGRESSIVE

> "I didn't know I'd have to follow up with the legal department so many times to get what I needed."

DO STATE THE FACTS OBJECTIVELY AND DESCRIBE WHAT YOU ARE DOING TO REMEDY THE SITUATION.

> "I didn't do the necessary follow-up to get the contract finalized in time. I'm sorry that my mistake lost us the venue. I've already started to look into alternative venues in the area and I have a couple of promising options to show you."

This shows that you're aware—and sorry—that you made a mistake, but just as important, that you're taking a proactive step to correct the problem.

Another tip: Apologies are always best delivered in person or, if necessary, on the phone. It might seem easier to hide behind an apology email than acknowledge a mistake face-to-face with your boss or team members, but that's exactly why it's so important to step up to the plate and have a conversation; it shows courage, character, and that you care so much that you're willing to endure some social discomfort to make things right. Your audience will also get to observe your genuinely apologetic tone and demeanor—things you can't convey through email. By all means, take a little time and make notes to yourself about what you want to cover in the conversation. But deliver the message in person (or as close to in person as you can get).

We know it can be hard to shake loose the guilt of making a mistake. But it's important to move on. Getting caught up in the repercussions of your error doesn't benefit you or your company. Once you've taken responsibility and apologized, it's time to look ahead and get busy working to rectify—and learn from—the mistake.

HANDLE CONFRONTATION LIKE A PRO

Conflicts and disagreements at work are inevitable, so one of the most important things you can do for your career is to learn how to resolve them professionally. Not every conflict requires a confrontation; it's up to you to decide how to best address the issue, and how to best position yourself for a constructive encounter.

When conflicts arise, it's easy to let our emotions get the better of us. But before getting fired up, make sure you have enough information to assess the situation—and keep in mind that the information you have might be limited, incomplete, or skewed, particularly if it's been passed through several people before making its way to you. Whenever possible, seek clarification directly from the source of the issue. In some cases, the issue may simply be a misunderstanding. For example, if you hear through the grapevine that you were moved off of a prize account, you might be upset and assume your boss doesn't trust you; you could storm into your manager's office pointing fingers, or you could say calmly that you heard some accounts were moving around and ask for clarification. Little did you know, there's a big new project coming up that they want you on instead, or some other context that you're not yet aware of. For a real-life example, a friend of Kathryn once became furious when his manager mentioned something offhand that another colleague had said. Kathryn's friend heard it as criticism, but in actuality, it was a taken-out-of-context comment that was part of a larger and highly laudatory piece of praise for his work, and once he heard the full story he was embarrassed to have flown off the handle.

That said, if there truly is an issue, your next step is to determine if a confrontation is necessary. First, it's key to separate personal feelings from professional actions. Remember, you don't have to be best friends with—or even like—everyone you work with, but you *do* have to work effectively with them. So before engaging in any work confrontation, do a thorough self-examination of your motives. Are you upset at Bill from accounting simply because he gets under your skin, or did his email to your client really cross the line in a way that hurts business results? This step is especially critical if the person at the focus of your potential confrontation is someone you dislike.

Next, ask yourself: How important is this issue to me, my team, and the company? How likely am I to have an impact on the issue at hand? Am I willing to contribute to changing the situation? The more important and higher-stakes the issue is, the more necessary it will feel to pursue a discussion, even if it's less likely that you'll be able to change the circumstances in a significant way. For example, maybe your direct reports are coming out of your company-wide training program without key knowledge that they need to perform their roles. A single confrontation may not lead to an overhaul of the established training program—not immediately, at least—but considering the effects on your team, it would still benefit you, your team, and really, the rest of the company to have a conversation with the person in charge of it.

If you determine a confrontation of some sort is necessary, it should go without saying that you need to approach it with respect and professionalism. That means keeping your cool, making smart communication choices, and planning ahead for the discussion, rather than relying on improvisation. And, as when you apologize for a mistake, avoid conducting these conversations over email. Remember that email communication is notoriously easy to misinterpret, which can escalate an issue rather than resolve it. It's also easy to get carried away when crafting an email, letting the anger or frustration of the moment overtake you and causing you to send an over-the-top message that you'll later regret. As intimidating as it may be, confronting a co-worker about an issue that's bothering you is something best done face to face.

Who needs to be present for the conversation? The answer: it depends. Small disagreements between colleagues can usually be worked out between just the individuals who are directly involved, and looping in a manager or higher-up before it's absolutely necessary can make the other person feel like you're tattling. However, if the situation escalates, or if you're broaching a more serious conflict that dramatically affects your work or the work of your team, don't hesitate to involve your manager or someone in HR. They can provide the support and guidance you need to handle the situation appropriately.

BE A STRAIGHT SHOOTER—BUT AVOID BEING PERCEIVED AS AGGRESSIVE

At The Muse, we're big fans of being direct. It's efficient. It reduces misunderstanding. Over the long term, it builds trust. That said, not everyone is used to or comfortable with such straightforward communication, which means it can sometimes get misinterpreted as overly harsh or aggressive. And, at times, when you're trying to be direct, it is possible to be perceived as excessively forceful, rather than polite, respectful, and constructive.

How can you be frank without sounding like a know-it-all or a bully? First, remember that the goal is not to be unkind—it's to clearly convey information for the benefit of all involved. Attempting to be direct does not give you free rein to toss out criticism left and right. If you have feedback to give, stay focused on the issue and how to solve it. For example, if a co-worker flubs a presentation that ends up costing you a client, you might be tempted to say something like "You're never prepared for client presentations. You're always rushing to finish your portion of the PowerPoint minutes before the client arrives, and it's obvious to everyone that you didn't invest enough time in it. You really make us look unprofessional." A more effective (and less critical) way to phrase your confrontation would be "I've noticed that you typically don't complete your portion of client presentations until the last minute. I really want us to come across as professional as possible. Moving forward, can we agree to have the PowerPoint finished three days prior to the client meeting? That will give us time to polish our presentation and make sure we make a great impression."

Oh, and definitely make sure you're paying attention to body language here. Think about how this message would come across if you had a furrowed brow and crossed arms—versus if you were leaning forward with a calm, relaxed demeanor.

START LEADING—BY LEARNING TO DELEGATE

You probably know by now that leadership isn't about job title; leaders can exist anywhere in an organization, regardless of their role or the number of employees they supervise. But in our experience, all effective leaders do have one important skill in common, and it's one you can practice now, wherever you are in your career: delegation.

At The Muse, we've been growing our team at a rapid pace, and as we bring on new employees and mentor our new managers, one of the most common concerns we encounter is how best to delegate tasks.

Through lots of trial (and some error) we've come up with what we consider to be the ten commandments of delegation. Whether you're an expert exec or a novice manager, keep them in mind the next time you hand off an assignment.

1. BE PATIENT

The first time you delegate any task, it is almost certainly going to take longer than doing it yourself. That's normal. So don't throw in the towel right away. Over time, it will get done faster.

2. DON'T SIMPLY DELEGATE THE THINGS YOU HATE

Delegation is not shifting work you should be doing to someone else's plate—it's getting those tasks you shouldn't be doing off yours. It's important to know the difference. If you ask someone else to take on writing the employee newsletter because you need to focus on external, client-facing communication, that's okay. If you ask someone to take it on simply because you don't enjoy doing it, it isn't.

3. PICK THE RIGHT PEOPLE

Make sure the person you're delegating to is qualified to do the task. Better yet, try to match the tasks you delegate with each of your team members' best skills and strengths. Then . . .

4. EXPLAIN WHY YOU'RE DELEGATING

When you select people to delegate a task or project to, tell them why you chose them specifically, and how you hope to see this help them grow. Help them see each delegated task as an opportunity to take on more responsibilities or grow new skills.

5. BE SPECIFIC

Be specific with your asks, including why a task needs to be done, the deadlines, and the expected results. Vague instructions can beget terrible output.

6. PROVIDE TRAINING

Delegation doesn't just mean handing off a task—you need to also make sure your team members have the resources and training they need to do the job. A good rule of thumb when training someone at a task is "I do, we do, you do" (in other words, watch me do this, then let's do it together, now you try).

7. TOUCH BASE

Throughout the course of the project or task, always schedule time to touch base. The more complex the task, the more often you may need to check in.

8. BUT DON'T MICROMANAGE

Once you've delegated, trained, and set up a schedule for touching base, back away from the project. To succeed (and to help your employee succeed), you have to let go. Your employee may approach the task differently from how you would do it, and that's okay.

9. OFFER FEEDBACK

Any time you delegate something, provide feedback on the end result (both positive and constructive). It's an extra step, but making sure you'll get exactly what you need going forward—and helping others get better over time—will only help you in the long run.

10. SAY THANKS

Hey, your employee or colleague is saving you time and providing value. Say thank you!

MANAGING UP

There's a lot of talk in the business world about the importance of "managing up." And we're on board with the buzz—in fact, we think managing up is so important, we're going to spend the rest of this chapter talking about what it means and how to do it effectively.

Managing up is a strategy for interacting with your superiors in a way that positions you as a future leader—someone who's proactively in charge of his or her career. Of course, those goals are nothing new—

not at this point in the book! But here we want to get into the details of what this strategy entails and how you can effectively use it to achieve those goals.

Here's the basic idea: Managing up is all about understanding how your role supports your manager's goals and objectives, and how you can do your job in a way that makes both you *and* your boss more effective. When you help your boss meet her goals, even when she hasn't asked you to do so directly, you not only position yourself as a stellar employee; you also demonstrate that you see the bigger picture and truly understand your boss's job—maybe even well enough to do it yourself someday (or another senior position).

Figuring out how to help your boss meet his or her goals will help you transition from an individual who can follow directions to a self-starter who's an integral part of the future of the company. Mastering this, however, is not about just adding more items to your to-do list. It's not really about doing more things at all—it's about *what* you choose to do and *how* you do it. And this is where the soft skills we've been talking about come in. To manage up effectively, you need to build the kind of relationship with your boss that allows you to add value; one in which you can intuit her needs and priorities without being told explicitly, find ways to take work off her plate and make her life easier, and finally produce the kind of results that make *her* look good to *her* superior.

Let's break down the strategy for managing up into four steps:

STEP ONE: KNOW YOUR OWN FUNCTION AND ROLE

We covered this during your job search process, but even after you've been in your role for a while, it's important to be aware of exactly what you're being paid to do. As you think about taking steps to move ahead in your career, understanding how you fit into your team and your company or organization isn't just important: it's critical. But understanding the nature of your role and what is expected of you isn't just about taking inventory of your daily to-do list—it also means keeping track of your accomplishments and communicating them to your superior. This will not only help both you and your manager stay aware of the new responsibilities you are taking on over time; it will also give you plenty of accomplishments to point to when your annual performance review rolls around.

If your role begins to change—for example, if colleagues or managers ask you to take on additional projects or tasks outside your original role—you should bring this information to the attention of your boss. Taking on greater or more senior responsibilities than you were initially hired to do is a great way to position yourself for a promotion—but only if your boss is aware that you're doing them!

Kathryn once had a direct report who was phenomenal at this. After a particularly impressive quarter and a lot of growth both in her role and at the company, she booked time with Kathryn to share some of her key accomplishments, the ways in which her role had evolved over the past few months, and her aspirations for the future. Once Kathryn was aware of all the wins this person had already scored—and where she was looking to go in the future—she was able to funnel even more new opportunities her way.

STEP TWO: UNDERSTAND YOUR BOSS'S ROLE AND GOALS

In part, managing up is based on the premise that you should become integral to helping your boss achieve his or her own goals, and the larger company's goals as well. Rather than just succeeding within your own job, you need to make an effort to understand your manager's role and objectives and how your job fits into helping her meet them.

Let's say, for example, that as an analyst on a marketing team, you're in charge of projecting the financials for various marketing initiatives. You could ask your boss detailed questions about the costs of each objective and build the corresponding financial models. Or you could take a step back and look at the bigger picture. What is your boss really aiming to achieve? Is she trying to reach as many people as possible with the lowest possible spend? Or is she responsible for ensuring the new product launch makes a splash, and she wants your projections to help her request an adequate budget to make that happen? Once you know what her end goals are, you can do more than just build your models—you can make suggestions to tweak marketing initiatives in ways that would help her succeed in those longer-term objectives. Suddenly her job is easier, and you've made yourself way more valuable.

The same idea applies to the small things, too. Let's say you typically give your boss a summary report on Wednesdays, and she uses it in her presentation to the executive team on Thursday mornings. Yes, she asked for it by EOD Wednesday—but by getting that report to her on Wednesday morning, instead of right before you leave the office at 6 p.m., you know you'd make her life a whole lot easier. Try it. Your attention to the bigger picture won't go unnoticed.

STEP THREE: IDENTIFY YOUR BOSS'S LEADERSHIP STYLE

Managing up requires constant communication and interaction with your boss. To do that most effectively, you have to be aware of his leadership style—the way he prefers to communicate, manage, and interact with others. For example, he might prefer to be directly involved with employee projects and receive daily updates on their progress. Or he might have a more hands-off style, opting to let direct reports take projects and run with them. Similarly, maybe your boss prefers email to keep electronic records of every conversation—or maybe he'd rather you just pop by his office, rather than send him a message from two doors down the hall.

These might seem like minor details, but by interacting with your boss in the way he or she prefers, you'll be more effective—with the ultimate goal, of course, of making your *boss* more effective.

Below, we outline a few of the most common leadership styles, inspired by Daniel Goleman's work in *Leadership That Gets Results,* and tips to help you identify and "manage up" to each.

THE DIRECTOR

Leaders with this management style expect their employees to do what they tell them to do—period. Often, they motivate with consequences, rather than incentives. If you report to this type of boss, make sure to not only follow his instructions but also communicate that you're following his instructions—tell him exactly what you've done and how you did it. Once he trusts that you respect his authority, you can start to introduce your own ideas.

THE AUTHORITATIVE LEADER

This manager focuses on the big picture—both for the company as a whole and your individual career. She motivates her team to work toward a unified objective, but doesn't necessarily give each employee much guidance in how to get to that point. When you communicate with this kind of leader, she'll want to hear less about the specifics of what you did, and more about how it fits into the ultimate goal, so it pays to focus the conversation on the results rather than the process.

THE PEOPLE PERSON

For this manager, people come first. This boss cares deeply about keeping his or her employees happy and making them feel like they belong. With such an emphasis on relationship building and maintaining a positive environment, however, this leader can have a hard time managing healthy conflict or providing constructive criticism. To succeed under this type of manager, you should clearly communicate how you're feeling—but you may have to specifically ask for feedback on ways you can improve.

THE TEAM PLAYER

Leaders in this category prioritize teamwork and consensus. Rather than telling employees exactly what to do, this leader would ask, "What do you think we should do?" If you have this type of boss, don't shy away from offering up your opinions and suggestions—keeping in mind that your ideas should benefit the team as a whole.

THE PACESETTER

This type of manager is a high performer and, often, an overachiever. Her priority is excelling at her own job, which means she can have a hard time delegating tasks to her employees. With this type of manager, you have to proactively ask to take charge of projects and tasks. By following through and consistently delivering great work, your boss will realize she can trust you to make her look good—securing your spot as an integral member of her team.

THE COACH

This leader has his eye on the future. Rather than only focusing on the tasks at hand, he helps employees develop new skills and improve over time. To succeed under this type of boss, you need to be open to feedback and willing to look at every task as an opportunity to grow—rather than something to check off your to-do list.

STEP FOUR: ASK FOR FEEDBACK

Most bosses give their employees occasional feedback—whether informally or during your annual performance review. But to effectively manage up, you need to proactively ask for more. We recommend scheduling a regular meeting with your boss—weekly, biweekly, or monthly, depending on your manager's preferences and schedule—to discuss his or her thoughts on your recent performance and ideas for how you can improve. This will help you keep a pulse on how things are going and how you *and* your boss are progressing toward your goals.

When you do sit down for these meetings, brace yourself: feedback can be tough to hear. Your boss may share opinions that you don't agree with, and you might find yourself getting defensive, wanting to make excuses for why you didn't hit a goal or perform your best. But step back for a minute. This is feedback *you asked for*—and to get better at your job and move up in your career, you need to hear and act on it. Rather than get defensive and insulted, look at the situation as an opportunity to grow.

Maybe, for example, you're in charge of the company newsletter. Because you're juggling several other projects, you got behind schedule on the most recent edition, forcing your entire team to jump in and help you finalize it by the deadline. As a result, your manager suggests that you should work to improve your time management skills. Your first reaction might be to burst out with "Look at my overflowing to-do list! I thought the newsletter was my lowest priority!" But instead, try to see the situation through your boss's eyes: the team had to devote an entire day to helping you get the newsletter out, taking everyone else away from their own priorities. To be an effective team member, maybe you *do* need to work on your time management.

If you don't agree with or understand the feedback, don't be afraid to ask for more information. In this situation, you might ask, "What do you think would be a better way for me to prioritize projects?" or "Should the newsletter have taken priority over the client escalation that I handled on Monday?" (Just watch your tone—your questions should convey that you're genuinely interested in understanding the feedback, not that you're combating it.)

Your boss's own behavior and work style can also help you come up with tangible ways to improve. If you ask her how she manages her time, for example, she might have a strategy or an app that you could adopt. Then start your next meeting by explaining what you've done to incorporate her suggestions into your daily routine. You'll prove that you take her feedback—and your career advancement—seriously.

THE ONE QUESTION EVERY EMPLOYEE DREADS HEARING FROM A BOSS

If you've followed the advice in Step 4 and set up regular meetings to sit down with your boss and talk about your performance, there's one more potential pitfall to avoid. Since these meetings revolve around feedback, at some point you might encounter a question from your boss that can easily throw you off guard: "How can *I* improve?" It can be pretty intimidating to tell your superior what he or she is doing wrong, but with the right approach, it can actually give a boost to your own effectiveness and your career growth.

The most important thing to remember in this situation is to provide specifics. Vague statements (e.g., "It's hard to get your approval

THE NEW RULES OF INTERPERSONAL SKILLS

on client contracts") typically won't yield great results; instead, try to (respectfully) point to specific examples: "Last week, I needed approval on the Smith contract by Wednesday, but by the end of the day, I still hadn't received anything from you—even though I emailed and stopped by your office." Then throw in a suggestion for how you think the situation could improve: "Going forward, would it be easier if I scheduled fifteen minutes on your calendar so we can both set aside the time to review and approve the contract?"

In general, and though it might not always seem like it, your manager *wants* to make your job easier—because that's going to allow him or her (and the company as a whole) to be more successful. By taking and offering feedback gracefully, you'll get a reputation as a straight shooter—strengthening your position as a leader and integral part of the company's future.

All the strategies we've discussed in this chapter for building, maintaining, and growing your relationships with colleagues and managers are key to thriving in your current role and setting yourself up to take your career to the next level. But of course, the specific circumstances and nuances differ from person to person and job to job—and we couldn't possibly come close to covering them all. So here's one general tip: as you manage the sometimes rocky waters of interoffice dynamics, always think about how your interactions serve yourself and others. Remember that people are social creatures, and no job exists on an island—so it's important to understand that interpersonal skills (relationship building, managing up, collaborating, leading, and mentoring) are vital to the trajectory of your career. Focusing on them will keep you working at the top of your game while also preparing you to move up to your next role.

CHAPTER TWELVE

The New Rules of Productivity

THE OLD RULE: Our work lives were compressed into a 9-to-5 schedule that pretty much everyone adhered to; being productive was measured as what we got done in the time frame determined by our superiors. We were not expected to work on the weekends or, unless on some sort of deadline, into the wee hours—either in the office or at home. The pace was set by our companies—who opened their doors at 9 a.m. and closed them at 5 p.m.

THE NEW RULE: Being productive is now a personal quality that we all define for ourselves—and that we all need to become experts in. Technology has created the expectation that we are always connected, available, and reachable, which often feels like we are supposed to be working all the time. As a result, we have to manage our time with the exactness of a samurai warrior.

No matter what field we work in or what role we have, high productivity is often what differentiates top performers from average ones. Indeed, we think that mastering your time—learning to use your time and energy to its utmost effect—is one of the most crucial aspects of enjoying a successful, lifelong career, no matter what form that takes or how it twists and turns along the way.

And at the same time, productivity is what makes work-life balance possible. Why? Because being more productive gives you options by giving you back time—time you can spend getting ahead on work or developing new skills, but that you can also spend with the people you love, on your hobbies, or (our personal favorite) getting more sleep. So whether you're in your first job or your fifth, you will need to understand these productivity rules so you can master your time—instead of letting your time master you.

In our age of distraction, this is no easy task. Moreover, demands on a professional's time are vastly different than even just ten years ago. At a time when we are all tethered to our iPhones and reachable 24/7, the lines between work and life have blurred dramatically, to the point where it's hard to know when work hours end and personal time begins. In this chapter, we are going to share our best tips and secrets to streamline your to-do list, minimize distractions, stoke your motivation, and resist procrastination. And when you put these techniques to work for you, guess what happens? Yes, you will become more productive and get more work done. But you will also learn how to get more time for the things you enjoy.

GETTING STARTED: MASTERING YOUR TO-DO LIST

Winning the war against time isn't about trying hundreds of online tools claiming to help professionals be more productive. Yes, those tools can help, but fundamentally, it's about rethinking how you use time. And this starts each and every day with how you organize your tasks.

In 2012, LinkedIn released a survey revealing just how much our professional to-do lists are in need of a makeover. It turns out, we're great at *listing* the things we need to do, but not so good at actually *doing* them. In fact, almost 90 percent of professionals admit they're unable to accomplish all the tasks on their to-do list by the end of an average workday. So if you're sick of tackling the same stale to-do lists every day—and coming up short—here are four key strategies to change all that.

KEEP A SINGLE MASTER TO-DO LIST FOR WORK

Let's be honest: if you wanted to get a complete view of all the tasks you had to get done for work right now, chances are you couldn't find it all on a single list. Instead, you probably have a few Post-its here, a saved draft in your email there, notes jotted in stickies on your computer, and maybe a checklist app or two on your phone, right? But if the goal is to actually get everything done, having a single place for your work-related tasks is a must. So pick your method of choice, and start consolidating. It can be a handwritten list inside your trusty planner, a document you keep on your desktop, an app on your phone, or whatever else; this isn't about the medium, it's about the thought process. Just make sure that whatever method you use, you can add to your list from anywhere—which means that if you use a desktop app, you'll want to set up a system to capture to-dos that crop up while you're away from your computer, such as assignments you get while in a meeting, or the phone call you remember suddenly, during your commute home, that you need to make tomorrow. Personally, we like to email these reminders to ourselves, then delete the email once we've transferred them to the master list, but writing them down on sticky notes and transcribing them to the file works, too.

FOLLOW THE 1-3-5 RULE

One of the ways that we have transformed not only our own productivity but also that of our entire team of Musers is by following the 1-3-5 Rule, which Alex developed. Here's the gist: on any given day, assume that you can only accomplish one big thing, three medium things, and five small things, and narrow down your to-do list to those nine items.

Sound scary? Well, it is, at first. But like it or not, you have only so many hours in the day, and the reality is that you're going to get only a finite number of things done. Forcing yourself to prioritize by creating 1-3-5 lists means the things you accomplish will be the things you *chose* to do—rather than those that *happened* to get done.

Of course, the number of tasks themselves can be flexible. If you spend much of your day in meetings, for example, you might need to reduce the number of tasks a bit. Or if your position is one where each day brings lots of unexpected to-dos and assignments, you might try leaving one medium and two small tasks blank in preparation for the last-minute requests from your boss.

But the point is, prioritization works. So, give it a whirl—we've even created a template below that you can use to try it out!

1-3-5 TO-DO LIST

TODAY
_____

I WILL ACCOMPLISH...
_____
_____

1 BIG THING
_____
_____

3 MEDIUM THINGS
_____
_____
_____

5 LITTLE THINGS
_____
_____
_____
_____

High five!

Note that this doesn't mean you need to limit your master to-do list to just nine things—rather, you should keep two kinds of lists: one large "kitchen sink" comprehensive list of everything you have to do at some point (all in one place, see strategy 1!), and another that is shorter and gives you your marching orders for what needs to get done *today*. We recommend that before leaving work in the evening, you take a few minutes to define your 1-3-5 for the next day, so you're ready to hit the ground running in the morning.

Planning ahead like this also means you'll be able to have more informed conversations with your manager when he or she drops something new on you that needs to be done right away, as well as the tools to reprioritize your other work. For example, when a surprise presentation falls on your lap, try: "Sure, I can get that to you by three p.m., but the Q1 reports won't be ready until tomorrow then, since I'd scheduled time to work on that today."

COMPLETE ONE SIGNIFICANT TASK BEFORE LUNCH (YOUR LEAST FAVORITE ONE, IF POSSIBLE)

Okay, this one can be tough, but it works. Take one of your big or medium tasks and tackle it first thing in the morning, even before checking email, if you can. Trust us, there's no better feeling than crossing off a major task before lunch. Author Brian Tracy calls this "eating your frog," a nod to the famous Mark Twain quote: "Eat a live frog first thing in the morning and nothing worse will happen to you the rest of the day." Kathryn often identifies her "frogs" for the next day—that is, the most difficult tasks, or the ones she knows she'll least enjoy—the night before; that helps mentally prepare her to tackle them in the morning, and it keeps her from pushing them off until the next day, then the next day . . .

BLOCK YOUR CALENDAR

If you find that you always overestimate how much you can get done in a day, try allocating time for each of your to-dos on your calendar, just like you would a meeting. Once you've defined the tasks on your to-do or your 1-3-5 list, try scheduling them, blocking off the appropriate amount of time for each.

The important thing is to be realistic about how long each will actually take. Writing that important email to a client might take fifteen minutes, for example, while preparing the Q1 strategy for your team may require a few hours.

It's easy—but dangerous—to fall into the trap of letting critical work products be relegated to moments left over between meetings. As economist John Kenneth Galbraith once said, "Meetings are indispensable when you don't want to do anything." Unless your job description is *just* to take meetings (and we are guessing it's not), time blocking is a great way to ensure you're making time for real work: the things that move the business forward and that your clients pay the company to produce.

When you try this approach, also make sure you block time in your calendar for catching up on email, brainstorming, or other important-but-not-deliverable-oriented tasks. If your responsibilities allow it, try blocking an hour in the morning and an hour in the afternoon to work through your inbox—and then discipline yourself not to spend time in between trying to handle emails the minute they come in, when you'd planned to be working on something else.

REALLY STRUGGLING TO CROSS OFF THOSE TO-DOS? USE YOUR FEELINGS (YEP, SERIOUSLY)

If you're really struggling to get things done that needed to happen yesterday, you may need to try a different approach in your battle with your to-do list. This one is a little out there, but stick with us for a minute. We learned this trick from entrepreneur Robyn Scott, who suggests appealing to how completing that task will make you *feel*.

You've already created a list of actions you need to accomplish above. Now move your hard-to-complete tasks into categories based on how that action typically makes you feel. Here's Robyn's list of categories, with some examples of what she puts in each:

- **Triumphant:** Client pitches, investment presentations, hiring plans. Mission-critical stuff.
- **Supremely satisfying:** Inbox zero (aided by Tony Hsieh's lovely "Yesterbox" technique—more on this later), making a tricky phone call, research.
- **Massive relief:** Tax return, sorting out insurance, booking flights.
- **Highly helpful:** Intros, advice, intros, intros.
- **Basic decency:** Thank-you notes, keeping promises, which helps avoid overpromising and jeopardizing integrity.
- **Delight:** Finally getting that print of Raphael's *School of Athens* for my office, calling a friend out of the blue.
- **Fit for Battle:** A daily run, ten-minute morning meditation.

When we got a bit overwhelmed during a particularly busy time at The Muse, we tried this trick ourselves. And when we did we found that appealing to emotions helped us avoid procrastination *and* increased our satisfaction. Why? Because it forces us to think about *why* we're doing the task, rather than just the action item itself. Just those few little words help harness a different kind of motivation, and with it, a promise of emotional rewards. This isn't a solution for everyone, but if you need help shaking things up and finding motivation to take control of your to-do list, it can be a great strategy to deploy.

LEARNING TO SAY NO

Managing your time more efficiently is not only about organizing your to-do list. It's also about learning to think differently about the value of your time. Often, this mind shift means knowing what not to do and what to stop doing. Saying no, giving yourself boundaries, and under-standing whether all the tasks on your to-do list are really necessary or important can make a huge difference in your productivity *and* your happiness. Try testing yourself with this list of five questions to make sure you're investing your time well.

1. ARE YOU "YESING" YOURSELF TO DEATH?

Most people have a deep need to be liked. As a result, we say yes to al-most everything that's asked of us. The problem is, this makes it impos-sible to do everything well, and zaps our time and productivity. Take a look at the last ten requests you received (except assignments from your boss, which you may not have control over). If you said yes to more than half, it's probably time to push yourself to start saying no.

2. ARE YOU DELEGATING ENOUGH?

Whether or not you're a manager, there are opportunities to delegate to colleagues. If you're doing everything yourself, and think "it's just faster for me to do it," you may be a delegatophobe. Take a good look at your tasks over the last week—are all of those really your job description? If not, then you want to begin to delegate more. (Refer back to page 262 for more on how to delegate.)

3. IS EVERYTHING ON YOUR TO-DO LIST NECESSARY?

Don't look at an endless to-do list as a challenge to get it all done—but instead as a challenge to prioritize. If you haven't tackled a certain task for weeks, or if you keep pushing it to a later date, that might be a sign that it's not actually necessary. Use your manager and colleagues as sounding boards to try to remove unnecessary items from your to-do list, so you can dedicate more time to high-priority items that will move your goals forward. Pro tip: Having trouble removing to-dos at work? Go through each one and write down the impact it will have (e.g., "revenue opportunity" or "user growth"). You'll be surprised how many items aren't aligned with your company or personal goals. If this is the case, let them go.

4. DO YOU *REALLY* NEED TO BE AT THAT MEETING?

News flash: You do not need to agree to be at every meeting you're asked to attend. Don't think you have to be a slave to those people who inconsiderately add meetings to your calendar without asking (every workplace has them!)—know that you have permission to decline anything that isn't critical to your job. Set a high bar for giving people your time, and you'll find that some questions can actually be sorted out more effectively via email or by picking up the phone—in a fraction of the time they would take to address in a meeting. Try "Thanks for the invite, but I'm not sure this is the best use of my time, and I'm confident that the rest of the parties can move forward without me" or "In the interest of time, why don't we try hashing this out over email? Here are the next action steps on my end."

5. ARE YOU A SLAVE TO YOUR INBOX?

Speaking of things you don't need to do: you do not need to answer every email that comes in. Give yourself permission to archive irrelevant and FYI emails you're cc'd or bcc'd on. And while you're at it, unsubscribe from any newsletter you signed up for and don't read (trust us, if don't have time to read it now, you probably never will).

We know this can feel harsh, but ask the people you admire and aspire to be if they answer every email they get and the answer will be no. As a wise person once told Kathryn, "My inbox isn't a to-do list that anyone can put items on. And that sometimes includes the hundred-plus cold inbound emails I get every month. If I wrote back to everyone, that's all I'd be doing!" Saying no to email is key to making time for real work.

HOW TO BE PRODUCTIVE WHEN YOU FEEL OVERWHELMED, OVERWORKED, OR JUST PLAIN OFF

Even equipped with the best productivity strategies, you'll have times when you feel overwhelmed. Your to-do list has gotten out of control, you're missing deadlines, and your inbox is full of emails from co-workers following up on things you promised them weeks ago. When things are really dire, a quick fix or new productivity app isn't going to cut it. To take control again, you'll need to take a step back, assess the situation, and make some more strategic moves to clear your plate.

First, grab that "kitchen sink list" and block out time on your schedule for a reality check with yourself (Alex likes out-of-office solo breakfasts). Yep. We know that means putting off other things that seem pressing, but this will help center your mind so you can think clearly about what you have going on right now and how to tackle it. At that "meeting with yourself," write down absolutely everything on your plate. Most of it is likely on your list already, but being as busy as you have been, it may not be up to date. Now is your time to get it there.

Next, identify the major categories of work (e.g., client communications, internal reporting, meeting follow ups), making sure to add an "Other" bucket for all the miscellaneous items that inevitably make it onto the list. On a piece of paper, place each of your tasks into the appropriate bucket. You may think of additional to-do items as you're writing—don't panic, just add them. No item is too small or too insignificant to make this list. It's important to face the reality of exactly what you need to get done to determine the seriousness of the situation—and how extreme a strategy you're going to need to put in place.

Typically, after going through your kitchen sink list, you'll find it lies in one of two camps: long but doable, or overwhelming and unfinishable. If the latter, don't despair. Whether you just have a bit of catch-up work ahead of you or you've truly bitten off more than you can chew, here are several strategies that can help get your frazzled work life back under control:

1. PRUNE THE TREE
Look at the tasks on your list and decide which ones can be taken off entirely. I know, it sounds scary—even impossible. But we're willing to bet that there are a few things that don't *really* need to get done right now (at least not by you). Anything noncritical should get the ax.

2. USE THE 80/20 RULE

Are there any tasks or projects for which 20 percent of the effort would yield 80 percent of the impact? For example, let's say your boss wants a competitive analysis for a new product she's thinking of launching. Before handing her a novel on the competitive landscape, would one page on each serious competitor be enough to help make that decision? If so, do that instead. Or, if the majority of the revenue you bring in as a sales rep comes from bigger deals, but you spend half your time on small deals that barely move the needle, could you shift your time and attention to the bigger deals instead? Yes? Then do it.

3. AUTOMATE OR OUTSOURCE

Productivity expert Steven Robbins wrote a great piece explaining that something that takes you thirty minutes each day adds up to three weeks a year. Whoa, three whole weeks! Get that time back by seeing if there are any smaller recurring tasks you can automate or outsource by hiring a freelancer or intern, or using third-party tools, such as Assistant.to for scheduling meetings.

4. ASK FOR HELP

If you're really underwater, there is no shame in turning to your boss, colleagues, employees, or even people in other departments for help. First, your teammates may have pointers on how they've dealt with similar challenges in the past. Or they may even be able to help take on some of the workload. Who knows—maybe your intern has been dying to get her feet wet in PowerPoint, or Dan from sales has an Excel model you could easily adapt to forecast your budget, or your boss no longer needs that document she asked you to draft. Look to areas where there is some overlap with colleagues' work for the most obvious handoffs. If you're concerned about seeming like a slacker, remember that it's in everyone's best interest for you to get some things off your plate so you can give everything else the full attention required to do your best work.

5. START PRIORITIZING

If everything left on your list at this point has to happen, and you're not going to get any more help, then it will all have to happen—just not at once. Look at your deadlines to determine which items are truly urgent and which timetables can be pushed back. Your manager can and should help you with prioritization and sequencing, so after you've ordered your list, consider discussing it with your boss. If you feel comfortable, simply approach her and say something along the lines of "I feel like I have a lot on my plate right now and would love your help figuring out the best way to tackle it all." Don't worry, this approach is proactive—and won't seem like you're complaining or trying to get out of work (so long as you aren't complaining and trying to get out of work).

6. PASS A MORATORIUM ON YES

As we mentioned above, saying no is an important strategy at all times, but right now it's mission critical for keeping your wits about you during this stressful time. Until things are under control again, you need to be the king or queen of "No!" Don't take on additional projects until you've gotten yourself out of this mess.

7. SUGGEST A HIRE

If you've tried all of the above and still find yourself swimming in to-dos with no end in sight, it may be time to request adding someone to your team. Depending on your company's culture and budget, consider a part-time hire, freelancer, intern, or temp as a lower-cost option.

8. TAKE A BREAK

Finally, don't forget that no matter how many things you have on your to-do list, you still need breaks—both throughout the day and at the end of it. We know it's tempting to think you have to work endless hours, pull all-nighters, or come in on the weekend in order to get it all done—we've been there, too! But you know what? When we take the time to take breaks, our minds and bodies function much better when we do get back to work. Give yourself the breaks you (and your brain) deserve.

MANAGING YOUR INBOX LIKE A PRO

Let's face it: even when you're on your A game, you likely get more emails than you can reply to each day, and being a slave to that inbox can seriously threaten your productivity and keep you from doing your "actual job." At the same time, in this modern world, staying on top of your inbox is a must if you're going to impress your boss and get ahead.

Moreover, it's important from a personal standpoint to keep email from taking over our lives. Most months, Alex receives and processes more than ten thousand emails (eek!), so finding the right way to manage all this correspondence has been critical for her day-to-day sanity.

Turns out that the "right way" to manage email depends a lot on your own personal style. Here we've rounded up some of the most popular and successful strategies so that you can decide which one is best for you:

1. START WITH THE ROCKS FIRST

We've heard people judge how well they handle their email by the number of emails they crank through. "I spent three hours this afternoon and answered 120 emails!" But in most cases, that line of thinking is a huge mistake. We believe that to handle your email well, you need to get smart about your strategy. Not every email needs the same attention—consider which of your emails fall into each of these categories:

- Emails that are a quick read and can be answered right away (Reply time: less than five minutes)

- Emails that require some thought or careful writing, but limited extra "work" (Reply time: 5–30 minutes)

- Emails that require research or an output to be created (Reply time: 30 minutes or more)

When faced with a block of time to attack your inbox, it can be tempting to start with the quickies. It's satisfying to get them out of the way, you feel like you're making rapid progress, and firing off the quick answers doesn't require too much brainpower. But we recommend taking the opposite approach. It's the old rock, pebble, sand metaphor: Imagine that you're given a glass jar you need to fill with rocks, pebbles, and sand. The only way to get it all in is to start with the biggest things: your rocks. If you fill your jar with sand first, you'll never have room to fit those big rocks in.

In email terms, that jar is your time and the quick and easy emails are the sand. If you're answering those first, you'll never have time to get to the big, important ones.

The easiest way to implement this strategy in your daily life is to get into the habit of automatically sorting your emails into the three buckets listed above. Each time an email comes in, put it into one of the three following folders or give it one of the three following tags (or filters in Gmail): "quick reply," "needs some thought," and "requires focused time."

Then, when you know you have a solid block of uninterrupted time, start with the "rocks"—emails that you flagged as requiring focused time—and get at least one or two of those done before doing any quicker ones. Once you've gotten some of those rocks out of the way, you can tackle the sand, so the next time you have a couple of minutes to spare before your next meeting, or while waiting for the bus or in line for coffee, use the time to get your "quick reply" emails out of the way instead of checking Instagram.

2. LIFO: LAST IN, FIRST OUT

This technique is the most common way that people deal with their inbox, and it simply means working through their inbox from top to bottom (aka, starting with the most recent email received).

This strategy is highly convenient and intuitive, but there are two primary risks. The first risk is inconsistent responsiveness. On days that you have a lot of time to spend on email, you'll reply to contacts lightning-fast. On days that you're busy and in meetings, you'll have messages pile up and get buried under newer emails, and people who got that instant response from you yesterday will wonder why it's now taking you so long to get back to them.

The second risk is that you may miss out on good opportunities because you didn't follow up in time. If you choose to use this strategy but want to mitigate these risks, we recommend blocking an hour or two once a week during which you switch to the reverse chronological approach (conveniently, the next strategy outlined below). This way, you'll catch anything old that might be important.

3. REVERSE CHRONOLOGICAL

The opposite of LIFO, taking a reverse chronological approach means dealing with the oldest emails first. The easiest way to do this is to simply switch the sorting of your inbox to go from oldest to newest (if you use Gmail, you can do this by just clicking the email counter in the top right corner). With this strategy, you'll often be confronted with harder emails you've been putting off, which is great for any chronic procrastinators. However, if you work someplace where you constantly receive urgent emails that really do need to be answered right away, taking a reverse chronological approach might be risky. If that's the case, you can definitely create a hybrid strategy—try using the reverse chronological approach when you check your email in the morning and then switch to LIFO for the rest of the workday.

4. YESTERBOX

Famously used by Zappos CEO Tony Hsieh, the Yesterbox technique focuses on dealing today with all of the email you received yesterday. Hsieh explains:

> *Your to-do list each day is simply yesterday's email inbox*
> *(hence, "Yesterbox"). The great thing about this is when you*
> *get up in the morning, you know exactly how many emails you*
> *have to get through; there's a sense of progress as you process each*

email from yesterday and remove it from your inbox, and there's actually a point when you have zero emails left to process from yesterday. There is actually a sense of completion when you're done, which is amazing.

This is a great strategy for anyone who feels like they're constantly drowning in email. Unlike other methods, your target remains the same as the day goes on, which can help you from feeling overwhelmed, and you'll also find over time that you get a better handle on how long email will take you to get through. Did you receive 25 emails yesterday? Okay, that might take you a little over an hour. Have a big day with 70 emails coming in? You can plan ahead and block additional time to manage the volume. Plus, this strategy guarantees that no one will ever be left waiting more than twenty-four hours for a response.

5. INBOX ZERO

A term coined by Merlin Mann, Inbox Zero is an email strategy whose goal is to always keep your inbox 100 percent empty. There are some big benefits to this: everything is always handled, and you don't waste time rereading an email for the third time before actually taking action. This strategy is good for Type-A list makers (like Alex!) who like to have complete control over their inboxes. But from our experience, it's easy to let your inbox dictate your life if you take this too far. And for less structured types like Kathryn, it's a "nice" but pretty much inconceivable idea!

Pro tip: Couple Inbox Zero with Boomerang for Gmail, an app that lets you file messages out of your inbox until the date and time of your choosing, so you can decide between answering immediately and delaying for later, while still keeping your inbox looking nice and empty.

KEEPING TECH DISTRACTIONS UNDER CONTROL

The irony in this age of distraction is that the most common sources of our distraction are the same technologies we need to keep up with the new world of work. Whether you're skimming Facebook, refreshing your inbox again, or checking that chat message that just came in, staying focused is hard. But there's no substitute for focused, truly uninterrupted time if you're going to actually get things done. So, in addition to our favorite productivity tools, we want to give you some strategies for keeping your own self-distracting impulses under control.

USE AN APP LIKE STRICT WORKFLOW

This Chrome plugin is based on the Pomodoro technique—a proven method that has you take 5-minute breaks after 25-minute focused work increments. Once installed, a simple click on your browser bar starts the timer for a 25-minute, interruption-free work session. During this time, the plug-in blocks common distracting sites (like Facebook, Twitter, YouTube, and Reddit), and you can customize your settings to add your personal guilty pleasures. If you try to visit those sites, you'll get a gentle reminder to get back to work. At the end of the 25 minutes, a timer rings and starts a 5-minute break. Rinse and repeat for a productive day!

SET YOUR CURRENT WORK TO FULL SCREEN

Every computer has the ability to take the tab or program you're working in and make it the only thing you can see. This is perhaps the most overlooked and underutilized tool for limiting distraction, and yet it's so easy! Working on a computer is distracting in the first place because of all the tabs and apps and bouncing icons with notifications. So sometimes all you need to focus your attention is to hide all that from your visual field. Whether working in Word, Chrome, or Photoshop, you just open the file you need (or just the one tab, if you're in a browser), and then enter full-screen mode.

TRY A TECH CURFEW

Sometimes the only way to free yourself from the haze of distraction caused by technology is to literally cut yourself off from it. Alex once gave herself a challenge that terrified her at first: a tech curfew. Though accustomed to answering emails well past 1 a.m. every night, she decided she would turn her laptop off at 11 p.m. and stop looking at any screens, including her phone and TV, until she went to bed. She forced herself to adhere to this strictly—she even closed her computer on a partially written email more than once! Guess what? No one died. No one even panicked. Giving yourself a hard cutoff time for being on your laptop (and phone) will help you get back in control by reminding you that the world won't stop if you detach for a number of hours. Alex found that her experiment made her more productive earlier in the day, and meant she had more time for other things—like reading—than ever before, and she *still* got more sleep. Crazy, right? Not to mention, having a daily deadline helped her prioritize better when she knew her "bedtime" was fast approaching. We can't recommend enough that you at least give this strategy a try.

———

If you take away just one thing from this chapter, we hope it's the understanding that at its core, productivity rests firmly on one singular principle: mindset. If you treat your time as something that's in your power to control and organize, you'll be able to set goals, prioritize them, meet them, and feel great about your progress. You have many tools and strategies to choose from—the ones we've given you are just the beginning!—and at the end of the day, the most important thing is that you choose the ones that work for you. We highly recommend experimenting, because there's no one-size-fits-all solution, and you can't always know what works for you until you try it. Plus, what works best may also change with the demands of your job and as you strengthen your time management muscles.

And remember, you don't have to be tied to your work 24/7 to be an effective employee, team member, or boss in today's world. In fact, you shouldn't be. Under the Old Rules, you would have been out of the office by 6 p.m. and unreachable the rest of the evening. While technology has improved our lives in so many ways, it's important to set boundaries so that you're not constantly working—and are more rested and engaged when you are. We are fully confident that a little effort in organization will help you become your most productive self—on a schedule that leaves plenty of room for having a life outside of work.

CHAPTER THIRTEEN

The New Rules of Career Advancement

THE OLD RULE: You relied on your employer to invest in and steer your advancement. If you did your work satisfactorily, receiving a promotion after a set number of years was more or less a given. And since average job tenure was high, good employees could expect professional development in return for their dedication and commitment.

THE NEW RULE: Companies realize that today's employees often aren't looking for a long-term relationship with one company or position—in fact, it's not unusual for an employee to stay in a role for just a year or two before moving on. Because of this, many organizations have done away with set promotion schedules and minimized or completely opted out of professional development programs and training. Which means that to get promoted within your organization or set yourself up for a more advanced position at another company, you need to take charge of your own professional growth and learning.

So far in this book, we've shown you that you can no longer approach your job search the way you might have ten years ago—and here we're going to talk about why you can't approach career development the same way, either. As we've seen, today's workplace is radically different, especially when it comes to career paths within companies.

Years ago, it was common for a company to provide employees with a clear, vertical path upward, based on an established timeline. Prove your competence by working as an assistant for a year, then get promoted to associate. Hit your company's defined metrics as an associate, and in four to five years, move into a manager or director position. And so on.

But it's no longer so clear-cut. Career paths today look more like a series of zigs and zags. Sure, you might take a traditional promotion. But to achieve your unique career goals, you might also make a lateral move or step into a lower role—often at a different company—in order to move up in another capacity.

Advancing in this kind of professional environment is both exciting and, well, terrifying. When there is no one obvious next step—but rather, dozens of possible next opportunities—how do you know which to pursue? And when there are no set timelines or metrics for promotions, how do you know when it's time to make the next move—or if you're qualified for the position you want?

It's a little overwhelming to consider. But before you freak out, take a deep breath and consider the upside. This flexibility gives you more choices and opportunities to find the right next step for you, without any limits on how long you have to wait to take it. Your potential is unlimited. You can and will advance—you just need to figure out where you want to go and how to successfully plot the path to get there.

In the new world of work, your advancement at your company and beyond is determined primarily by the skills you bring to a job and the competencies you learn and develop once you're there. But that introduces an important question: How do you go about acquiring skills that you don't yet possess—or even figure out which skills you need in the first place?

The answer *isn't* to rely on your boss or employer to set you up for future success. In today's workplace, it's not your manager's job to make sure you have the necessary skills you need to advance; it's yours. Understanding this and proactively pursuing the learning you need to take your career to the next level is what differentiates great professionals from average ones.

Professionals who stay upwardly mobile don't let years go by without thinking about the next step; they constantly keep their career trajectory at the front of their mind. They actively connect with their network, continuously broaden their skills, and regularly ask for feedback from their superiors. They are committed to personal growth, and they work at it consistently—and as a result, they keep advancing.

In this chapter, we are going to help you figure out how to be one of these people—how to take charge of your professional development, position yourself for advancement, and actually take that next step in asking for a promotion or strategic lateral move. In the short term, these strategies will help land you the next role you want, but over the long haul, they'll also be the key to meeting your overarching goal of thriving and flourishing in your career.

TAKING CHARGE OF YOUR PROFESSIONAL DEVELOPMENT

With the lack of clear vertical opportunities in today's workplace, it's not always obvious what skills you should be actively developing. Figuring out what will position you for advancement takes some detective work (but by now, you should be used to that!). In this section, we've laid out a few strategies for anticipating, identifying, and learning the skills you need to take your career to the next level. And even if you're new at a job and aren't yet thinking about your next step, read this chapter anyway! It's never too soon to start thinking about the skills that will enable you to advance and take advantage of new opportunities.

IDENTIFY THE SKILLS YOU NEED

Maybe you're starting to feel a bit antsy at your current job. The work is no longer exciting or challenging, and you feel you're ready for a new role and new responsibilities. Or maybe you're happy where you are right now but are looking ahead to where you want to be six months or a year from now. The skills you need to get to that next step may not be obvious at first, but they're also not a secret. In fact, you've probably come across them already—in your research, job postings, and informational interviews. So where do you begin?

A great place to start is the Muse Grid you created at the beginning of this book. Take a look at that very first version you drafted, which included your potential functions and industries, as well as your list of dream companies. Did you write down any skills that you might need to break into those fields or companies? Maybe you wrote down a skill that you didn't have while you were interviewing for your current position—that's a perfect candidate for the "Skills Needed" list we're going to help you create in this section. Perhaps you were interested in business development jobs, for example, but steered away from them because you didn't have any financial or negotiation experience—yet. Well, maybe you've now been in your current position for a year or two, during which time you've had some practice in putting together project budgets, or gained some exposure to different styles of negotiating. Or maybe you've been in your job only a few months, but now that your job search is over, you have some extra time. What's to stop you from building a practice financial model for one of your current projects, asking to sit in on a partnership negotiation with your boss, or taking a nighttime accounting course? (And if you don't feel you have time? Finding a way to invest in your career on an ongoing basis—even if it's in small, bite-size chunks—is critical. As time goes on, it's one of the biggest things separating those who move forward quickly from those who feel themselves stalling.)

Another way to identify skills you might need is to look through job listings (even though you aren't actively looking right now) and read the job descriptions of roles you think you might like to have in the future. Make notes of the skills that crop up most often in those descriptions, especially those that could be critical barriers between you and a job you'd love to have. One of our longtime Muse editors, Erin Greenawald, suggests creating a living document or folder (Erin uses Evernote, but you could use something as simple as Microsoft Word) for keeping track of the job descriptions that interest you—regardless of how out of reach those roles may seem at the moment.

Your network, of course, is also a valuable source of information for future skills. By perusing your contacts' LinkedIn profiles, you can easily make connections between the positions or titles that appeal to you and the skills those people have. At networking events, talk to people with interesting jobs and ask what skills they use most often or what they had to learn to get where they are.

As you do this research, keep a running list of skills you want or need to acquire (don't worry, you aren't going to tackle them all at once—more on that in a minute) in the space below.

SKILLS NEEDED LIST

_____   _____
_____   _____
_____   _____
_____   _____
_____   _____
_____   _____

PRIORITIZING YOUR SKILL LIST—WHAT TO TACKLE FIRST

You may now be looking at your list, thinking—understandably—that there's absolutely no way you could ever learn all those skills. Your list probably includes skills that range from simple (that is, something you could pick up in a couple of weeks with a little practice, like a few advanced functions in Excel) to complex and long-term (like learning to code or mastering a new language). Before you dive in and risk becoming frustrated or overwhelmed, take a few minutes to prioritize, thinking both about a realistic time frame to learn that particular skill and whether it's a short- or long-term goal. Some will fall into the "now" category—these are skills that can immediately impact your ability to do your current job. Some may fall into the two- to three-year category, which would be skills that prepare you to move up to the next level. And some may fall into the long-term, four- to six-year category. Then, in the right-hand column, jot down your best estimate of how long you think it will take to achieve the level of proficiency you want.

By prioritizing the skills you need, you'll know what to tackle first and what to keep on your radar as you consider professional development opportunities in the future.

NOW	

2 TO 3 YEARS	

4 TO 6 YEARS	

THINK ABOUT YOUR LEARNING STRATEGY

Armed with the knowledge of the skills you need and their priority within your career plan, you can now create a strategy to acquire them. Depending on the specific skills you're focusing on, the strategy for each could be very different. In some cases, it may be a matter of absorbing knowledge—say, getting up to speed on trends in a particular market— and a simple strategy of regularly reading industry blogs and news will get you a long way. In other cases, the only way to learn will be to roll up your sleeves and get your hands dirty; for example, if your goal is to be able to build a website or learn how to write advertising copy, you probably need a class or other hands-on experience. Don't forget that many skills can be learned on the job if you actively ask for these opportunities. Still other skills might require an official certification, a specific degree, or another form of higher education.

How can you figure out what it'll take to acquire your target skill? Again, go back to the LinkedIn profiles of the people in roles you aspire to, and see if they list any relevant courses, internships, apprenticeships, or certifications and degrees they've acquired along the path to that job. Also consider asking for an informational interview with a mentor, boss, or other contact in your network who excels at your desired skill. Most people will be happy to spend ten or fifteen minutes sharing how they developed their talents and experience. In the absence of face-to-face time, an email response might even be enough to point you in the right direction.

Here are some common methods or resources they're likely to recommend, and how to pursue them:

1. GO BACK TO SCHOOL

One of the most straightforward ways to learn or refresh a skill is to take classes—online or in person. We don't necessarily mean going back to get an advanced degree (unless that's what it will take to get you to the next step in your particular industry), but rather, taking advantage of universities and community colleges that offer one-off classes in practical, professional, and technical skills, such as accounting, computer programming, and business writing. Most of these classes are offered at night to cater to busy professionals like you!

Of course, you can also find free or low-cost classes online. Good sources for online courses include Coursera and EdX, as well as platforms such as Udacity, Udemy, Skillshare, Open2Study, and Lynda, which offer quick but excellent deep dives delivered by experts on literally thousands of topics—including data sciences, graphic design, social media marketing, negotiation, and problem solving. We believe in this so much that we launched an entire section of The Muse dedicated to classes—see some of our top, up-to-the-minute recommendations at www.themuse.com/courses. Many top universities are even starting to offer their course content online; try googling "MIT OpenCourse-Ware" or "Stanford OpenCourseWare" to see a few examples.

Don't limit yourself to traditional schools, either. For example, General Assembly (a coding boot camp founded in New York City) offers in-person classes—both full- and part-time—in major cities across the country, covering programming topics from user experience to web development to visual design. Do a quick Google search for your city and you're likely to find other unconventional educational opportunities—like the Brooklyn Brainery in New York City, or Workshop in San Francisco, which both offer classes on nearly everything you could imagine, from floral design to proofreading.

For specific functional areas, ask around to find out what's particularly popular in your field. For example, Adobe KnowHow offers highly specialized classes in design and the Iron Yard offers immersive, twelve-week coding courses at several campuses across the United States. If you don't think you need a full course but still want to get a basic understanding of the nature of a skill, try listening to class lectures online through Apple's iTunes U.

But before signing up for anything, do your homework to make sure it's a good match. For example, if you're taking a programming class with the goal of learning how to code in Python, but the instructor's experience is in JavaScript, that class might not be the best choice. Or you might have found an online marketing class that seems like a great deal at ninety-nine dollars—until all of the online reviews you find say it's a complete waste of time. Take a close look at the course description, syllabus, and background/professional experience of the instructor and then search for reviews online (including those available on The Muse) to see what comes up. Even if it's free, a subpar or irrelevant course is a waste of valuable time you could have spent *actually* learning the skill you're after.

2. GO TO CONFERENCES

Another great way to pick up new skills or knowledge is to attend conferences, events, or meetups. Many professional conferences host panels, lectures, and skills-focused workshops that might fit your needs. But even if you scan the schedule and don't see a session for the particular skill you're pursuing, conferences can be a great way to expand your understanding of your industry and the current issues and challenges in the marketplace. These events are also great networking opportunities, giving you a chance to talk with people in your field about their own professional development strategies.

3. TAP RESOURCES AT YOUR COMPANY—OR OTHERS

There may be professional development resources closer than you think. Check with your manager or an HR representative to see what your company offers, which could be anything from comprehensive training programs to a library of online courses to quarterly lunch-and-learns.

If you don't find anything that meets your needs, talk to your manager or HR rep to see if you can put together a proposal for a new learning opportunity at the company. If you can demonstrate the value of the course by outlining exactly what you'd like it to cover, the various roles (in addition to your own) in which the skill can be put to use, and how it will benefit not just you but other employees and therefore the company more generally, HR may agree to make it happen.

Still can't find what you're looking for? Venture outside your own organization. Many companies have begun offering open (and mostly free) webinars on topics in their field with the goal of establishing themselves as thought leaders—and you can take advantage of that knowledge. Again, as with courses, make sure you do your research on the company and speakers to determine if the webinar is worth your time and energy.

4. BE A JOINER

Another way to gain new skills (and expand your network) is by joining a professional organization. These groups, which exist for nearly any industry and career path, generally exist to help their members advance and succeed in their careers. As a member, you'll gain access to a range of benefits—anything from access to publications and journals to the opportunity to attend exclusive conferences. Joining an organization is generally fairly straightforward (although some require exams), but membership fees can vary. If you're looking for a more budget-friendly option, consider looking at local organizations, rather than national groups—they typically have lower dues.

If you're not sure what organization would benefit you the most, go back again to the LinkedIn profiles of your contacts or talk to your co-workers—they'll likely be able to provide some recommendations.

5. GET YOUR HANDS DIRTY

Classes and trainings are great, but there's often no substitute for taking on real-life opportunities at work that will force you to develop and master new skills. In an ideal world, any time you wanted to learn a skill, you'd have the opportunity to shadow a pro, learn from him or her, and then try your new skill out on your own. Sometimes great opportunities like that pop up, especially if your manager and other colleagues know that you're looking for, say, a chance to build client management or event organization skills. Other times you'll have to be a little more creative. For example, you might ask your boss to let you spend a week "interning" in another department or ask your team to let you test out your budding marketing skills on one of the company's latest projects.

In many cases, if you're open with your manager about your goals, he or she will be more than happy to help you build skills that will make you more valuable to your company. Keep in mind that your boss may not want you spending too much time away from your core responsibilities, but if you identify one or two key skills that you are hoping to develop over the next six to twelve months—and suggest a way to practice those skills without neglecting your existing job—chances are you'll be able to get him or her on board.

MOVING UP: ACTING LIKE A LEADER, NOT JUST AN EMPLOYEE

Working toward your next career move doesn't stop at developing new skills. Simply put, the best way to prepare for your next step up is to start thinking and acting like a leader, rather than an employee.

What's the difference? Employees strive to do their job well, focusing on completing their individual tasks. Leaders think and act outside of their individual roles, basing their actions on what will benefit the entire team and company. At its core, leadership isn't about a formal role or title, it's about mindset. We've seen it again and again: people who get promoted to management positions are those who think like managers, even if they don't yet have any direct reports.

What does this mean for you? You should be striving to think and act like a leader, no matter where you are in your organization today. Below, we've outlined a few actions you can take now that will help you stand out as a go-getter and prove that you're ready for the promotion you have your eye on.

DO A JOB BEFORE YOU HAVE IT

Today, it's rare to get promoted to a position on the assumption that you'll learn your new responsibilities once you're in that role. Instead, you have to prove you can do the job *before* you get that new title. How? Again, this takes initiative. When you face an opportunity to push yourself to go above and beyond in your current role—like when you encounter a project that needs extra hands on deck or unexpected work gets dumped on your plate—take it! For example, if a client meeting pops up unexpectedly, offer to create the first draft of the agenda or presentation—a task that might otherwise fall on your boss's already full plate. Situations like these are a perfect chance to demonstrate your leadership potential.

Don't feel ready to take on that kind of responsibility? Worry that you don't have what it takes and will be exposed as a fraud and a fake? These feelings are normal. But instead of focusing on your self-doubt, ask yourself: *What will happen if it's not perfect?* In most cases, the answer is you can get feedback, learn from it, and be that much more prepared to execute in the future. To prove you're ready for the next step, you don't have to demonstrate that you're superhuman, simply that you have initiative and that you're capable of performing beyond your job description.

THE NEW RULES OF WORK

HELP SOLVE PROBLEMS

Anyone can drop a complaint into the metaphorical suggestion box, but the mark of a truly brilliant employee is coming up with *solutions* to those problems. Becoming a problem solver shows that you care—not only about your own career, but also about the long-term health of the entire business. And don't sit back and wait for problems to find you; even if there aren't big crises staring you in the face, there's *always* something that could be done better or more efficiently, in every workplace.

Maybe in your role as a project manager, for example, you spend a huge portion of your day documenting what you did on each project, which is limiting your ability to make much progress on the project itself. And you know this doesn't only affect you; you've heard similar complaints from the rest of your team. It would be easy to bring up the problem to your boss and wait for him or her to come up with a solution. But it would be a true sign of leadership to not only bring up the issue, but also present a solution—like an idea for templates that would significantly cut down on the time you spend documenting each project. Better yet, offer to create those templates yourself if your manager likes the idea!

If you're the one who identifies workplace challenges *and* suggests a way to fix them, you won't only make your life easier; you'll prove to your boss that you're ready to solve the bigger and thornier problems that fall to a manager or leader.

FIND PLACES TO LEAD

It's been said that you can't lead without followers—so until you're in a supervisor position, how are you supposed to prove that you are ready to lead? Ask your boss for additional leadership responsibilities and create opportunities to mentor. Whether you offer to manage a project team, volunteer to mentor a junior employee, or take the lead to train the new interns, don't wait for a leadership opportunity—create one! Yes, sometimes taking on these opportunities might require you to stay late, catch up on a bit of work on weekends, or shift some of your other responsibilities around, but if you can make it work, it's usually worth

302

it. Finding opportunities to mentor or lead others can demonstrate your leadership potential to your superiors and give you the experience and confidence you'll need if this is something you hope to do later in your career.

DEVELOP INTERNAL ALLIES

Most people work hard to impress their bosses. And that's important (hence all the talk in Chapter 11 about managing up). But as you begin to think like a leader and position yourself for advancement, you need to go beyond that. Smart leaders know they're nothing without the team that supports them. Which means that you should work to impress *everyone*—from the mailroom clerk and receptionist to your peers and superiors.

What many people don't realize is that getting a promotion often requires having a number of people on your side, not just your boss or manager. For example, let's say you're part of a marketing team and work closely with the sales department. If, when you're up for a promotion, a sales manager can speak up about how well you've listened to his department's needs and constantly delivered quality, on-time materials, it will make an even more convincing case that you deserve the position.

We stressed this in the networking chapter, but we'll repeat it again: your commitment to networking shouldn't stop once you've landed a position. In fact, you are networking for life—it's an ongoing process, not one-and-done. Continue to look for opportunities to build relationships within your own company or organization. Make an effort to attend social events or group outings with your co-workers. Ask your colleagues to lunch or coffee. Use those interactions to ask questions and make real connections. As you strengthen these relationships, you'll turn co-workers and contacts into allies who will have your back when an opportunity comes your way.

SHOW THAT YOU'RE A TEAM PLAYER

You might assume that senior leaders only know (and care about) what's happening in their own functional area. Not true! They make it their business to know what's going on in every area of the company so they can understand and contribute to the big picture. By pitching in and participating outside your own realm of responsibilities, that perspective will become clear to you, too. So if an opportunity comes up to join an interdepartmental committee or help plan a company-wide event, offer your services! Your participation will show that you're looking beyond your role or department and thinking about how you can serve the company more broadly, and, as an added bonus, it'll give you the opportunity to create those internal allies that are vital to your advancement.

KEEP TRACK OF AND COMMUNICATE YOUR PROGRESS

Remember, *you're* in charge of you, so it makes sense that it's your job to stay aware of where you are on your path to promotion. This part is easy: all it takes is a spreadsheet or notebook (or the pages of this book!) to keep track of the skills you've mastered and what you still need to work on. However, all the work you're doing to position yourself for advancement won't yield much if no one knows about it.

Earlier, we suggested that you set up regular meetings with your manager. As part of those meetings, we recommend that you ask for feedback about your goals and promotion plan. Do you know exactly where you need to grow and what your boss sees as realistic goals for your future? Are you aware of the timing of your next review and the process to ask for promotions and raises? This information is incredibly helpful no matter where you'd like your career to take you.

Here are some questions to guide your next sit-down with your boss:

1. What are your objectives for the next year or two? What are the goals of the company?
2. How might the company change in the coming year? Is there anything coming down the pike that would be helpful for me to anticipate?
3. How do you think I can better prepare for these changes or goals?
4. I'm looking to move into a management role within the next

year or two [or whatever your goal is]. Can you identify any specific skills that might help position me as a good candidate?

5. How do you see my role within the organization evolving in the next two to three years?

These questions can open up a valuable dialogue and provide an opportunity for you to receive helpful feedback. Yes, feedback can be tough to take, but it's crucial that you take it seriously (without taking it personally) and work to understand how to put it into action. So don't just ask for feedback; use it. This one little thing often differentiates those who sputter from those who soar.

You can also use these meetings to remind your boss of your achievements. Keep track of your sales numbers, project results, or client feedback—whatever metrics and results are most important for your role—in a running document or folder in your email. Then, at your regular check-ins, share them.

For this to be most effective, mention specific metrics and couch your achievements in the broader scope of the company's success. For example, rather than telling your boss, "The prospect event went smoothly," try something like "We got a great response rate from our prospect event—eighteen prospects requested a follow-up meeting, which added $30,000 to my pipeline and will make a big dent in the company's Q3 sales goal."

Lastly, you can even work with your boss to get a job description of the role you'd like to grow into, so you can compare it with your current role and work on closing the gaps.

Your measurable successes will show—again—your commitment to the company, which can only make things easier when you get to the next step: asking for the promotion.

IT'S GAME TIME: ASKING FOR THAT PROMOTION

So, you've been learning new skills, showcasing your leadership abilities, and working on the goals that you and your manager have set together.

And now you feel ready to take that big step and ask for a promotion—that's great news! Before you move forward, though, ask yourself a few questions, to make sure the time is right and you've laid the necessary groundwork to set yourself up for success:

___ As you've been developing professionally over the last months or years, have you kept your manager or boss informed of your progress, accomplishments, and newly acquired skills?

___ Looking ahead, have you researched your goal position and made sure that you have the hard and soft skills required for the role?

___ Is your company doing well overall? Is it growing, expanding, or evolving?

If you've gone through the steps described above, and you've answered these questions in the affirmative, then we're confident that you're ready to ask for that promotion—as long as the timing is right. Now, you don't have to necessarily wait for your annual performance review to ask for a promotion (although if the timing aligns, that's a great opportunity to discuss your achievements and where your career is headed). But there are a few factors to consider before you pop the question.

Has your department been hiring recently, bringing on new team members to help with your team's surplus of work? Has your team recently separated into two smaller groups because the department had become so large? Big changes like these are a good sign that the company is in growth mode, giving you an opportunity to ask your manager about the future of the company and how your role might grow and change with it.

On the flip side, if there have been recent layoffs or cutbacks, or belt-tightening (such as limits on travel and expenses), that's a clear sign that the company isn't in the best place financially, which means the leadership team may not be in the position to promote *anyone,* especially if it comes with a big pay bump or if they'll have to hire someone new to fill your position.

If you decide the time is right to move forward but don't have a regular performance review scheduled in the near future, then you need to request a meeting with your boss. In your email, make sure to be clear and direct, so your boss understands the purpose of the meeting. For example:

> *Hi Bob,*
>
> *I'd like to get on your schedule to discuss my current position and prospects for advancement at the company. Do you have 30 minutes within the next week to meet one-on-one with me?*
>
> > *Thanks so much,*
> >
> > *Jen*

Keep in mind that asking for and actually getting a promotion might not happen in one conversation or meeting. Be prepared to ask for the promotion during that first meeting, but understand that it might take some back-and-forth between the higher-ups over a few days or weeks to get an answer.

When you do sit down with your boss, open the conversation with a reminder of how long you've been at the company and in your current role. Mention how much you like the company, envision a future there, and are motivated to continue to add value to the business.

Then spit it out: you want to be considered for X position for Y reasons (this is where you cite the contributions to the company we talked about above). At this point, you don't need to talk about a raise. It's implicit, but not the right time to start negotiating. And then? Be patient. You might be in a rush to get an answer. Who wouldn't be? Asking for a promotion is stressful and your adrenaline will probably be pumping. But look at the situation from your boss's point of view: she will need time to digest the idea and discuss it with her superiors and other members of the team.

But while you probably won't get a firm answer during the course of that meeting, there will be clues in the response you receive that will provide valuable feedback for determining your next steps.

If your boss asks for time to think about it and then schedules a follow-up meeting, it's probable—though by no means certain—that he or she is at least seriously considering your proposal. If that happens, you need to go into that second meeting prepared with your target raise so you can begin negotiating your bump in salary. How do you know what to ask for? Research what others in a similar role, industry, and geographical location are earning to know your market value—just like you did in Chapter 9. Then it's a matter of articulating the value you can bring to the role. (Review our tips for negotiation on pages 203–208.)

If your manager's response indicates that she has doubts that you're ready or qualified for the new job, dig into that feedback a little more. Ask what you need to do to gain the experience and skills required for the promotion, and about a realistic timeline for reaching that point. Then act on it immediately. And don't wait until your next performance review to tell your boss how you've implemented her suggestions. Follow up with your boss regularly—during monthly one-on-ones, for instance—to provide updates on how you've taken her advice and begun to acquire the necessary skills and experience for the role. And when you reach the end of your agreed-upon timeline, gather your most recent achievements and ask again.

If, however, your boss turns you down again, it may be time to take a step back and evaluate. Self-awareness is key here. It could be that he or she is right, and you're not yet ready, or aren't a great match for this particular role. In that case, you can continue to build your skill set and work toward the position you want or consider whether another opportunity might be better for you. Or you may be working under someone who doesn't see your value—and that may be a sign that it's time to move on.

LIFELONG LEARNING

If you follow the advice we've laid out in this chapter, chances are you will get that promotion—maybe not tomorrow or next week, but within a reasonable time frame. And when you do, we know that you'll be prepared to thrive in that new role, continue to grow your skills, and begin to set yourself up for your next move, even if it won't happen for a while. To do this, we can't stress this point enough: no matter where you are in your career, constantly striving to learn something new will be your ticket to something bigger and better. As we've built The Muse from a few people in an apartment to well over one hundred employees in New York City, our mantra (when it came to learning and personal growth) has been "Our job is to grow faster than the company." The more you consider yourself as (and act like) a lifelong learner, the better you'll be positioned to be happy, fulfilled, and successful in whatever you choose to do.

Musers are always learners. When people across all different industries and stages in their careers share their stories with us, they often speak about how their advancements and successes have happened over time because they were open to learning new skills, exploring different industries, making lateral career moves, and developing deep, broad networks. Those are the keys to carving out a path to a fulfilling career.

Hey there—you made it! Congratulations! Armed with the best of The Muse's tools, tips, and advice, you're now ready to go out and conquer the next phase of your career.

As you do, remember that as Musers, we believe that term—your *career*—is about so much more than your day-to-day work. Instead it's a lifelong process of honing skills, developing self-awareness, and understanding what really makes you tick—and how you can best apply all of that to your work. It's a journey, and an adventure—one that we hope we've made a little less scary, a little more accessible, a bit more exciting!

And what if you've gotten to the end of this book and you still feel unsure about something? *Wait!* you might be saying. *We haven't covered everything I wanted to know!* There may be specific questions that we haven't tackled, or areas where you doubt your own ability to level up. We wish we could wave a magic wand and take away those fears, but what we'll do instead is tell you this: You're not alone. We've been there, too.

In fact, we promise you: every single person in a position you admire—the television news anchor, the tech start-up founder, the genius PR wizard or marketer, the high-powered lawyer or investment banker with the great suits, even that #boss woman or man in your department whom you've always looked up to—we promise you, they have all dealt with doubts, with setbacks, with insecurities, and with questions for which there weren't easy answers. They've felt deep-seated career insecurity, nerves, or anxiety. But they pushed forward—and you will, too.

The amazing, deeply human thing about finding the right career is that the journey itself often becomes a critical part of your success, even if you can't see it at the time. And just because you're uncertain about where you are right now doesn't mean you can't get to exactly where you should be. Sometimes it just takes the right support and guidance.

That's why we started The Muse, and that's also why we wrote this book. We hope you know how much we believe in your ability to find your path, to discover a career that fulfills you and that you can throw your true self into. A career that you can thrive in, and that gives back to you, too—not just in the form of a paycheck, but in the form of learning, growing, and making an impact on the world. It might not happen immediately, but anything worth having takes time to build, and your career is no exception.

Brick by brick, step by step, job by job, we're here to help you through it. So don't put this book down forever. Revisit these exercises from time to time, and see where your skills, values, and preferences may have changed as you have grown—both as a person and in your career. Go ahead and scratch stuff out that no longer applies, keep scribbling new stuff in the margins, or go to TheMuse.com/thenewrules to download new, clean worksheets for all the exercises in the book and start them anew. And once you've conquered the "101"-level tips in some of the chapters on communication, workplace relationships, and more, know that we're still here for you: visit TheMuse.com for the advanced ninja-level advice on all these skills.

And remember, a career is not a solo journey, so we hope that you will also use the advice in this book as the basis for discussion with some of your colleagues, peers, or mentors; use it as a tool to understand where each of you is going and how you can help one another along.

And while it's not a solo journey, it is *your* journey, and you're in the driver's seat. And it's going to be a wonderful ride.

Muse on, dear readers. We're with you every step of the way.

—Kathryn and Alex

ADDITIONAL TOOLS

Here are the content and articles that were referenced throughout the book. Access or download all of our favorite resources at TheMuse.com/thenewrules, including:

The 11 Best Career Quizzes to Help You Find Your Dream Job (page 25)

These fun quizzes will help you hone your work style and figure out the type of career that may be best for you.

https://www.themuse.com/advice/the-11-best-career-quizzes-to-help-you-find -your-dream-job

185 Powerful Verbs That Will Make Your Resume Awesome (page 136)

Wanna wow a hiring manager? Update your resume with these action words to make sure your resume stands out in a crowd.

https://www.themuse.com/advice/185-powerful-verbs-that-will-make-your-resume -awesome

7 Tips to Help You Nail That Interview Presentation (page 178)

You're moving along in the interview process but were just told that the next stage is a presentation. Don't panic; read these tips to make sure you're ready to nail it!

https://www.themuse.com/advice/7-tips-to-help-you-nail-that-interview-presentation

Your All-in-One Interview Prep Guide (page 179)

Interviewing can be stressful, especially if you're juggling several companies and interview rounds. This handy prep guide will ensure you've got all the details covered.

https://www.themuse.com/advice/the-allinone-interview-prep-guide

A Better To-Do List: The 1-3-5 Rule (page 274)

Do you struggle to stay productive but want to make the most out of each day? Download this simple to-do list to help you tackle all of the items on your agenda in a strategic way.

https://www.themuse.com/advice/a-better-todo-list-the-135-rule

Want to redo some of the exercises? Go to TheMuse.com/thenewrules to download new, clean worksheets for all the exercises in this book, and start them anew!

Finally, for further advice on the topics covered in the book, here are a few of our all-time favorite Muse articles.

PART ONE: WHAT DO I ACTUALLY WANT

4 Ways to Figure Out What You're Good At, Not Just What You're Passionate About

So many professionals get stuck when they focus only on uncovering their passion. Sure, passion matters, but sometimes a better starting place is your strengths.

https://www.themuse.com/advice/4-ways-to-figure-out-what-youre-good-at-not -just-what-youre-passionate-about

3 Ways to Figure Out If You Just Need a New Job or an Entirely New Career Path

Is your unhappiness at work due to your employer, or is it because you're in the wrong career? Here are a few questions that will help you find the answer.

https://www.themuse.com/advice/3-ways-to-figure-out-if-you-just-need-a-new-job -or-an-entirely-new-career-path

Start-up or Corporate: Which Is Better for Your Career?

It's not just about perks versus a steady salary—if you're choosing between these two paths, consider your long-term career goals, too.

https://www.themuse.com/advice/startup-or-corporate-which-is-better-for-your -career

PART TWO: MAKING YOUR MOVE

43 Resume Tips That Will Help You Get Hired

Need more help putting together your resume? This article rounds up even more of our expert-backed tips.

https://www.themuse.com/advice/43-resume-tips-that-will-help-you-get-hired

31 Attention-Grabbing Cover Letter Examples

If you're struggling to write your cover letter, get inspired by these opening lines from great cover letters that made a strong impression.

https://www.themuse.com/advice/31-attentiongrabbing-cover-letter-examples

30 Behavioral Interview Questions You Should Be Ready to Answer

"Tell me about a time when you made a mistake at work." Open-ended interview questions like these can be tricky, so practice your responses using this helpful list (and a friend!).

https://www.themuse.com/advice/30-behavioral-interview-questions-you-should -be-ready-to-answer

51 Interview Questions You Should Be Asking

When the tables turn and it's your turn to ask questions, be prepared for the conversation by drawing from this list.

https://www.themuse.com/advice/51-interview-questions-you-should-be-asking

PART THREE: CHARTING YOUR COURSE
THROUGH THE MODERN WORKPLACE

3 Ways to Prove You're a Leader, No Matter What Your Position

Even if you're not officially in a leadership role yet, you can show that you've got the chops for it using these strategies.

https://www.themuse.com/advice/3-ways-to-prove-youre-a-leader-no-matter-what -your-position

7 Free Ways to Continue Your Education If You Have a Job (and No Free Time)

While the New Rules of Work are all about learning, that doesn't mean you need to (officially) go back to school right now. There are lots of ways to build your skills if you get creative and look for the resources around you.

https://www.themuse.com/advice/7-free-ways-to-continue-your-education-if-you -have-a-job-and-no-free-time

45 Productivity Tips for Extremely Busy People

Even more productivity advice for getting even more things done!

https://www.themuse.com/advice/45-productivity-tips-for-extremely-busy-people

Thank you again for joining us on this journey! Stay tuned for new advice and resources on TheMuse.com, and let us know what you think on Twitter at @DailyMuse, @KMin & @ACav!

ACKNOWLEDGMENTS

It would have been impossible to complete *The New Rules of Work,* or to build The Muse itself, without a million instances of kindness and support along the way.

While it would be impossible to acknowledge everyone, it would be a crime not to specifically call out a few.

First, to The Muse community: Thank you for being a part of our journey and for letting us be a part of yours. A special thank-you to those of you who have been fans since the early days, and who shared us with friend after friend, and colleague after colleague. It's because of you that a little bitty company and three people in a Brooklyn apartment have grown to a, well, a substantially larger company with dreams of even bigger heights.

Secondly, thank you to the Muse team. You took a chance on us. You joined the company early on—in some cases when it probably seemed like a risky career move! You put your heart, soul, and sweat into building a legacy we're proud of, and we would gift you each a baby giraffe if we could!

Thanks to Melissa, our brilliant third cofounder and original editorial mastermind. Yes, we forgive you for leaving to cure cancer. But you'll always be a Muser.

We have been grateful through this journey to have had so many incredible people believe in us: We want to thank Rachel Sklar, one of our earliest advisers; Y Combinator, who backed us financially when most thought we were crazy; the women of TheLi.st, who provided much-needed moral and financial support; and other early advisers, investors, and backers. Your support then and now means the world to us.

As you can imagine, this book was the product of extensive collaboration with our Muse editorial team, writers, and editors. We can say for sure that we wouldn't be as proud of it as we are without the editorial leadership and brilliance of Adrian Granzella Larssen, The Muse's first employee and editor in chief. Thanks also to Kat Boogaard, Aja Frost, Jessica Solloway, Katie Wolf, Lily Zhang, Lily Herman, Erin Greenawald, Stacey Lastoe, Jenni Maier, and Elliott Bell for contributing such great career advice to *The New Rules of Work*. Thanks also to Laura Du and Patrick Morley for their suggestions and feedback on the manuscript.

Then there are a set of people who became our partners and guides in this crazy process they call publishing a book:

Thank you to our editor, Talia Krohn, who has been incredible to work with. She saw the vision for this book from the very beginning and made sure every word was imbued with the mission and ethos of The Muse. Thank you to the whole team at Crown Business—Tina Constable, Campbell Wharton, Ayelet Gruenspecht, Owen Haney, Julia Elliott, Christine Tanigawa, Andrea Lau, Philip Leung, and Dannalie Diaz—who worked so hard to make this book a reality.

Thanks to our literary agent, Kristyn Keene, who has been a partner and fellow #ladyboss throughout this process. Thanks also to the whole team at ICM for their hard work.

And finally, we want to thank our family and friends, for supporting us through thick and thin. To our friends Mark, Nick, Joy, Sarah, Jocelyn, Alison, Alex T, Bea, Christina, Gesche, and Christie, and so many more than we can name here. Thank you for being the best (and for forgiving us for being MIA sometimes).

From Kathryn: I want to thank my parents, Steve and Terri Minshew, for teaching me pretty much everything I know and backing me wholeheartedly through some of my craziest endeavors (including leaving a great job to try a start-up and losing all of my money the first time around!). Thank you to my not-so-little brother, William, who's still probably the smartest person I know. And finally, to my husband, Jeremy: superhero or sidekick, there is no one I'd rather ride into battle with. You're my other half, and I feel so blessed every day to have found you on that mountain. Excited to take the next fifty years by storm ;)

From Alexandra: Thank you to my parents, Alix and Panos Cavoulacos, for always believing in me, even when I was a handful of a five-year-old. To my siblings, Sophie and Dimitri, you are a constant source of love and inspiration; I'm so proud of you both. My grandparents have given me the values and true north that make me who I am, particularly my two incredible grandmothers (darling Yaya et ma Grandmami adorée, plein de bisous d'amour), who modeled strength, humor, and kindness. To Regina, Jay, Karen, Vincent, and Melissa, who have made me feel more welcome than I could ever have imagined. And my biggest thanks of all is to my husband, Anthony: You've been by my side since before The Muse was even a dream. You've been through the highs and lows, the months without a salary, the nonstop work to make this company a reality, and you are always there for me. I love you, always and forever.

INDEX

skills:
  gaps in ("Skills Needed" list), 59, 293–95
  keywords on resume, 131, 149
  mentioned in cover letter, 144, 149
  prioritizing, 295–96
  transferable, 57
Skype interviews, 176–78, 192
smiling, 176, 177
Snapchat, your profile on, 80
social anxiety, 89
social media:
  company "personality" in, 128, 172
  industry-specific, 121–22
  and job search, 120–22
  networking in, 86–87
  your brand profiles on, 67, 72–80
soft (interpersonal) skills, 244–71
solutions, suggesting, 302
speakerphone, 240
speech, preparing, 229
stand tall, 176
stereotypes, 31
strengths, recognizing, 59, 68
stunt double, 103
switching tactics, 158–59

talking too much, 181
team player (management style), 268
teamwork, 251–52, 253–54, 303–4
technology:
  controlling distractions of, 287–89
  meet-ups, 87–88
  and productivity, 272
telling your story, 145–46
test-driving career paths, 53–56
thank-you notes, 96, 100–101, 112, 118, 183–85
TheMuse.com, 5–6, 312
  additional tools, 313–15
  Coach Connect, 56
  image and video search of companies via, 129
thinking outside the box, 36, 150–56
time management, 273–80
  blocking your calendar, 276–77
  delegating, 279
  learning to say no, 278–80
  managing your inbox, 284–87
  1–3–5 rule, 274–76
  using your feelings, 277–78
to-do list, 273–80
  last in, first out, 285–86

outsourcing tasks, 282
prioritizing, 283
pruning, 281
reverse chronological approach, 286
yesterbox, 286–87
tuition reimbursement, 206
Twain, Mark, 276
Twitter:
  chats, 90
  following new connections on, 101
  and job search, 120–22
  your bio on, 80

understanding your audience, 154

vacation days, 202, 206–7
values, 20–23
  accountability to, 60
  on Muse Grid, 34–35, 37
  and Muse Method, 28
  and negotiation, 198
  passion vs. profession, 35–37
  priorities, 43
video assessments, 178
video interviews, 176–78
volunteering, 55, 131

wardrobe, for interviews, 171–73, 175, 177
websites:
  building your network, 82
  creation platforms, 83
  easier to find you via, 82
  freedom and control via, 82
  helping you stand out, 81–82
  keywords for, 82
  landing page, 83
  personal, 67, 80–83, 81
  studying others, 40
what are you seeking?, 19
who are you now?, 17–25
wingman or -woman, 91, 106–7
Wordle (word cloud generator), 82
words or phrases, importance of, 68–69, 76, 78, 82, 135–36
work:
  learning about vs. performing, 18
  values related to, 20–23
  and your current frame of mind, 23–25
work matchmaker, 106
Workshop, San Francisco, 298

yesterbox, 286–87